P9-DZA-536

Praise for *The Cello Suites*:

Mavis Gallant Nonfiction Prize Winner
McAuslan Best First Book Prize Winner
Governor General's Literary Award Finalist
Writers' Trust Nonfiction Prize Finalist
BC National Award for Canadian Nonfiction Finalist
One of The Afterword's Best Books of the Year (National Post)

"Vividly chronicles [Siblin's] international search for the original, and unfound, Bach score . . . Mr. Siblin's book is well researched, and filled with enough anecdotes to engage even the classical-music aficionado . . . but the book is best distinguished by its writing. To vivify music in words is not easy. But Mr. Siblin rises to the task. . . . Read *The Cello Suites*—preferably with their melodious hum in the background—and you will never look at a cello in quite the same way again."
—*The Economist*

"This is rich terrain, and Siblin's book is an engrossing combination of musical and political history spiced with generally vivid descriptions of the cello suites themselves . . . [Siblin] has given us a compelling portrait of a passionate, prickly Bach, of Casals, a musician who was also politically engaged, and an engrossing cast of secondary characters. Best of all, *The Cello Suites* makes us want to pop in a CD and really listen to those cello suites. Awesome."
—Wynne Delacoma, *Chicago Sun-Times*

"A work of ever-percolating interest. Mr. Siblin winds up mixing high and low musical forms, art and political histories, Bach's and Casals's individual stories and matters of arcane musicology into a single inquisitive volume."
—Janet Maslin, *The New York Times*

"Pitch-perfect. *The Cello Suites* is, on all counts, a superior book."
—McAuslan First Book Prize jury citation

"This is one of the most extraordinary, clever, beautiful, and impeccably researched books I have read in years. A fascinating story deftly told—and, for me at least, ideally read with Bach's thirty-six movements playing softly in the background; a recipe for literary rapture."
—Simon Winchester, author of *The New York Times* best seller *The Professor and the Madman*

"It's not often that one begins reading a book with mild interest and then can't put it down, which happened to me with this beautiful book."
—Diana Athill, author of *Stet* and *Somewhere Towards the End*

"Cothen, Barcelona, Prades, Berlin, Montréal—Eric Siblin's *The Cello Suites* reads with the page-turning urgency of a mystery novel, breathing new life into some of the most profound music to flow from the human imagination."
—Matt Haimovitz, internationally renowned cellist and professor of cello at McGill University

"An ambitious, carefully researched, and inventively constructed book written with clarity and verve."
—Mavis Gallant Prize for Nonfiction jury citation

"A delightfully quirky quest . . . Eric Siblin seamlessly weaves together the tale of how Bach's lost and mostly forgotten manuscript came to be discovered a century later by Pablo Casals, and finally became Siblin's personal passion."
—Governor General's Literary Award jury citation

"A book of extraordinary charm, insight, and widespread literary appeal."
—BC National Award for Canadian Nonfiction jury citation

"Engaging and imaginative . . . a charming narrative."
—Melinda Bargreen, *The Seattle Times*

"The author has done a wealth of research in pursuit of his new passion, and he writes engagingly. . . . this intrepid writer has worked hard to interest readers in his musical obsession, and there is a great deal to chew on here."

—Priscilla S. Taylor, *The Washington Times*

"The ironies of artistic genius and public taste are subtly explored in this winding, entertaining tale of a musical masterpiece. . . . Siblin is an insightful writer with an ability to convey the sound and emotional impact of music in words."

—*Publishers Weekly*

"Included in his thorough research are interviews with cellist such as Mischa Maisky and Anner Bylsma. . . . In Siblin's history of the composer, Bach is far from the stuffy image often applied to classical music; he appears restless, brash, and proud. . . . Siblin's writing is most inspired when describing the life of Casals, showing a genuine affection for the cellist."

—Elliot Mandel, *Booklist* (starred review)

"A winning combination of music history, biography, and whimsy."

—*Library Journal*

"Siblin firmly believes 'Bach is what you make of him'—and his book represents just that. . . . No matter what the great composer means to readers, they will surely enjoy Siblin's fun, fast-paced journey from pop-music scribbler to Bach afficionado."

—*Christian Science Monitor*

"Superb . . . there is something almost magical in how Siblin is able to bring the music alive . . . Indeed, I will never listen to any composition by Bach in quite the same way again. . . . In a sense, *The Cello Suites* is a triple biography—we learn about the lives of Bach and Casals and the music itself. Siblin cuts back and forth between these three narratives in a kind of dazzling verbal counterpoint, and he manages to touch on almost everything there is to know or say about Bach . . . but he always brings us back to the "Cello Suites" in all of their richness, power, and subtlety."

—Jonathan Kirsch, *Jewish Journal*

"A passionate ode to the joy of discovery . . . genuine and well researched . . . The charismatic power of [Casals] comes across in Siblin's descriptions, which are beautifully interspersed with reflections on the tumultuous times through with Casals lived. . . . Prose of cinematic quality . . . Siblin artfully conjures a sense of nostalgia for all that has been without it becoming cloying, and his is a touching and occasionally lonely presence, one that we sense is still searching."
—*The Times* (UK)

"Eric Siblin is in many ways just the kind of listener whom musicians love to find in their audiences: an open-minded voyager who's trying something new."
—Susan Tomes, *The Independent* (UK)

"Eric Siblin's first book joyfully and informatively mixes anecdote and biography—of both Bach and Casals—with just the right dose of his own voyage of musical discovery. . . . That these personal jottings never outstay their welcome is testament to the author's skill and warmth; the rest of the book, meanwhile, is fitting tribute to one of the classical canon's cornerstones."
—Metro.co.uk

"Siblin's enthusiasm for his subject is boundless and, as a newbie in a foreign land, he brings an unstuffy freshness to the often staid world of classical music writing. . . . *The Cello Suites* [celebrates] the good fortune of discovering great works of art. . . . This book reminds us of the joy of exploration, of finding glorious things in the least likely places."
—Suzy Klein, *The New Statesman* (UK)

"A well researched, highly enjoyable exploration of both the suites and their 1980 rediscovery . . . readers won't need a classical music background in order to enjoy this book, but listening to these suites compounded my pleasure. But even for those who read in silence, Eric Siblin connects the dots well: two great men, six great suites, and one engrossing story."
—Bob Sanchez, Internet Review of Books

"The quest was part Homer but also part George Plimpton . . . Everywhere Siblin went, every door he opened, was *worth* opening. Bach's mysterious life unfolded before him, prompting more questions about the mystery of these cello suites. Where and when were they written? Why was the manuscript lost? Might he be the one who actually finds the original? It all becomes part of his magnificent obsession . . . The way the doors opened onto other doors in this quest makes Alice's seem one-dimensional by comparison. . . . This book shouts life and also a future for our music."

—Eric Friesen, *Queen's Quarterly* (Canada)

"Succinct but wide-ranging . . . vivid travel writing . . . an erudite and immensely readable miscellany that will give you the sensation of having consumed a library over a weekend or less. . . . Concise yet richly detailed, Siblin's summary of Bach's life is reason enough to read the book. . . . Siblin maintains interest with writing that is accurate, colorful, and personal. Conveying in mere words sounds as rich and multifarious as those that comprise the "Cello Suites" takes no small literary gift. To say the author has done justice to his subject is the highest praise of all."   —Arthur Kaptainis, *Montreal Gazette*

"Fascinating . . . *The Cello Suites* is a satisfying and sustaining read. Highly recommended for music fans and lay people alike."

—*Montreal Review of Books*

"A rare combination of history and a journey of self-discovery and self-fulfillment written for a general reader . . . Insightful [and] engaging . . . Eric Siblin puts us in touch with the joy of discovering a new passion in life."   —*Toronto Star*

"Eric Siblin's new book is at once a study of music, a work of history, and a passionate tribute. . . . Meticulous in his research, Siblin makes convincing connections and offers possible answers to the questions surrounding the suites . . . If Siblin is correct that 'Bach is what you make of him,' then *The Cello Suites* has made him, if possible, yet more legendary."   —*Quill & Quire*

"An utterly fascinating new book . . . I could not put it down."
—Mike Duncan, Classical 96.3 FM

"Siblin is right that the "Cello Suites" provide a perfect entrée into the sound world of Bach. He provides a delightful and illuminating journey into that world."
—The Whole Note

"A delightful whirlwind tour through the two different ages of musical history . . . The book's greatest triumph is its structure, which borrows from the music . . . with the stories of Bach, Casals and Siblin's personal search rotating throughout, creating a thematic counterpoint that cleverly suggests the timelessness of the music it explores."
—The Walrus

THE CELLO SUITES

J.S. BACH, PABLO CASALS,

and the search for

A BAROQUE MASTERPIECE

THE CELLO SUITES

ERIC SIBLIN

Grove Press
New York

Copyright © 2009 by Eric Siblin

All rights reserved. No part of this book may be reproduced in any form or by any electronic or mechanical means, or the facilitation thereof, including information storage and retrieval systems, without permission in writing from the publisher, except by a reviewer, who may quote brief passages in a review. Any members of educational institutions wishing to photocopy part or all of the work for classroom use, or publishers who would like to obtain permission to include the work in an anthology, should send their inquiries to Grove/Atlantic, Inc., 154 West 14th Street, New York, NY 10011.

Originally published in Canada in 2009 by
House of Anansi Press, Inc., Toronto, Cananda

Printed in the United States of America

ISBN 978-0-8021-4524-6
eISBN 978-0-8021-9797-9

Grove Press
an imprint of Grove Atlantic
154 West 14th Street
New York, NY 10011
Distributed by Publishers Group West
groveatlantic.com

19 20 21 22   11 10 9 8

To my parents, Herbert and Jacqueline Siblin

CONTENTS

SUITE NO. 1
(G major)

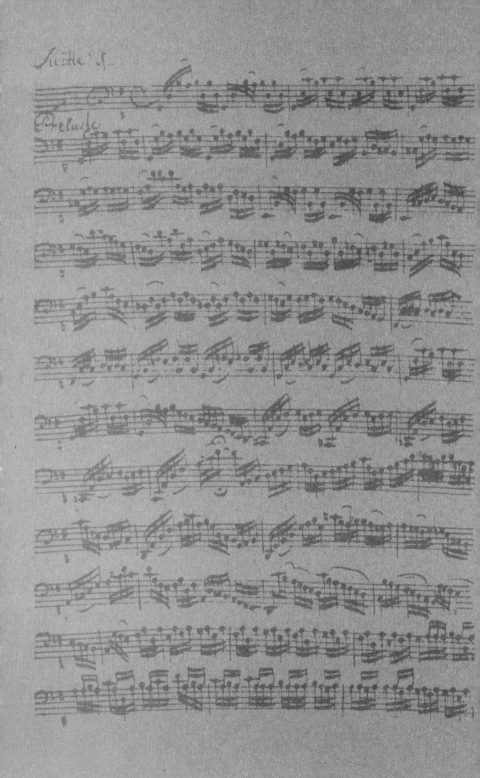

PRELUDE

We find a world of emotions and ideas created with only the simplest of materials. LAURENCE LESSER

THE FIRST MEASURES unfold with the storytelling power of a master improviser. A journey has begun, but it's as if composition is taking place on the spot. The deep-toned strings take us back to the 1700s. The soundworld is happy. The jauntiness youthful. Discovery is in the air.

After a pause that contemplates the future, the cello resumes with aching soulfulness. Things will not come easily. The notes are murmured, stated with courtly purpose, and blasted through with rapture. We peak higher. A new vista opens up, rhapsodic resolution, the descent a soft landing.

This is how the opening notes of Bach's Cello Suites sounded to me as I sat in the courtyard of a seaside villa in Spain that once belonged to Pablo Casals, the Catalan cellist who discovered the music as a boy one afternoon in 1890. As I listened to the music on headphones, shaded by the palms and pines of a lush garden, the shimmering waves of the nearby Mediterranean seemed to roll perfectly in time with the prelude of the first cello suite.

There was no more fitting place to appreciate the music. Although the Cello Suites first flowed from the composer's quill sometime in the early 1700s, it was Casals who, two centuries later, made them famous.

My own discovery of the Cello Suites had taken place one autumn evening in 2000, a "Bach Year" marking two and a half centuries since the death of the composer. I was in the audience at Toronto's Royal Conservatory of Music to hear a cellist I'd never heard of play music I knew nothing about.

I had no reason to be there aside from a concert listing in a local newspaper, idle curiosity, and the fact that I was staying at a nearby hotel. But I might have been searching for something without knowing it. Sometime earlier I had ended a stint as pop music critic for a daily newspaper in Montreal, *The Gazette*, a job that had filled my head with vast amounts of music, much of which I didn't want to be there. The Top 40 tunes had overstayed their welcome in my auditory cortex, and the culture surrounding rock music had worn thin. I still wanted music to occupy a central place in my life, but in a different way. The Cello Suites, as it turned out, offered a way out of the jam.

The program notes for the recital by Laurence Lesser, a distinguished cellist from Boston, explained that "amazingly, for a long time," the Cello Suites were seen as only a collection of exercises. But since Casals had started playing the suites at the dawn of the twentieth century, "we now know how lucky we are to possess these extraordinary masterworks. What most music-lovers don't know, however, is that no known composer's manuscript of these works exists... There exists no truly reliable source for the suites." This got the journalistic wheels in my head turning: what had happened to Bach's manuscript?

It was in the small German town of Cöthen in 1720 that the Cello Suites were said to have been composed and inscribed by Bach's raven-quill pen. But without his original manuscript, how can we be certain? Why was such monumental music written for the cello, a lowly instrument usually relegated to background droning in Bach's time? And given that Bach regularly rewrote his music for different instruments, how can we even be sure that the music *was* written for the cello?

From my seat in the Royal Conservatory concert hall, the lone figure producing this massive sound with such modest resources seemed to defy the musical odds. Only one instrument, and one anchored to a very low register, the cello appeared unequal to the task, as if some supreme composer had devised an overambitious score, an ideal text, with little regard for the crude vehicle that was to carry it out.

Watching Laurence Lesser expertly play the suites, I was struck by the bulkiness of his instrument—in former times called the violoncello, or 'cello for short—bringing to mind some lumbering peasant from a medieval string kingdom, rough-hewn and primitive, nowhere near sophisticated enough for the refined music it was playing. But on closer examination I could see the intricately carved wooden scroll and the curvaceous sound holes, shaped like some exquisite baroque time signature. And what was coming out of those sound holes was music more earthy and ecstatic than anything I'd ever heard. I let my mind wander. What would the music have sounded like in 1720? It was easy to imagine the violoncello proving itself in aristocratic company and seducing the powdered wigs.

But if the music is so uniquely captivating, why were the Cello Suites virtually never heard until Casals discovered them? For nearly two centuries after this baritone masterwork was composed, only a small circle of professional musicians and Bach scholars knew of this epic music. And those who did thought they were more technical exercises than anything fit for the concert hall.

The story of the six suites is more than musical. Politics shaped the music, from the Prussian militarism of the eighteenth century to the German patriotism that propelled Bach's fame a century later. When European dictatorships ruled in the twentieth century, the notes became so many bullets in the anti-fascist cello of Casals. Decades later, Mstislav Rostropovich played the Cello Suites against the backdrop of a crumbling Berlin Wall.

After Casals gave the music mass appeal — which happened long after his discovery of the music — there was no stopping the suites. There are now more than fifty recordings in the catalogue and upwards of seventy-five performance editions of the music for cellists. Other instrumentalists found they could transcribe and tackle the Cello Suites: the flute, piano, guitar, trumpet, tuba, saxophone, banjo, and more have all essayed the music with surprising success. But for cellists the six suites quickly became their alpha and omega, a rite of passage, the Mount Everest of their repertoire. (Or the Mount Fuji: in 2007 Italian cellist Mario Brunello climbed to the summit, nearly 3,750 metres above sea level, where he played selections from the Cello Suites, declaring that "Bach's music comes closest to the absolute and to perfection.")

The music is no longer considered overly challenging for the average listener. New recordings of the suites regularly win "disc of the year" honours. And the scratchy old mono recording made by Casals continues to be a top seller among historical titles.

But it is not lighthearted music. A cursory scan of recent performances shows that the suites were played at two major memorial services in England held in honour of the victims of 9/11, at another memorial marking the Rwandan genocide, and at various high-profile funerals, including the massive one held for Katharine Graham, former publisher of *The Washington Post*. More recently, at Senator Edward Kennedy's stately funeral, the sarabande from the sixth Cello Suite was performed with aching beauty by Yo-Yo Ma.

If the music has often been employed for sad occasions, it is in large part explained by the dark, moody tones of the cello, plus the fact that the Bach suites require one lonely instrument. Yet the cello is the instrument that most closely resembles the human voice; it is capable of more than just doom and gloom. The Bach suites, most of which are written in major keys, have their fair share of upbeat merrymaking, devil-may-care attitude, and ecstatic abandon. The roots of the music are in dance — most of the movements are in fact old European dances — and dancers have been quick to choreograph the suites. Mikhail Baryshnikov, Rudolf Nureyev, Mark Morris, and Taiwan's Cloud Gate Dance Theatre, among others, have all moved to its propulsive rhythms.

The music gets around. Yo-Yo Ma produced six short films that used gardening, architecture, figure skating, and kabuki to illustrate the suites. The rock star Sting made a short film in which he played the first prelude on a guitar while an Italian ballet dancer enacted the melody. And the suites have been heard in a number of films, most notably (and, alas, gloomily) in several by Ingmar Bergman, as well as in *Master and Commander*, *The Pianist*, and the television series *The West Wing*. The music can be found on discs as varied as *Classic FM Music for Studying*, *Bach for Babies*, and *Tune Your Brain on Bach*, not to mention *Bach for Barbecue*. The Bach suites have been cited by one opera singer as her favourite music for cooking. Snippets of the music are widely available as cellphone ring tones.

But the Cello Suites haven't quite gone mainstream. They remain "classical" music after all, and have the refined aroma of music for connoisseurs. They were considered exactly that by reviewers — "an item for connoisseurs" — when Casals' pioneering recordings were first released back in the early 1940s. "They are cool and pure and lofty," wrote the critic for the *New York Times*, "set forth with the simplicity that distinguishes searching art." They still have serious status, fuelled by highbrow reviews that suggest the suites "represent some sort of apex of Western musical creativity" or that the music "has a purity and intensity that approach the Japanese yet remains more accessible to Western ears."

The idea to write a book about the Bach suites, one that is not aimed at classical connoisseurs, came to me when I first heard three of the Cello Suites in that Toronto recital by Laurence Lesser. The idea was vague, but I had a strong sense there was a story there, somewhere, and decided to follow in the footsteps of the notes.

Since then I have heard the suites performed on Spain's Costa Dorada, on the grounds of Casals' former villa, now a lovely museum devoted to the cellist. I listened to a young German cellist play the suites in a Leipzig warehouse, not far from where Bach is buried. Matt Haimovitz, a one-time wunderkind, gave a rollicking account of the music at a roadhouse juke joint in the Gatineau Hills north of Ottawa. I attended a master class on the suites given by the eminent Dutch cellist Anner Bylsma at a music camp perched on the banks of the St. Lawrence River. I was at Lincoln Center for Pieter Wispelwey's marathon playing of all six suites, and at a Manhattan conference on Bach in the twenty-first century, where the suites were gorgeously performed on marimba (marimBach!). At a high-rise apartment building on the outskirts of Brussels, I heard a Russian émigré violinist play the suites on an intriguing five-string fiddle that he'd built, convinced it is the mysterious instrument lost to history that Bach really composed the suites for.

The compact discs have piled up — from the Old Testament recordings that Casals made back in the 1930s to the slickly produced discs of recent years, including "authentic" early music approaches and the suites rendered on any number of instruments, in jazzified form, or blended with traditional West African music. In 2007, three centuries after composition, the Cello Suites hit number one on the iTunes classical music chart with a recording by Rostropovich. (Bach seemed to be boasting to the iPod generation that month: another version of the

SUITE NO. 1 ～ 9

Cello Suites was on the same Top 20 chart, not to mention three other works by the composer.)

By then the music had become a story for me. And it seemed only natural for the story to be structured along the lines of the music. The six Cello Suites each contain six movements, starting with a prelude and ending with a gigue. In between are old court dances—an allemande, a courante, and a sarabande—after which Bach inserted a more "modern" dance, either a minuet, a bourrée, or a gavotte. In the pages that follow, Bach will occupy the first two or three movements in each suite. The dances that come afterwards are earmarked for Pablo Casals. And the gigues that close each suite will be reserved for a more recent story, that of my search.

If I've been on the trail of the music for this long it's because there's so much to hear in the Cello Suites. The genre may be baroque, but there are multiple personalities and mood swings within the suites. I hear barnstorming peasant tunes and post-modern minimalism, spiritual lamentations and heavy metal riffs, medieval jigs and spy movie soundtracks. The ideal experience for most listeners may be as I first heard the music, without preconceptions. But connect the notes, and a story emerges.

ALLEMANDE

*The elegant allemandes in the Cello Suites, each
preceded by a dramatic opening movement, have been
described as slow and pensive pieces of great beauty.*
OXFORD COMPOSER COMPANIONS: J. S. BACH

To piece together the story of the Cello Suites means getting
to know the music's composer. And for anyone born in the
past half-century, to become acquainted with Johann Sebastian
Bach—really acquainted—means to infiltrate another art form,
another era, another frame of mind. To get myself up to
baroque speed, I went about listening to massive amounts of
Bach's music, perusing second-hand music shops to build a
respectable collection, reading everything Bachian I could get
my hands on, from eighteenth-century accounts to glossy classical music magazines, and going to concerts bravo'd by mature
audiences that were a far cry from the rock circuit.

I also became a card-carrying member of the American
Bach Society. The main perk of membership was occasional
mailings of the ABS newsletter, which was emblazoned with
Bach's personal seal, his initials stylishly entwined and topped
with a crown. I scoured the handful of pages trumpeting the
latest scholarly research for clues about the Cello Suites. It felt
as if I'd joined a secret society. In high school during the 1970s,

when musical choice seemed to be between the enemy forces of disco and spaced-out synthesizer rock, being a Rolling Stones fan felt vaguely esoteric. At some point since then they became the band of choice for people practically in my mother's demographic, but back then true Stones fans were not numerous. Two decades later, finding fellow Bach enthusiasts in my social circles was more or less impossible.

So when I learned that the American Bach Society held conferences every two years, and the next one was to take place not far away, at Rutgers University in New Jersey, I eagerly registered. Having done my homework on the Cello Suites I could qualify, sort of, as a bona fide Bachian and rub shoulders with my own people.

Thus in April 2004 I found myself walking across the emerald lawns of Princeton University with a gaggle of Bach devotees, nearly all of whom were scholars and an alarming number of whom were bearded and wearing dark blazers. We had just heard a very high-forehead lecture on Bach and were emerging from a university building, blinking in the sunlight, as a student event called "Spring Fling" was noisily underway. There was face-painting and Hacky Sack, football, a barbecue, and a garage band cranking out REM's rock anthem *It's the End of the World As We Know It (and I Feel Fine)*.

This was so much white noise for the Bach scholars, who were at Princeton on a musicological mission, a colourful field expedition in the otherwise staid world of Bach research. The world's finest portrait of Bach, almost never accessible to the public, was being made available for delegates to the 2004 American Bach Society conference. Only two authentic portraits of Bach are known to exist, both by the same artist, the Saxon court painter Elias Gottlob Hausmann. They are nearly identical, both in oil, and show the composer in the same serious pose. Despite their similarity, they are thought to have been painted on separate occasions. One of the portraits today hangs in the municipal museum of Leipzig, the city where it was painted in 1746. It is in poor shape because of repeated over-painting, as well as having been used once upon a time for target practice by bored students armed with crumpled paper.

The other portrait, painted two years later, is in pristine condition. It is this one that half a century ago made its way into the hands of William H. Scheide, an independently wealthy Bach enthusiast with a long history of studying, performing, and collecting the works of his favourite composer. Normally the portrait hangs in Scheide's Princeton home, but he agreed to display the portrait for those attending the fourteenth bien-nial meeting of the American Bach Society.

The Hausmann portrait has, more than anything else, fleshed out the popular image of Bach—that of a severe-looking, bewigged, and somewhat corpulent German burgher. It is an image that graces countless CD covers, concert programs, and festival posters, and has gone a long way towards helping lis-teners imagine a composer for whom scant biographical detail exists.

So, as the Bach scholars made their way across the Princeton campus, their excitement was palpable. The Bach portrait and William H. Scheide were waiting in the special collections room of the John Foster Dulles Library of Diplomatic History. The Bach crowd, eighty-five strong, filed into the wood-panelled room and clustered around the portrait.

"Oooh!"

"Stunning."

"Like the *Mona Lisa*."

"So serious."

"It sort of hits me in the stomach, right inside there, like, whoa!"

"It has a kind of energy."

"Should we bow three times or something?"

The portrait did have a convincing intensity. The buttons on the composer's coat glistened, his white shirt sleeves radiated crispness, the wig was springily soft and his complexion flushed, as if the composer had drained a few glasses of the Rhineland wine he favoured. From inside the thick gold frame Bach seemed to be casting an all-knowing, wary eye over the proceedings.

William H. Scheide, ninety years old, wearing a powder-blue jacket and a red tie patterned with music notation (which may or may not have been from a Bach cantata), gave a brief talk on the other Bachiana in his collection—original manuscripts in the composer's hand and a rare letter. Then he was asked the question on everyone's mind: how he came into possession of the portrait. "A long time ago," he replied, leaning on a cane with a ski-pole grip as a handle. "I can barely remember it anymore."

The upshot is that Scheide, whose family made its fortune in the oil business, heard about the portrait sometime after the Second World War and arranged for an art dealer in London to purchase it from its owner, a German musician by the name of Walter Jenke. The owner had left Germany in the late 1920s, settling in Dorset, England; he returned to Nazi Germany a decade later to retrieve the portrait, which had apparently been in his family since the nineteenth century.

The Hausmann portrait has helped cultivate an image of Bach that is far more severe and serious than he probably was. "Part of the reason that people think of Bach as an old fuddy-duddy," music commentator Miles Hoffman once observed on National Public Radio, "is because there's only one fully authenticated portrait of him, and it shows him as an old guy with a powdered wig looking very stuffy and stolid." Hoffman made a point of saying that Bach was in fact a man of passion, the sort of man who got into a sword fight with a bassoonist, was thrown into a duke's prison at one point, and fathered no less than twenty children.

The viewing of the portrait fit nicely with the theme of the biennial conference, which was titled "Images of Bach." Along with concerts and cocktails, scholarly papers were delivered with titles ranging from "When an Aria Is Not an Aria" to "'I Must Live Amid Almost Continual Vexation, Envy, and Persecution': A Psychological Reading of J. S. Bach's Relationship to Authority." The keynote speech was delivered by Christoph Wolff, a German-American musicologist and Harvard professor who is the world's foremost Bach expert. In his lecture, Wolff suggested that the iconic Bach portrait should not be seen as some sort of casual snapshot. "It is an official pose," he said. "The sitter likely wanted to be painted in this way. We can assume that Bach wanted to shape the image."

In the portrait, Bach is holding a sheet of music: a highly complex piece, his own composition, known as the "triplex canon." By doing so, Wolff argued, "Bach tried to avoid his fame as a virtuoso, playing down his (professional) office... and taking a backseat as a human being... all deferring to his oeuvre."

By saying that Bach had his portrait painted with an eye towards posterity, controlling his posthumous image as he wanted it to appear, Wolff was challenging a common impression of Bach. The conventional image of the baroque master is that of someone who worked day to day without any thoughts of posterity, cranking out masterworks as a matter of course and not being overly concerned about his popular reputation or the shelf life of his music. In Wolff's view, Bach in fact took an active role in "promoting his afterlife." He did what he could to safeguard examples of his art and to secure his place in history. Even in the Hausmann portrait, by holding a highly complicated piece of music (a "puzzle canon" that is like a mathematical riddle), "the man with the restrained smile wanted the viewer to feel challenged. It worked in 1748 — and it works today."

Wolff then took questions from the audience. One questioner, a heavy-set man with his hair in a ponytail, sporting a bow tie and peering through oversized tortoiseshell glasses, took Wolff's comments a step further. He accused Bach of being behind "a concerted campaign to control everything he could about what posterity thought of him."

This was the amateur Bach expert Teri Noel Towe, well known in Bach circles and, despite being a self-described "passionate and obsessed eccentric," well respected by the nine-to-five scholars. A New York City lawyer specializing in intellectual property law, Towe said he was outraged that Bach's first biographer, Johann Nikolaus Forkel, did not manage to get more in the way of personal details about the composer. Although Forkel was writing decades after Bach's death in 1750, he was in touch with Bach's sons, especially Carl Philipp Emanuel (C.P.E.). "I would love to put C. P. E. Bach on the witness stand," Towe said. He complained that there is no mention in Forkel's biography, published in 1802, of what Bach looked like, his height, his weight, or what his favourite dessert might have been.

"At the same time," Wolff replied, "eighteenth-century biographers were not interested in desserts."

"We don't know what he ate," piped up a musicologist in the audience, "but we know what he drank!"

"And smoked!" added another scholar.

The debonair silver-haired Wolff agreed, noting that when Bach travelled he was put up in the best hotels and consumed the highest-quality beer and pipe tobacco. "It is quite clear that he indulged. He liked the good things in life."

But all Bach scholars bemoan the lack of hard historical information available on their subject. Aside from Shakespeare, there is probably no other towering figure in modern art about whom we know so little. There is nothing like the heartfelt letters Mozart wrote to his wife, or the stream-of-consciousness notebooks that Beethoven left behind. When documentary signs of life occasionally pop up for Bach—and they do pop up— it makes the search for an elusive personality all the more enticing. But Bach's biographers have their work cut out for them.

"It is difficult," Wolff said, "to see the man behind the portrait."

COURANTE

[Louis XIV] danced it better than any member of
his Court and with quite an unusual grace.
PIERRE RAMEAU, 1729

THE MAN BEHIND the portrait was born on March 21, 1685, in the small German town of Eisenach. Nothing is known of Johann Sebastian Bach's early years, though it can be safely assumed that he was raised to be a musician. His father, Ambrosius Bach, was a musician who was the son of a musician who was the son of a musician and so on, going back to the sixteenth century. The patriarch of the family, one Veit Bach, was a "white-bread baker" who moved from Hungary to Germany to escape religious persecution against Protestants. Veit was known to pluck his cittern, a guitar-like instrument, while the millstone turned grain into flour, pounding out a steady rhythm. As time went on, the Bach clan—staunchly Lutheran, rooted in the central German region of Thuringia—produced a distinguished line of professional musicians similar to the Couperins in France, the Purcells in England, and the Scarlattis in Italy.

There was no Germany in the modern sense of the country. The only central authority speaking for Germany was the Holy Roman Empire, an empty shell of an empire dating from the time of Charlemagne. It had virtually no army, no revenue, and no working machinery of government. To quote Voltaire, it was neither holy, Roman, nor an empire. This phantom empire encompassed a number of significant states such as Austria and Prussia, both of which would gain substantial power after 1700. But the Holy Roman Empire itself was a jigsaw puzzle of some 300 entities: dukedoms, principalities, imperial free cities, some encompassing barely more than a few acres—a mosaic shaped by the ups and downs of dynastic change and the fortunes of war.

No dot on the map, though, was too minuscule for German absolutism. Most of Germany was ruled by petty princes, most of whom were not substantial enough to pursue an independent foreign policy or employ a standing army. But they built ostentatious palaces and adorned their small courts with ceremonial guards, dancers, fencing masters, and musicians, imitating the great absolutist power of the period—the Sun King, Louis XIV of France. The petty rulers of German lands looked to Versailles as a role model, conjugating their verbs and powdering their wigs accordingly.*

In Bach's native town of Eisenach, 6,000 people lived in the shadow of a minor duke whose palace staff included a French elocution master, numerous pages headed by a page-master, a gaggle of ladies-in-waiting, and a master of the hunt who presided over eighty-two horses and coaches. Bach's father, Ambrosius, was a prominent town musician who became director of the municipal orchestra in Eisenach and a member of the duke's orchestra. He was first and foremost a violinist, but proficient on several other instruments such as the trumpet, which

---

* When the Holy Roman Emperor, for example, responded to a French invasion of the Rhineland in the 1670s by declaring war against France, about 20,000 German troops were serving in the French army, and six of the German empire's eight "electoral" princes remained clients of Louis XIV. "Not a dog barks in Europe," boasted one French diplomat, "unless our king says he may."

he played in a brass band that performed twice daily from the town hall balcony overlooking the market square.

A vivid portrait of Ambrosius, now housed in the Berlin State Library, shows him posing in a Japanese kimono, a fashion statement in the late seventeenth century. He has shoulder-length dark hair, a slightly exuberant moustache, and a proud but easygoing, affable expression.

Less is known about Bach's mother, Elisabetha. What we do know is that her father was a wealthy furrier and a member of the town council in nearby Erfurt, and that she was twenty-four when she married Ambrosius in 1668. They had eight children, seven of whom were given the first name of Johann, Johanne, or Johanna. Four died early on.

Johann Sebastian was the youngest child and grew up surrounded, like all the other Bachs, by music. He presumably received lessons from Ambrosius on violin, viola, and probably cello. And he would have accompanied his father when he performed at church, castle, and town hall, joining in on various instruments as soon as he was up to the task.

At St. George's Latin School, where Sebastian (like Martin Luther two centuries earlier) was a pupil, the perfection of God's will was never doubted. Yet creation was a coin tossed in the air, forever on the verge of landing on its dark side. At the age of six Sebastian was standing by the graveside of his older brother Balthasar. Two years later his father's twin brother died. Then, when the boy was nine, his mother died. Ambrosius remarried a twice-widowed woman, but within three months he too died, leaving Sebastian an orphan before his tenth birthday.

The family unit was broken apart and relatives picked up the pieces. The Bachs' seventeen-year-old daughter, Marie Salome, moved to Erfurt to be with her mother's family, while Sebastian and his older brother Jacob went to live with their newlywed brother Christoph, twenty-three, an organist in Ohrdruf, a small town at the northern edge of the Thuringian Forest.

With Christoph serving as music teacher as well as caregiver, Sebastian regained his emotional footing and channelled his grief into learning the keyboard.

Later in life Bach told the story of being denied a certain collection of Christoph's sheet music that was locked away every night in a cupboard. Sebastian apparently managed to slip his small hands through the grilled doors of the cupboard, roll up the music, and funnel it out. He'd copy out the scores by moonlight, so the story goes, until Christoph got wind of this and confiscated his treasure. The tale of the "moonlight manuscript," whether or not it really happened, was recounted in later years to give the impression of a young musician who'd stop at nothing to educate himself. That much was true.

After five years Sebastian had risen to the top of his class and was old enough to strike out on his own. In March 1700, a couple of weeks before his fifteenth birthday, he set out on a journey of more than 300 kilometres, apparently on foot, perhaps toting a violin inherited from Ambrosius. He was accompanied by an older schoolmate named Georg Erdmann (who, far in the future, would provide precious clues about his travel companion). Their objective was the north German town of Lüneburg, where high school scholarships offered to boys with singing talent awaited them.

In Lüneburg Sebastian soaked up every musical influence in the vicinity, from a French orchestra employed by the local duke at his imitation-Versailles court to Hamburg, the largest city in Germany, where he travelled to hear the renowned organist Johann Adam Reinken. He also had access to the school's library, which contained more than a thousand scores. After two years he had completed the equivalent of high school and, either not wanting to go to university or lacking the funds, he was ready to start his professional career as a musician.

Bach's first job took him to the minor court of Weimar in 1703, where he was hired as a violinist and "court lackey." Despite his low employment status (the job entailed non-musical tasks and valet services), Sebastian's musicianship must have been obvious. The teenager was soon contracted to evaluate an organ in the town of Arnstadt, and in the process so awed the authorities with his playing that he was offered on the spot a job as church organist.

His new employer was Count Anton Günther II, ruler of the main town in the territory of Schwarzburg-Arnstadt. A certificate of appointment is the first historical document that sheds any light on Bach's professional life:

> Whereas our Noble and Most Gracious Count and Master, Anton Günther, one of the Four Counts of the Empire, has caused you, Johann Sebastian Bach, to be accepted and appointed as organist in the New Church, now, therefore, you are to be true, faithful, and obedient to him, His above-mentioned Noble Grace, the Count, and especially to show yourself industrious and reliable in the office, vocation, and practice of art and science that are assigned to you; not to mix into other affairs and functions; to appear promptly on Sundays, feast days, and other days of public service in the said New Church at the organ entrusted to you; to play the latter as is fitting; to keep a watchful eye over it and take faithful care of it.

The job contract continued on a moral note that the organist was also expected "...in your daily life to cultivate the fear of God, sobriety, and the love of peace; altogether to avoid bad company and any distraction from your calling; and in general to conduct yourself in all things toward God, High Authority, and your superiors, as befits an honour-loving servant and organist..." This would challenge the most upstanding of teenagers, and it soon challenged the eighteen-year-old organist. On an August evening in 1705, Bach allegedly drew his dagger and brawled with a student bassoon player named Johann Heinrich Geyersbach.

With so many dry facts and question marks surrounding Bach's life, every shred of documentary evidence that exists, direct or indirect, is pored over by scholars desperate for insight. Colourful accounts from his life that have survived the centuries, being few and far between, are cause for biographical excitement.

One such account, recorded in the minutes of the Arnstadt consistory, the church governing body, begins by summarizing Bach's complaint that, as he passed the town hall late at night, Geyersbach (who despite being a student was in fact three years older than Bach) followed him into the market square, brandished a heavy stick, and wanted to know why Bach had made an "abusive" remark about him. The derogatory remark in question, *"Zippel Fagottist,"* has traditionally been translated by Bach scholars as "nanny-goat bassoonist." But in recent years it has spawned alternative translations thought to be more accurate, among them "greenhorn bassoonist," "rapscallion of a bassoonist," "prick of a bassoon player," and "bassoonist breaking wind after eating a green onion."

The bassoonist understandably took offence. According to Bach's testimony, Geyersbach proceeded to strike him, forcing Bach to draw his sword in defence, but Geyersbach jumped him and the two tussled until finally being separated by other students. Bach requested that the town council punish his assailant and that he be "accorded respect by the others, so that henceforth they would let him pass without abuse or attack." The town council later heard from Geyersbach, who

...denies that he attacked the plaintiff Bach. Rather...Bach, tobacco pipe in his mouth, was crossing the street, whereupon Geyersbach asked same whether he admitted having called him a greenhorn bassoonist. Inasmuch as he could not deny this, he, Bach, proceeded to draw his dagger, he, Geyersbach, had to defend himself; otherwise he would have suffered some harm.

After hearing from Geyersbach and calling other witnesses to the scuffle, the town council rebuked Bach: "He might very well have refrained from calling Geyersbach a greenhorn bassoonist; such gibes lead in the end to unpleasantness of this kind, especially since he had a reputation for not getting along with the students." In a more philosophical vein, the authorities had some advice for Bach: "Men must live among the *imperfecta.*"

Two months later, Bach requested a month-long leave to visit the great organist Dietrich Buxtehude, apparently walking more than 400 kilometres to Lübeck. Four months passed—three months more than he'd been granted—before Bach finally made it back to Arnstadt, leading to reprimands from the town council. Summoned before the local church governing body to account for his transgressions, Bach showed unusual cockiness for a twenty-year-old at risk of losing his first real job. He justified his extended absence as a trip undertaken to "understand various things in his art." When reminded that he'd been away three or four times the agreed period, he dismissively replied that he'd delegated someone else to do the job.

More complaints followed. The choir prefect testified that after Bach was reprimanded for playing the organ for too long during church services, he started to play exaggeratedly short pieces. He was also slapped on the wrist for inserting "strange notes" into hymns at church. And he was scolded for allowing a "strange maiden" into the organ loft in church.

Bach finally managed to get away from Arnstadt and its *imperfecta*, courtesy of a job offer to become church organist in the "imperial free city" of Mühlhausen. He brought the strange notes and the strange maiden along with him.

Bach got married after the move to Mühlhausen. Some biographers have identified his bride as the unknown maiden from the Arnstadt organ loft. Maria Barbara Bach was a second cousin, the daughter of a church organist in Gehren, and five months older than the groom. After her mother died she had gone to live with her uncle, the mayor of Mühlhausen, in whose guest house Bach happened to be living.

There was no salary increase for the newly married organist in Mühlhausen, but it was an improvement over Arnstadt.* The picturesque town was the second-largest in Thuringia, boasting no less than thirteen churches within its turreted walls. And as one of those curious anomalies of the Holy Roman Empire, it had been free of princely rule since the thirteenth century, answering directly to the emperor in Vienna.

But very quickly Bach found his musical possibilities restricted. His nineteenth-century biographer Philipp Spitta observed that town council and church authorities in Mühlhausen

> ...clung to old fashions and customs, and neither could nor would follow Bach's bold flights, and even looked askance at the stranger who conducted himself so despotically in a position, which as far back as the memory of man extended, had always been filled with a native of the city and for its sole honor and glory.

In the early eighteenth century a musician in Germany could work for three kinds of employers: a town, a church, or an aristocratic court. Given Germany's fractured political condition, with a large number of miniature princes vying for prestige, there was strong demand for court musicians. The pay was generally good, and it offered the chance to work with high-calibre musicians. And in an age when the public concert had not yet come into being, elaborate performances at court were the big-ticket entertainment items of the day.

The ducal court of Weimar was Bach's next employer. Weimar was where he'd started his career a few years earlier as

---

* Bach negotiated to keep his salary at its previous level of 85 gulden, and his new employer threw in some perks: two cords of firewood, six bundles of kindling, fifty-four bushels of grain, and a wagon to transport his belongings.

a court lackey. This time around, Bach became organist and a member of the Weimar court band, playing violin in the mandatory hussar's costume for performances at the castle of the rigidly pious Duke Wilhelm Ernst. For nearly a decade, starting in 1708, Bach worked in Weimar, polishing his compositional skills and mastering especially the rhythmic concerto style of Vivaldi, which was influencing musicians across Europe. And he began to toy with some ambitious ideas.

Bach more than likely thought about the idea of solo cello music for the first time in Weimar. The inspiration was probably the solo works for violin by Johann Paul Westhoff, a virtuoso violinist and linguist at the Weimar court. His violin works, published in 1696, are the earliest known multi-movement compositions for solo violin. Bach would have met Westhoff when he was briefly employed in Weimar back in 1703. Five years later, Westhoff was dead but his solo violin works were probably circulating at court.

Bach moved up the professional ladder in Weimar, receiving two promotions and eventually becoming concertmaster. In 1717, enjoying a local reputation as an organ virtuoso, he had his first brush with the glittering world of music at a major court. In Dresden, the headquarters of August the Strong, France's leading organ and keyboard virtuoso Louis Marchand was visiting to perform before the Saxon king. It occurred to a member of the Dresden court orchestra, perhaps wanting to upstage an insufferably famous Frenchman, that Bach might engage in a keyboard contest with Marchand — a musical duel was a common device for pitting great virtuosos against one another. Bach journeyed to Dresden, where he would have been struck by the dazzling entertainment infrastructure at the court, the most ostentatious in the Holy Roman Empire. Huge sums were being spent on an Italian opera company and a French ballet, while Bach's counterparts in the court orchestra were pulling in three times his salary.

Bach sent a polite note to Marchand inviting him to "a musical trial of skill," offering to improvise on the spot using whatever piece of music the Frenchman threw his way, and requesting that Marchand be prepared to do the same. The challenge was accepted and King August the Strong gave royal approval. The duel was set to take place at the mansion of Count Flemming, where "a large company of both sexes and of high rank assembled." But if Bach sensed that, after a career in the provincial shadows, his moment of destiny had arrived, he would be disappointed. An acquaintance of his, Johann Abraham Birnbaum, writing many years after the fact, outlined the story:

> The hour arrived when the two great virtuosi should match their strengths. The Honorable Court Composer [Bach], together with those who were to be the judges of this musical contest, waited for the other contestant anxiously, but in vain. It finally developed that he had vanished from Dresden early in the day by the fast stagecoach. Doubtless the famous Frenchman found his talents too weak to withstand the powerful assaults of his expert and valiant opponent.

Although formal triumph—and apparently the prize money—had slipped through Bach's hands, his reputation as a keyboard master had received a major boost, as did his desire to work where his talents might be better appreciated.

That same year, the Capellmeister of the Weimar court band died and was succeeded by his son, a move that disappointed Bach (now the father of four children), who'd hoped for the job. The situation had him pondering his career options. An offer to become Capellmeister for a small court came from the Prince of Cöthen, who had heard Bach's music and was impressed. Bach was enthusiastic, but his employer was not. When Bach asked Duke Wilhelm Ernst for permission to leave and take up employment at Cöthen—apparently pressing the issue—he was unceremoniously thrown in the castle jail.

AN OLD ACCOUNT handed down from one of Bach's students says that the composer began writing *The Well-Tempered Clavier*, that monumental work for solo keyboard, during his imprisonment in Weimar, a time when he had limited resources and lots of time on his hands. The beginning of *The Well-Tempered Clavier*, with its simple unfolding of chords, sounds unmistakably like the opening bars of the prelude for the first cello suite.* Forced to fall back on his most basic creative tools and yearning for freedom from within the confines of a rigid structure, Bach quite possibly started writing the first cello suite in jail. But was the music designed for cello? Deprived of anything other than quill and paper in prison, he could have meant the composition for some other instrument. Or for the ideal of pure music.

Because Bach's original manuscript of the Cello Suites has disappeared, dating its genesis is a guessing game. The traditional assumption is that he composed the work in the years following his imprisonment, sometime around 1720, when he was focused on instrumental music. But some of the suites seem to have been composed separately and only later combined into a set. The gestation could have been over a long period of time.

Whenever it was that Bach first dreamed up the novel idea of music for solo cello, his blueprint was highly symmetrical. It would take the form of a suite, one of the most popular structures of instrumental music in Europe. A loosely structured collection of dance movements, the standard suite in Germany grouped together an allemande, a courante, a sarabande, and a gigue. But the layout of the suite varied, with an improvisational

---

* An intriguing recording titled *Gamba Sonatas, Riddle Preludes, Baroque Perpetua* by the Dutch cellist Pieter Wispelwey illustrates how much the beginning of the first cello suite resembles that of *The Well-Tempered Clavier*.

prelude sometimes introducing the music, and other dances thrown into the mix.

Bach decided to kick off each suite with a *prélude* (the name is taken from the French), a dramatic introduction with improvisation woven into its fibre. Bach's preludes are virtuosic scene-setters that give each suite personality. They are fantasias that operate outside the rigid tempos governing the other movements; they stop, start, and stray, soar to dizzying heights, hold their breath, and come crashing down. The essence of the story told by each suite is concentrated in the prelude.

The allemande, occupying the second position in every cello suite, was a popular dance that first appeared in Germany early in the sixteenth century. In Bach's day it had outgrown its function as music that was actually danced to and had become serious and solemn. In the Cello Suites the allemandes tend to be elegant and slow. Johann Mattheson, a contemporary of Bach's, described the allemande as "the image of a content or satisfied spirit, which enjoys good order and calm."

The French version of the courante (*courir* means "to run") was an aristocratic dance associated with the court of Louis XIV, who apparently danced it with impressive skill. But most of the courantes employed by Bach as the third movement in the Cello Suites are in fact *correntes*, inherited from Italian composers. Full of hops and springs, the *corrente* was danced in many parts of Europe in the late sixteenth and early seventeenth centuries. The effect is cheerful and sprightly.

After the courante comes the sarabande, the spiritual centre of each cello suite. The sarabande was at one time a hot-blooded Iberian dance that was as quick in tempo as passion. In the words of musicologist Peter Eliot Stone, it began its career as a "fast, lascivious dance, sung to obscene words, with dancers striking indecent poses and men and women dancing the 'last fulfillment of love'." But by Bach's time the sarabande had been stylized by the French court and mellowed to become the most languid of movements, a work of aching melancholy more than wanton release.

The fifth movement varies from suite to suite—Bach uses the minuet, bourrée, and gavotte, all popular French court dances. In Bach's lifetime they were considered "modern" dances, unlike the other movements in the suites, which by 1717 were for the most part no longer danced. The minuet, by contrast, said to symbolize Versailles' ideals of elegance and nobility, was danced well into the eighteenth century.

These so-called *galanterie* movements—the minuet (in suites one and two), as well as the bourrée (in suites three and four), and the gavotte (suites five and six)—are less intense than the other movements but by no means lightweight. There is a tunefulness in these dances that often makes them the most memorable parts of the whole. And there is a spring in their step, a joyous bounce, especially coming as they do on the heels of the wistful sarabande.

Every suite ends with a gigue. It is the sound of jaunty exclamation marks, a fiddling ditty. The French gigue takes its name from the English jig, which in turn was borrowed from the Old French *giguer,* "to dance," or the German *geige,* "fiddle." It is faster-paced than any of the other movements. One hears the devil-may-care merriment of a tavern player: here is the tune; dance to it—tomorrow another Thirty Years War may be upon us.

A MONTH AFTER he was thrown into the duke's jail for "too stubbornly forcing the issue of his dismissal," Bach was finally released. A report by the Weimar court secretary noted that on December 2, 1717, he was "freed from arrest with notice of his unfavourable discharge." Bach was free now to switch jobs, and promptly shook the dust of Weimar from his boots, making his way to the town of Cöthen, the tiny capital of a German territory ruled by a young prince.

His new employer was Prince Leopold, a twenty-three-year-old bachelor, well travelled and himself an amateur musician. Although Cöthen was a mere speck in the aristocratic universe, Leopold had adorned his miniature court with a first-rate band that had few equals anywhere. Bach was hired on as Capellmeister—leader of the *Capelle*, the princely orchestra.

Coming to this remote town after Weimar may have seemed hardly worth the move, much less risking one's liberty for. Surrounded by a medieval wall and dominated by the prince's castle, Cöthen was a marginal court located deep in a rural area; its detractors mocked it as "Cow-Cöthen." But in his new position of Capellmeister, Bach had reached the highest rank in the musical hierarchy at court. His only superior was Prince Leopold, who eagerly awaited the creations of his prized Capellmeister.

Leopold himself had studied music in Italy and could hold his own as a bass singer and viola da gamba player. He did not use music superficially to showcase his greatness; he "both understood and loved the art," as Bach would write in a rare letter years later. The prince, for his part, was clearly under the spell of Bach's talent.

It did not take long before Bach's music echoed from the candlelit rooms of Leopold's castle, his lush harmonies drifting across the sparkling moat and manicured gardens. An uncommonly friendly bond apparently developed between His Most Serene Highness and the master musician a decade his senior. Leopold and his Capellmeister would most probably be found in the ground-floor music room of the palace, the prince playing the viola da gamba and Bach leading the way on a wing-shaped harpsichord, their spirits refreshed from the castle's supply of brandy and tobacco.

Tranquility and contentment governed Bach's life during his first years at Cöthen. The prince was made godfather when Maria Barbara gave birth to a seventh child, Leopold Bach, who was baptized in the austere palace chapel. Bach was a highly valued member of the Cöthen court; he earned 400 thalers before bonuses and was given a generous budget for new instruments, music paper, copying, binding, and purchasing scores. Guest musicians were hired for special events, among them the famed bass Johann Gottfried Riemschneider, trumpeters to perform what became known as the *Brandenburg Concertos*, a lutenist, and a foreign musician who played a mysterious guitar-like instrument that might have given Bach ideas about just how far he could push notes on simple strings.

Bach's creative powers benefited from the small-scale aristocratic atmosphere in Cöthen. Supported by an encouraging patron, freed from deadline pressures and church demands, far removed from the intrigues of more important courts or the distractions of larger towns, the new Capellmeister was able to stretch out in breathtaking directions. But if some of the world's greatest instrumental music was the result of Bach's years at Cöthen, the Cello Suites among them, the world would not hear a single measure of it for a long time to come.

SARABANDE

Its movement is quiet and solemn, suggesting Spanish haughtiness, and its tone is grave and calm.
PHILIPP SPITTA, 1873

DOWN THE COAST from Barcelona, on a stretch of beach filled with vacationers, the austere notes of a solo cello can be heard. The sound of Pablo Casals performing Bach feels oddly out of place amid the sunbathing, paddleball, and sandcastles here on the Costa Dorada, Spain's golden coast. Yet a recording of his cello playing belongs nowhere more than here, the Villa Casals, a seaside museum that was once the home of the twentieth century's greatest cellist.

Searching for the man behind the Cello Suites meant not only J. S. Bach but also the cellist who discovered the music and hand-delivered it to the world. I took a summer vacation in Europe at the start of my search, aiming to learn what I could about Casals. The museum in San Salvador seemed a natural place to start.

The Villa Casals, enclosed by a peach-coloured wall with an iron gate, stands out in the down-market beach district of San Salvador. Its whitewashed façade is embellished with whimsical blue squares beneath a red-tiled roof. Classical sculptures eye the Mediterranean from atop the second-storey balustrade behind the villa. The seaside courtyard, full of meditative calm, contains a formal garden shaded by pines and palm trees, a reflecting pool of water, and an assortment of marble statues, including Apollo, god of light, inspiration, and music—all of which the villa has in abundance.

The Pablo Casals Museum has a highbrow aesthetic at odds with the beach-resort tourism that now surrounds it. Yet musical endeavours and seaside pleasures blended effortlessly for Casals. He cherished the sand and sea at San Salvador, which is not far from the Catalan village where he was born.

The museum is a seductive space, with the beach and the Mediterranean visible through its ample windows, but there's a ghoulish feel to much of the contents: pipes he smoked, ashtrays he filled, eyeglasses he peered through, the bed he slept on. Relics that Casals himself collected include a Beethoven death mask set on a rough stone that was taken from the room where the composer died; a piece of paper containing a few measures of music scrawled by Brahms; and in a gilt frame, a lock of Mendelssohn's hair.

As I meandered through the villa, a curtain suddenly rose electronically on the far side of a dining room, opening the way to a dimly lit salon. The room was arranged for concerts, with dozens of crimson upholstered chairs, a cello on display, and an eerie bust of Casals. Without warning a film materialized on a large screen and I took a seat. Casals emerged as if from the grave, in black and white, serious, sombre, with utter focus on the music that channelled through him. He was performing the allemande of the first suite, looking equal parts Zen master and Victorian solicitor: round glasses, unflinching gaze, left hand mapping out perilous archipelagos on the fingerboard, right hand moving the bow vessel-like, perfectly calm on a stormy sea of notes.

About four kilometres inland from the museum is the small, dusty Catalan town of Vendrell, where Casals was born in 1876.

His father, Carlos, was musical and political, qualities the son easily absorbed. Musically, Carlos was parish organist, choirmaster, and teacher. Politically, he was a Catalan patriot and an ardent republican.

Being a republican in Spain meant first and foremost opposition to the Bourbon monarchy, which got its blue blood from France's Louis xiv. Madrid had learned its royal lessons directly from the court of Versailles. At about the same time Bach was composing the Cello Suites, Spain's first Bourbon king, Philip of Anjou, grandson of Louis xiv, was abolishing Catalonia's autonomy. A ruggedly individualistic province like Catalonia stood only to lose from the Spanish Crown's centralizing rule. By the early nineteenth century, Madrid had outlawed Catalonia's penal law, coinage, and tribunals, even the right to speak the Catalan language in schools.

For a Catalan patriot like Carlos Casals, republicanism made perfect sense. He dreamed of a republic that did not exist: a federalist Spain composed of semi-independent states. Spain had on one occasion experienced a republic—the First Republic—but it lasted only a few months in 1873 before a pro-monarchy revolt broke out. During the monarchist uprising, Carlos Casals took to the hills with a small band of republicans to protect his village from the royal threat. But his efforts were in vain. He'd risked his life for a cause that was defeated, and Spanish generals put the monarchy back in power. Two years later, Pablo was born.

When Pablo came into the world on December 29—perilously, with the umbilical cord twisted around his neck—the Republic was a thing of the past. The young Alfonso xii was on the throne and Catalonia's autonomy was doomed. Catalan nationalism came as naturally as musical talent to Pablo.

Pablo's first music teacher was his father, who taught him piano, violin, flute, and—once his feet were able to reach the pedals—organ. He took to the instruments in no time and was able to carry a tune before he could string words together. When at the age of eight he heard some itinerant musicians in a street performance, he was awestruck by a one-stringed instrument made from a bent broom handle. Carlos, with help from a local barber, obliged Pablo by building an instrument out of a hollowed-out gourd, adding a string, a scroll, and a fingerboard. It was on this crude instrument that Pablo performed for a saint's day one evening at a crumbling twelfth-century cloister, somehow conjuring music out of the gourd by moonlight.

A few years later Pablo encountered his first real cello when a chamber trio from Barcelona performed in the village Catholic centre. He was instantly won over. From the moment he heard the first notes, the future virtuoso was overwhelmed, could barely breathe on account of the tender beauty of its sound. "Father, do you see that instrument?" he said. "I should like to play it." Carlos managed to find a junior-sized cello for Pablo, but he really wanted his son to become a carpenter.

While Pablo received his musical talent from his father, the push to succeed as a musician came from his mother, Doña Pilar, who decided to take the gifted boy beyond the provincial horizons of Vendrell. Doña Pilar herself did not quite fit into the village and was perhaps eager for a change of scenery. Her own parents had left Barcelona in the 1840s for Cuba and Puerto Rico, where she was born. But after both her father and brother committed suicide, Pilar's mother returned to Catalonia with her two children.

Pilar was a conspicuously independent woman, with a regal bearing and long, dark hair coiled neatly in two braids around her head. When her music lessons with the handsome church organist took a romantic turn, she married Carlos. But she would experience considerable heartache and pain, losing eight children to premature death. Pablo was her eldest, and intensely close to her heart.

Over the objections of her husband, Pilar arranged for the eleven-year-old boy to enrol in Barcelona's Municipal School of Music. In 1888 she moved to Barcelona with Pablo. Carlos, unhappy over the arrangement, stayed behind to make his living in Vendrell. Pablo flourished in Barcelona, excelling at school and progressing quickly on the cello. He was soon moonlighting in a café as part of a trio to help pay for his education. And within a couple of years he would discover something that would capture his heart and alter the course of music history.

MINUET

*This stately walking dance was the most popular
and widespread social dance at European courts
until well into the late eighteenth century.*

THE CELLO SUITES (BÄRENREITER EDITION, 2000)

IT WAS A leisurely stroll through the streets of Barcelona, past
the heroic monuments and flower stalls, the Gothic arches
and fashionable cafés, that rescued the world's greatest cello
music from obscurity. To imagine the scene, which took place
one afternoon sometime in 1890, we have to picture Pablo and
his father walking along the Ramblas, the city's most celebrated avenue, shaded by plane trees, lined with neoclassical
mansions, and teeming with markets selling fresh flowers,
local produce, and birds in cages.

At thirteen, Pablo was small for his age, shorter even than
the cello he was carrying, with close-cropped black hair, searching blue eyes, and a serious expression out of synch with his
youth. His father, visiting from Vendrell, had a few hours to
spend with the young cellist who was making a name for himself in the big city—they called him *el nen*, "the kid." Pablo,
who preferred his Catalan name of Pau, was working seven
nights a week in a trio at the Café Tost, which was well known
for its coffee and thick hot chocolate beverages. Earlier in the

day Carlos had bought Pablo his first adult-sized cello, and the two had their eyes open for sheet music the boy could use for his café concerts.

They strolled in the vicinity of the Columbus monument, towering sixty-two metres above the eight bronze lions at its base. It was a fiercely proud Columbus, the world's highest, clutching a parchment in one hand and pointing to the Mediterranean with the other, as if suggesting future discoveries. At some point Pablo and his father would have left the singing birds of the Ramblas and entered the tangle of narrow, twisting streets near the waterfront. Ironwork balconies were draped with laundry and flowers. The occasional stone gargoyle screamed mutely. There was a faint smell of the sea.

Father and son made their way through the cramped streets to one second-hand store after another, rummaging for cello music. On Carrer Ample they went into another music shop. As they rustled through the musty bundles of sheet music, some Beethoven cello sonatas were located. But what's this? A tobacco-coloured cover page inscribed with fanciful black lettering: *Six Sonatas or Suites for Solo Violoncello by Johann Sebastian Bach*. Was this what it appeared to be? The immortal Bach composed music for cello alone?*

Pesetas were paid for the sheet music. Pablo could not unglue his eyes from the pages, beginning with the first movement, the prelude to everything. He glided home through the twisting streets to the rhythm of a music that was taking shape in his imagination, the sensual mathematics of the score filling him from footsteps to fingertips.

He would have heard the first prelude as an opening statement, improvisatory, like a leisurely stroll that ends serendipitously. The ground is prepared for all that follows: structure,

---

* The edition Casals found was titled in French: *Six Sonates ou Suites pour Violoncelle Seul*.

character, narrative. The comfortable pulse undulates into more intricate passages. The baritone soliloquy grows in intensity, solidifying, gathering strength, ascending a great height where a vast panorama reveals itself. Pause for one beat. The stakes are raised. Struggle is pressed into service. In time, a satisfying denouement.

Pablo looked again at the score. He would practise it every day for twelve years before mustering the courage to play the suites in public.

PABLO CASALS WAS discovered not long after he found the Bach suites. The great Spanish pianist Isaac Albéniz happened to hear the young cellist perform at La Pajarera, a fashionable Barcelona club designed to look like a birdcage. Albéniz, smoking his trademark long cigar, tried to convince Doña Pilar to let him take the teenager under his wing and relocate to London for serious lessons. But Doña Pilar, who attended Pablo's every performance in those days, sitting alone at her regular table nursing a cup of coffee, was not about to send him off into the world alone. She declined. But she did accept Albéniz's offer to write a letter of introduction to Count Guillermo de Morphy, chief adviser to the Queen Regent of Spain.

Two years later, after Pablo had finished his studies at the Municipal School of Music and won top prizes, the letter was finally used. Carlos had by then moved to Barcelona to join the family, which now included two more boys. He continued to oppose Pablo's career as a musician and, as usual, was outvoted. Carlos returned to Vendrell, and the rest of his family made the journey to distant Madrid in a cold third-class railway carriage.

Immediately upon arrival, the Casalses went to the townhouse of the Count de Morphy and presented the letter to his butler. Pablo and his family were ushered into an elegant drawing room, where they were warmly received by the count. After reading Albéniz's letter of introduction, the count asked

Pablo to play his cello. He was instantly won over. Soon Pablo was receiving instruction on how to conduct himself in the presence of royalty. He first impressed the queen's sister-in-law ("You were right. He is a marvel."). He was then summoned to the palace to play for Queen María Cristina, and by the time he lifted his bow from the strings, the sixteen-year-old café musician had won the highest patronage in the land. The little family was awarded a living allowance to support Pablo's education. Music lessons took place, though already by this time there was no one in Madrid who could teach Pablo anything about the cello.

Pablo became a fixture in the royal palace. There were weekly sessions with the Queen Regent in her private chambers. He played the cello, trying out his compositions; the two joined forces for duets on the piano, mostly four-handed Mozart; and Pablo played toy soldiers with Alfonso, the seven-year-old future king. "Does your Royal Highness like music?" Pablo once asked the boy. "Yes," came the reply, "it pleases me. But what I want most is to be given some guns."

Eighteen months went by, and Pablo, now seventeen years old, was fully formed as a virtuoso cellist. In the fall of 1894 he played some concerts in the provinces with a chamber ensemble. In Santiago de Compostela, one review praised to the moon "a violoncellist of such extraordinary merit that, hearing him play, one wants to examine his instrument to see if there exists inside some nest of spirits entrusted with producing such an outpouring of art." The writer for another newspaper, *El Alcance*, was no less effusive:

> His bow, sometimes sweet as a voice from heaven, at other times vibrant and robust, produces such a sonorous combination of voices and tones that it seems that the body of his violoncello is the magic secret of sublime harmonies capriciously transformed at the contact of that hand...the most

inspired muse, the most artistic intuition...his violoncello appears to speak, to moan, to whisper...to exhale sighs and to sing...

Pablo was by now recognized as the most impressive musical talent in all of Spain. But he was not impressed with what he considered the "airs and pretensions" of court. And politics, not for the last time, clashed with his cello. The Count de Morphy wanted to turn Pablo into a composer who would free Spanish audiences from the rage for Italian opera. There were royal designs on his cello for it to be patriotically enlisted to create great Spanish opera. The Queen wanted him to join the royal *chapelle* (or *Capelle*, as Bach would have called it). But Pablo and his mother followed their own agenda. He would not become a court-appointed composer; instead he would focus on playing the cello.

Once Pablo and his mother had made up their minds that his future was as a cellist, not as a patriotic instrument of the Spanish court, the family left Madrid, never to return. In 1895, after they had spent the summer by the sea at San Salvador, Pablo, Doña Pilar, and her two other sons, Enrique and Luis (without Carlos, who as usual stayed behind), made their way to Brussels. The Count de Morphy, wanting to keep as much royal control over the young cellist as possible, arranged for Pablo to enrol at the Brussels Conservatory in exchange for a royal allowance of 250 pesetas a month.

Doña Pilar rented a cheap *pension* and Pablo soon went off to the rococo conservatory building. The first day of study did not go well. In a class filled with French-speaking students wearing their hair fashionably shoulder length and decked out in velvet jackets and silk ascots, Pablo looked painfully out of place. He was not much taller than five feet, had short hair, wore a plain suit, and spoke only halting French. After the teacher, the esteemed cellist Edouard Jacobs, had ignored him for the better part of the day, finally some remarks were made to the class about "the little Spaniard" in their midst. Jacobs asked him what he would like to play. "Anything you like," replied Pablo, not meaning to be arrogant. But his remark drew chuckles from his classmates and sarcasm from Jacobs.

Pablo was asked to perform "Souvenir de Spa," a piece full of difficult pyrotechnics. He knew it well, having performed it in Spain the previous year. He poured all his fury into the piece, and when it was over, total silence hung over the class. Jacobs quickly reversed his attitude, fawning all over the "little Spaniard," beckoning him into a nearby office, accepting him into the conservatory, and promising him first prize in the annual competition. But it was too late. Pablo, incensed over the way he'd been treated, refused the offer and stormed out.

Within a few days the Casalses were on a train headed for Paris. The French capital seemed to offer more promise than a classroom at this stage in Pablo's career. He was hired by a second-rate music hall on the Champs-Élysées. Doña Pilar took in piecework sewing while looking after the two younger boys in their rented hovel. But Pablo was forced to leave his job after becoming ill with dysentery and gastroenteritis. His mother returned home without her hair one day after selling it for a few francs to a wigmaker. Leaving Brussels had meant that Pablo was stripped of his paycheque from the Spanish crown, and the family was on the brink of desperation. Doña Pilar dispatched a telegram to Carlos, who sent money to bring his family home.

Back in Spain, things rapidly improved. After a much-needed vacation in San Salvador, Pablo found himself benefiting from a scandal involving his former cello professor and a married woman. The professor fled Barcelona and Pablo took over his teaching position at the city's top music school. He quickly settled into the routine of a professional cellist, becoming lead cello for the Liceo Opera House, a member of national chamber ensembles, and star soloist at concerts across the country — a "national glory," in the words of one newspaper account.

There were also trips to Madrid and an emotional reunion with the Count de Morphy, who did not hold a grudge. Neither did the Queen Regent, who presented Casals with a small sapphire to remember her by, as well as funds to purchase his first serious cello, a Gagliano. He grew a moustache, let his hair get longer, and had the sapphire set into his bow.

Barcelona at the end of the century, with its lively cafés, *modernismo* architecture, and animated street life, no doubt had its charms for a young musician. "The Barcelonans," observed an early *Baedeker's* guide to the country, "combine the vivacity of the Gaul with the dignity of the Castilian, while their appreciation of music recalls the Teuton. In no town in the Iberian peninsula flows a more vigorous and cheerful tide of life; and none makes so cosmopolitan an impression."

But the political and economic atmosphere in Catalonia worsened badly during the 1890s. Barcelona itself was convulsed by political violence. There were bitter social divisions, new ideologies, and anarchist bombs, one of which notoriously exploded in the Liceo Opera House, killing twenty-four. The situation further declined after the pathetic defeat of Spain's armed forces in the Spanish-American War of 1898, which lost the country its remnants of empire: Cuba, the Philippines, and Puerto Rico. Casals would never forget the spectre of gaunt, hungry Spanish soldiers whose food and equipment had been sold by corrupt officers during the war, disembarking at the port of Barcelona like so many ghosts.

It is difficult to overstate the backwardness of Spain as the nineteenth century wore to a close and a sixteen-year-old was about to become king. Political and economic corruption was endemic. Life expectancy was about thirty-five years, no more than it had been when Christopher Columbus was setting sail.

Illiteracy rates averaged about sixty-four percent. In the first decade of the new century, more than half a million Spaniards, out of a population of 18.5 million, would emigrate to the New World.

In 1899, at age twenty-two, Casals saw no future in Spain. He left for Paris once again, this time without his mother or support from the Spanish crown—and this time in pursuit of an international career. He was a solo cellist, already the best cellist in Europe, though nobody yet knew it.

After arriving in Paris, Casals got in touch with the American soprano Emma Nevada, whom he knew from her frequent performances in Madrid. Nevada was on her way to London, where she had two concerts planned, and invited Casals along. She arranged for his London debut at a Crystal Palace concert, which led to positive reviews and invitations to play private recitals at the homes of wealthy music lovers.

One of those contacts led to the highest rung of the social ladder: an invitation to perform before Queen Victoria. Ruler of the British Empire since 1837, Victoria liked music, and on one memorable occasion half a century earlier had sung contralto while a visiting Felix Mendelssohn played along. At Casals' royal recital, which took place on the Isle of Wight, a turbaned Indian servant placed a small stool under the feet of the eighty-year-old monarch, who then raised a plump hand to signal the start of the music. Victoria wrote in her journal that evening of "a very modest young man, whom the Queen of Spain has had educated... He has a splendid tone and plays with much execution and feeling."

After returning to Paris, Casals went to see Charles Lamoureux, the foremost conductor in France. He carried a letter of recommendation from the Count de Morphy, but the French conductor, who was famously bad-tempered and suffering from rheumatism, was only irritated by the intrusion. However,

Lamoureux grudgingly read the count's letter and asked Casals to return the next day for an audition.

The next day, Casals played the first movement from Édouard Lalo's Cello Concerto in D minor. Lamoureux's disinterest melted away after a few bars; the ailing conductor got to his feet while Casals was still playing, making his way with difficulty to the young cellist. When the first movement was over, he embraced Pablo, tears in his eyes, declaring: *"Mon petit,* you are one of the elect."*

Within a few weeks Lamoureux had arranged for Casals' Paris debut. He joined Lamoureux's orchestra for its performance of *Tristan,* later taking the solo spotlight for the Lalo concerto. *Le Temps* praised the cellist for "an enchanting sound and a beautiful virtuosity." A month later, Casals played the Saint-Saëns cello concerto. The crowd erupted, and Lamoureux embraced the cellist. For Casals it was the start of an international career. "Almost overnight, following my concerts with Lamoureux, wide recognition came to me," he later recalled. "I was besieged with requests to play at concerts and recitals. Suddenly all doors were open to me."

---

* It was not by accident that Lamoureux employed the same French word (*predestiné*) that Schumann had famously used to describe a young Brahms.

GIGUE

Ends the suite in an atmosphere of optimism and cheerfulness. DIMITRI MARKEVITCH

IT WAS DRIZZLING and dark outside the Montreal restaurant when I asked the waitress for the bill, explaining that I was rushing to make a concert at 8 p.m. "U2?" she inquired. Virtually everyone under the age of fifty knew that the Irish rock band was playing at the Bell Centre that evening. Few were aware that the city's first annual Bach Festival was also underway. A gala concert was being held at a downtown Presbyterian church. The program seemed like a greatest hits list: a cello suite, a Brandenburg concerto, one tune from the *St. Matthew Passion*, an orchestral suite, including Air on a G String, a couple of cantatas, and a "new" Bach aria recently discovered in a shoebox.

U2, which has been performing since 1976, was showcasing its own new material and golden oldies. But will the rock band's oeuvre still be performed three centuries from now? And will music scholars be sifting through old shoeboxes in search of lost U2 compositions? It is very possible. One also expects that Bach will continue to be a major musical figure, but there's only so much music that posterity can possibly have time for.

The U2 concert drew more than 20,000 fans on two nights running, and chances are they would have continued to draw big numbers if more shows had been scheduled. Inside the Church of St. Andrew and St. Paul, the venue of the Bach concert, no more than 250 people sat quietly in the pews. The crowd, as usual for classical music, was composed mostly of elderly people and music students. The audience members studied their programs as if preparing for an exam.

A shroud of stuffiness surrounds classical music concerts. Nobody feels they have the right to speak; throat-clearing is meant to be done between movements, when, incidentally, we can't even applaud and are forced to sit on our hands until the entire opus comes to a close. It wasn't always this regulated. Until half a century or so ago crowds applauded after every movement. And why shouldn't the audience be able to unleash its bravos or reward a smoking instrumental solo in real time? In Bach's day there was no such hushed reverence. The audience—maybe not in church, but certainly at venues like Zimmerman's coffee house in Leipzig, where he performed many of his works—drank, smoked, circulated, chatted, and occasionally groaned that Bach was going off on one of his convoluted fugal tangents again, or burst into applause over one of his finger-sprinting solos.

The only way to take classical music out of the museum is to stop playing it in a museum. The adventurous cellist Matt Haimovitz said as much recently, when he toured dive bars, pizza parlours, and roadhouse juke joints with the Cello Suites. "People were reacting to the music as it was going by," Haimovitz told CBC Radio, "and if they really enjoyed something or were impressed by something, they howled or whistled or sighed, and yet they were totally riveted to the music. At first it was disconcerting because I'm so used to waiting until the end of the piece for a reaction, but having an immediate reaction like that was extraordinary, and in my opinion in character with these pieces—they should make you laugh and cry and everything else." Classical concert setups will have to get with the

program of the twenty-first century—get their listeners' heads
out of the programs and bring a little looseness to a rigid listening ritual—if younger music fans are ever going to shuffle
Bach alongside Bono, Beck, and Björk on their digital playlists.

In the meantime, inside a Presbyterian church, the gala concert for the Bach Festival kicked off with a solo cello. Phoebe
Carrai, a reputable Boston-based cellist with a bird's nest of
frizzy hair, launched into Suite No. 3 at high speed. The prelude's great downward scale was a Bachian blur that warranted a
traffic ticket for speeding. There were some nice touches—the
fat double stops of the sarabande, the jaunty barnstorming of the
bourrée, and the positively Zeppelinesque rock guitar riffs of
the gigue—but from twenty-three rows back the cello sounded
a bit muddy. Most of the credit belonged to the composer.

Next up, a baroque ensemble took its chairs to back up hometown countertenor Daniel Taylor. The piece was the famous
aria "Erbarme dich" from the *St. Matthew Passion*. It was spine-
shivering, a jewel-encrusted melody on a velvet swath of organ
and strings. To enjoy it one didn't have to think about Jesus,
though the stained-glass window towering above the musicians
depicted a benevolent Christ with arms outstretched. Instead I
contemplated Prince Leopold's funeral, how Bach reworked
this spiritual music to pay homage to his departed prince and
offer it up as a funeral dirge for a court in mourning. The flags
lining the church's stone side walls looked weather-beaten, like
medieval standards that had been carried into battle.

Elsewhere in the city, Bono may have been singing "Sunday,
Bloody Sunday," perhaps waving an Irish flag tossed onto the
stage. That's what happened when I reviewed the band's 1997
concert for the *Gazette*. It was one of the first concert reviews
I'd written for the daily newspaper, which meant exiting the
show halfway through and furiously typing on a laptop from
some high-altitude press room in the cavernous Olympic
Stadium. My review began: "Filter out the high-tech hoopla,

the muddy sound and dubious new songs, a rock show of the highest order was struggling to be heard at U2's Olympic Stadium extravaganza last night. Ignore the towering McDonaldesque arch, turn a blind eye to the world's biggest high-definition TV set blitzkrieging computerized animation, and avoid the industrial-sized olive atop a 30-metre toothpick... but who could? Beneath it all, somewhere, was U2. For those among the 52,000 fans who wanted to see more than four Lilliputian musicians' making huge noises in the Olympic Stadium Sunday night, technology blew everything out of proportion." (The hate mail rolled in soon after publication.)

There is little in the way of hoopla or technology at your average Bach concert. The church interior at the Bach Fest was austere. Amid the heavy stone walls and dark wood of the pews the musicians repositioned onstage for the piece at hand. The men were in tuxes, the women in black formal attire. The instrumentalists took their places, checked their scores, and emitted a drone of notes, moving first from the low-end registers of cello and bass to the violins and then to the winds, like a game of sonic tag, until all the instruments were on the same wavelength. (The squall of tuning always sounds fetching to me.) Then singers stood formally onstage, straight-backed, stiffly holding dark books that contained the German text, the content of which generally makes it easier to enjoy if one doesn't understand the language.

The concert also featured the local premiere of "Alles mit Gott," the aria in Bach's hand that had been discovered just a few months earlier in a shoebox. This charming music for soprano and harpsichord was composed in Weimar for Duke Wilhelm Ernst, the same duke who threw him in jail a few years later. The manuscript, written in Bach's swirling calligraphy, was stuffed in the shoebox with other poems and letters written to fete the duke's fifty-second birthday in 1713. The Weimar library, where the music was stored for three

centuries, had recently burned to the ground; by chance the
box containing the aria was removed before the fire.

The aria sounded immediately familiar and sweet in performance, with soprano Dominique Labelle doing the catchy
vocal melody justice. After each stanza of the poem the strings
would swell with gusto, led by violinist Cynthia Roberts, swaying in a sinuous and sexy way that embodied Bach's rhythm.
Meanwhile, cellist Phoebe Carrai, granny glasses perched on
her nose, intently concentrated on the score while providing
the low-end scaffolding of the piece. It was as if she were playing the cello suite again, but only a few phrases, extended ad
infinitum to buttress this pretty little ditty. The aria is not a
major work. Stretched to the max it lasts only about ten minutes. There is none of the high-minded contrapuntal intricacy
that became Bach's calling card; in its place is something more
human in scale and intimate. A beautiful melody that was shut
up in a shoebox for nearly three centuries had been released
back into the world. One couldn't help wondering what other
Bach treasures might be languishing in storage elsewhere.

SUITE NO. 2

(D minor)

PRELUDE

Should one, as a rare exception, add something here?
Add some notes in a text where the composer, in general,
is so clearly using as few as possible?
ANNER BYLSMA, BACH, THE FENCING MASTER

THREE NOTES ESTABLISH a gut-wrenching sadness. There's a slight tremor on the fingerboard, the bow a harbinger of difficult news. The cello, wavering at first touch, recovers its equilibrium and reports a painful chronicle. After the buoyancy of the first suite, the mood has shifted. The key is minor, the three notes a tragic triad. The tones move closer and closer to a harrowing vision, weaving spider-like, relentlessly gathering sound into tighter concentric circles that come to an abrupt stop. Nothing fills the empty space. A tiny prayer is uttered.

In May 1720, Bach and a handful of musicians from the court orchestra accompanied Prince Leopold on a trip to take the waters at a spa in Carlsbad, where the fashionable aristocracy summered along with their retinues. Carlsbad was situated in Bohemia, farther south than Bach had ever ventured. Its medicinal springs, popular since the fourteenth century, had become fashionable as an aristocratic vacation spot after the newly crowned Holy Roman Emperor Charles VI began regular visits from Vienna in 1711 to what became known as the "imperial spa."

When Prince Leopold and Bach visited, the spa was abuzz with nobility from Moscow to Venice. The casinos were in full swing. Aristocrats with frail constitutions debated the various spring-water cures. Music and theatre performances were staged. As servants carried around Leopold's new harpsichord, Bach and his five colleagues from Cöthen must have been in their element. The core members of the *Capelle* had been employed by the King of Prussia until 1713 and were comfortable in elevated aristocratic situations. The backwoods town of Cöthen was a provincial comedown from Berlin, and Carlsbad may have provided a welcome cosmopolitanism. The musicians likely traded stories about the peccadilloes of the nobility; the competition was eyed (other princes had dragged along their own retinues) and prospective employers contemplated.

For Leopold, his music-makers provided personal entertainment while flaunting his miniature court's sophistication. The jewel in Leopold's showcase was his Capellmeister. Now thirty-five years old, Bach had some brilliant compositions to his name, especially some secular instrumental works he'd been working on at Cöthen. He'd written a fair bit of unconventional music for the gut strings of a cello. What better venue than Carlsbad for a debut performance of a cello suite? It was easily portable music, requiring just one instrument. One of the Cöthen court musicians—either Christian Bernhard Linigke, a cellist, or the gambist and cellist Christian Ferdinand Abel—may have essayed the music for the prince and his guests.

After more than a month at the spa town, Leopold and his court musicians headed back to Cöthen. During the journey home, Bach's thoughts would have turned to his wife, Maria Barbara, and their four young children. But not long after the travellers had reached the prince's castle and Bach was approaching his house near the medieval walls, a foreboding took hold.

When he got home, Maria Barbara was nowhere to be seen. Who was it who revealed the devastating news when he walked through his front door? Was it twelve-year-old Dorothea? Her younger brother William Friedemann? Or was it some relative who was taking care of the children?

Maria Barbara was dead. The burial notice from the Cöthen register of deaths, one of the few mentions of Bach's presence there to have survived, was terse: "July 7, the wife of Mr. Johann Sebastian Bach, Capellmeister to His Highness the Prince, was buried."

One can almost hear the scene in this movement. The dread that begins this prelude in a minor key follows an initial suite — a lifetime — of joy. The last measures of the prelude could well depict Bach entering his home, heart racing, anticipation modulating into panic. What has happened? Where is she? And then a young child, a shadow of his or her former rambunctious self — small, alone, a broken chord. He won't see Mother again.

THE LISTENER IS forced to imagine what is going on. There are hints, gaps, half-uttered statements, and fragmented lines in the Cello Suites. This stems from the cello itself, which is a melodic instrument, melodic because no more than two strings can generally be bowed at the same time. That limits how much harmony — the simultaneous playing of different notes — can be achieved. Melody — successive notes strung out in a horizontal timeline — moves straight ahead chronologically. But harmony is a vertical stacking of notes.

Harmony was Bach's specialty. At the summit of his harmony was polyphony, the braiding of two or more musical lines that create a greater whole while at the same time retaining their separateness. So how does Bach accomplish harmony with just one cello? How does he compose for a situation in which he cannot stack the notes vertically and pull off his trademark polyphony? He does it by creating "implied harmony."

He hints at it, suggests it, plants the seed of harmony. He removes as many notes as possible to strip the polyphony down to its bare essentials and let the listener fill in the blanks. He alternates fragments of different lines from different registers and tricks the listener into thinking he or she is hearing more than one line at the same time. Bach *implies* harmony.

I once sat in on a master class given by Anner Bylsma, the Dutch cellist, who spoke about how "thrifty" Bach had to be in the Cello Suites, as he was working with only four fingers and four strings. "It's funny," said Bylsma, "how much you can leave out in music and still make the picture complete in the mind of the listener."

Chords are another occasion for implied harmony in the Cello Suites. The cello cannot produce full chords, which are formed by at least three notes played simultaneously. Now and then in the Cello Suites two notes are bowed together, which is called a double stop. Every time it happens, the result tickles some nerve endings in the listener that appreciate a fat low-end sound. It is as if the cello, limited for the most part to sounding single notes, is straining to couple two of them together, the solitude of individual notes finding momentary union.

It is not quite a chord. There are numerous chords in the Cello Suites, but since a chord is formed by striking three notes at the same time, they cannot be played as such on the cello. Instead they are broken, or to use the musical term, arpeggiated. The broken chord, or arpeggio, is instead played in staggered form, note after note—another way that Bach implies harmony.

Arpeggios can be played in various ways—in the absence of precise musical instructions from Bach, cellists trying to approximate chords in the music have to use their imagination. So do listeners. Hearing Bach's tragic loss in the prelude here may seem to be overly imaginative. But the elegiac mood of this suite fits with a sense of grieving, and the timing of Bach's tragedy overlaps with its possible date of composition.*

BACH COULD DO nothing more than visit his wife's grave. Thirteen years together, nine children, four of whom survived, and the relationship was terminated without warning, the most important person in his life transposed into memory. And if his grief needed a musical tonic, there were few outlets. The palace church in Cöthen was Calvinist, which frowned on any sort of elaborate music. The pastor at the Lutheran church was a dubious character, and the inferior organ there was not worth playing.

His mind may have wandered elsewhere, to nearby Dresden, not to mention to Rome or London or Paris—where music-makers were celebrated, vast numbers of listeners were packing opulent venues to hear opera, and lesser composers than Bach had become famous. And here he was, isolated, cut off from the musical world by the moat of a minor prince. What had life become?

And so in November, four months after Maria Barbara's death, Bach found himself in a stagecoach—first-class travel of the day—en route to the bustling metropolis of Hamburg. A church organist's job had become vacant at St. Jacobi's Church, which boasted a four-manual organ with sixty speaking stops,

....
* Other clues link this suite to the death of Maria Barbara. One theory holds that Bach composed his Partita in D Minor for solo violin as an epitaph for his deceased wife. The second cello suite, similarly for a solo string instrument and likely composed in the same period, is in the same key. And for the sarabande and minuet of this cello suite Bach may have borrowed music from the great keyboard player François Couperin. The opening of the sarabande is strikingly similar to Couperin's "La Sultane," also in D minor and thought to have been composed in 1712 in memory of Marie Adelaide, wife of the Dauphin of France, who died young. If Bach was borrowing some of these notes from Couperin it was likely with an overlapping sense of mourning.

and Bach was in the running. Bach tried his hand at the excellent organ there, as well as at St. Catharine's Church, where he played for more than two hours to an audience that included the famed organist Reincken.

Nearly two decades earlier Bach had journeyed from Lüneburg to Hamburg in order to see Reinken, an old man, kimono-clad, already appearing to be History itself. The organist, ninety-seven years old now, was impressed with Bach's half-hour improvisation on the hymn "By the Waters of Babylon." "I thought such art was dead," he is quoted as saying, "but I see it still lives in you."

In the end, Bach either experienced reservations about the job or was unwilling to pay the large sum to the church that employment there oddly required. There was some outrage that the job went to the son of a wealthy tradesman who could "prelude better with thalers than with his fingers." In any event, church records show that Bach was unable to stay in Hamburg for an audition, as he was obliged to "travel to join his prince."

But Bach continued to pull out all the stops to secure work elsewhere. His next bid for employment would focus on the mighty city that held political sway over minuscule Cöthen.

ALLEMANDE

Now the allemande is a broken, serious, and well-constructed harmony, which is the image of a content or satisfied spirit, which enjoys good order and calm.

JOHANN MATTHESON, 1739

IT DID NOT transpire until long after Bach's death, but the upstart kingdom of Prussia would ultimately take control of Germany. Its Hohenzollern-ruling dynasty, guided by Chancellor Otto von Bismarck in the nineteenth century, would annex all the lands between Cologne and Königsberg, and after 1871 rule as emperors of Germany.

But in the early eighteenth century, Prussia was just one of many German states comprising the crazy quilt that was the Holy Roman Empire. The idea that Prussia, with its capital, Berlin, would gain leadership of a greater Germany would have sounded highly improbable. If Bach's contemporaries ever contemplated pan-German leadership, they would have put their money on Austria, say, or Saxony. That would rapidly change. In Bach's own lifetime Berlin was transformed from a desolate backwater into a formidable power known as "Sparta of the North."

Bach never lived in Berlin. But after his death, the Prussian capital would be the springboard for his reputation. And Berlin played an instrumental, if not immediately obvious, role in Bach's life—and the Cello Suites.

Berlin's rise to power can be traced back to Bach's early years, when the Prussian ruler Frederick William of Brandenburg, known as the Great Elector, held power. By creating a granite-strong army, the Great Elector laid the foundation for the kingdom of Prussia. He died in 1688 and was succeeded by his son Frederick 1, a fun-loving ruler given to much wasteful pomp. Frederick's main accomplishment was obtaining the title of king. He managed this in 1701, by offering a contingent of much-needed Prussian soldiers to the Holy Roman Emperor during the War of the Spanish Succession. For the coronation, Frederick went all out to flaunt his newly acquired kingship—thirty thousand horses were required to transport the court from Berlin to the site of his crowning in Königsberg, where he donned a diamond-studded ceremonial robe that today would be worth several hundred thousand dollars.

Upon Frederick's death in 1713, his son, another Frederick William—this one known to history as the Soldier King—reshaped power in his own austere image. The Soldier King promptly rid his court of the unessentials: silk stockings, wigs, pearls, fans, delicate gloves, and twenty-course meals were all seen as decadent trappings of the *ancien régime*. Architecture, dancing, and painting were deemed useless. Intellectuals were no longer welcome at the Berlin Academy, where a court jester was appointed president.

The new regime put itself on a war footing. Order, efficiency, and cleanliness were the new priorities. In the realm of music, the court orchestra, the Berlin *Capelle,* was unceremoniously fired. There was no room for effete music-making in the Soldier King's realm.

The king's boorish move against music, however, proved a boon for one unintended beneficiary: J. S. Bach. Young Prince Leopold of Cöthen was soaking up everything musical on his

European "grand tour" when he learned that the excellent musicians of the Berlin *Capelle* were suddenly unemployed. Leopold prevailed upon his mother, the Queen Regent, to hire as many of the musicians as his court could afford. Six musicians were immediately engaged, to be followed a short time later by a former colleague, the cellist Christian Bernhard Linigke. In one bold stroke, Leopold's orchestra was transformed into a top-flight musical establishment.

When Bach was hired in Cöthen in 1717, the court *Capelle* consisted of sixteen musicians, the core of whom came from the disbanded Berlin *Capelle*, courtesy of rising Prussian militarism. The expertise of the *Capelle* was key—no run-of-the-mill string player could inspire Bach's pen or execute his ideas. Bach rose to the occasion of having the finest players under his command: he proceeded to compose technically demanding instrumental music. The Cello Suites could only have been written with a masterful string player in mind, either the cellist Linigke or the gambist Christian Ferdinand Abel. Berlin's loss was Bach's gain.

There is a straight line connecting Prussia's militarization with the six suites for solo cello.

Bach visited Berlin—for the first time, so far as we know—in March 1719. He was sent there, 165 kilometres from Cöthen, by Prince Leopold to oversee the purchase of a new harpsichord that had been commissioned to Michael Mietke, the renowned instrument-builder to the Prussian court. All that is known about the trip is that Bach spent 130 thalers from Leopold's purse on the two-keyboard harpsichord. The new instrument was in the Cöthen palace by mid-March. And Bach left Berlin with something else: plans to dedicate to a Prussian noble a composition that would one day be famously known as the *Brandenburg Concertos*.

Margrave Christian Ludwig of Brandenburg was a son of Prussia's Great Elector by his second wife, which meant that he was not in line to inherit the throne; it was the margrave's

half-brother who reigned as the first Prussian king. And it was
the margrave's nephew, the Soldier King, who fired the Berlin
Capelle. While the Soldier King obsessed over Prussia's military
might, Christian Ludwig kept culture alive in his own household. Music was one of his priorities.

It is assumed that Bach played for the margrave during his
visit to Berlin, because he later dedicated his *Brandenburg Concertos* to this member of the Prussian royal family. But he might
have met him earlier, during one of Prince Leopold's trips to
Carlsbad. In Bach's dedication of 1721, he refers to a performance before the margrave two years earlier and his request
for some of his compositions. His dedication is penned in
courtly French and styled in the exaggerated humility that was
typical for the times:

> To His Royal Highness
> Monseigneur
> Cretien Louis
> Margraf de Brandenbourg &c. &c. &c.
> Monseigneur

As I had the pleasure a couple of years ago of being heard by
Your Royal Highness, in accordance with your commands,
and of observing that you took some delight in the small musical talent that Heaven has granted me, and as, when I took my
leave of Your Royal Highness, you did me the honor of requesting that I send you some of my compositions, I have therefore
followed your most gracious commands and taken the liberty
of discharging my humble obligation to Your Royal Highness
with the present concertos which I have adapted to several
instruments, begging you most humbly not to judge their
imperfections by the standards of that refined and delicate
taste in music that everyone knows you to possess, but rather
to accept, with benign consideration, the profound respect and

most humble devotion that I attempt to show by this means. For the rest, Monseigneur, I most humbly beg Your Royal Highness to be so kind as to continue your good grace towards me, and to be assured that I desire nothing more than to be employed on occasions more worthy of you and your service, being with unparalleled zeal,

Monseigneur,

Your Royal Highness's
most humble and most obedient servant,
Coethen, 24 March 1721   Jean Sebastien Bach*

There is a clue in the *Brandenburg Concertos* that helps explain why Bach wrote the Cello Suites. The cello was a background instrument in 1720, expected to hug the shoreline of a tune's progression, not an adventurous solo vessel. The viola da gamba was a more popular, exciting instrument in the same range as the cello. So why did Bach write solo string works for the cello, and not the gamba?

In the Brandenburgs, Bach composed each suite for a different set of instruments (his actual title for the work was *Six concerts avec plusieurs instruments*, or *Six Concertos for Several Instruments*). The instruments employed were tailored to the musicians in the Cöthen *Capelle*. In the sixth concerto, the instrumentation turned conventional string wisdom on its head: the viola da gamba parts are undemanding, while the more modern viola and cello are called upon for solo duty. Bach shows a penchant in these concertos for juxtaposing instruments in novel ways, but there is another reason why the cello is given more demanding parts than the viola da gamba: the gamba was played by Prince Leopold. And while Leopold

....
* The archaic spelling, rendered in eighteenth-century courtly French, is in Bach's original dedication.

may have been a competent player, he would not have been in the same league as the virtuosos in his *Capelle*. Since Bach was writing for an orchestra that often included the prince on gamba, the composer did not want to embarrass Leopold, or make the music suffer.

The viola da gamba parts "are undemanding and may have been written for Leopold himself to play with [*Capelle* gambist] C. F. Abel," writes the Bach scholar Malcolm Boyd. The result is wonderfully effervescent music that makes only modest demands on the gamba player. The same logic applies to the Cello Suites. Composing extremely demanding music for the gamba at Leopold's court would not have been tactful, because it was the prince's instrument. With the cello, Bach could be as musically ambitious as he wanted.

COURANTE

The difference between the reputation that Bach enjoyed in his lifetime and that which accumulated posthumously is one of the remarkable phenomena in the history of music. PERCY M. YOUNG

BACH WAS NOT famous in his own lifetime. He was never a European sensation as was Beethoven or Mozart or his contemporary Handel. His low-profile career took place in the anonymous outskirts of Germany, before Germany was Germany. He never lived in a major city like Vienna, London, or Paris, which enabled other composers to become hugely famous in their lifetimes. He never wrote opera, never having worked in a city that had an opera house, and opera was the only road to musical fame in those days.

Bach's musical style didn't help his cause. Polyphony, the intricate blending of two or more musical lines, fell out of fashion. Many of his contemporaries and the generation that followed considered the polyphonic style burdened with excessive learning, convoluted and old hat, out of step with the lighter, gayer times.

Whatever renown Bach did enjoy as a musician didn't have much to do with his compositions, precious few of which were printed. Only nine works were published during his career, among them relatively minor items such as an early cantata composed for the annual changing of the town council in Mühlhausen.*

In the words of Bach scholar Friedrich Blume, any noteworthiness that Bach achieved in his day "was as an organist and harpsichordist, as a dreaded technical expert and adviser on the organ, as an uncanny master of the art of counterpoint, as a teacher, but not as composer... The silence could not have been any deeper if his compositions had never existed at all."

But the silence would not last forever. Four of Bach's sons became professional musicians, two of them famous in their own right, and they, together with a large number of his dedicated students, made sure that many of his compositions would be projected far into the future. In some circles, albeit small ones far removed from the mainstream, "Old Bach" was known and revered.

Four decades after his death, for example, Mozart heard a Bach motet at a church in Leipzig and was powerfully startled by the music, asking, "What is this?" When the double chorus was over he cried out, "Now this is something one can learn from!" Beethoven, who as a twelve-year-old first got attention in Vienna for playing The Well-Tempered Clavier, would call Bach the "progenitor of harmony." But these artists, part of a professional elite, were ahead of their time.

The first biography of Bach was published only in 1802, more than half a century after his death. The biographer was

....
* Other printed works included the Clavier-Übung, which included six keyboard partitas published in three volumes during the 1730s, as well as the Goldberg Variations (1741), and the Musical Offering (composed for Frederick the Great in 1747). Bach's monumental The Art of the Fugue was published one year after his death, but it sold a mere thirty copies and its plates were eventually melted down and sold for scrap by his son C. P. E. A handful of keyboard works were published with pedagogical objectives during the fifty years after Bach's death. And a few music dealers offered some Bach works for sale in manuscript form.

Johann Nikolaus Forkel, a shoemaker's son who went on to become one of Germany's most influential music historians and theorists. His slim volume was published at a time of political ferment in Europe, when the French Revolution and the Napoleonic Wars were acting as triggers for German nationalism. Forkel's biography is stamped with national pride. "The works which Johann Sebastian Bach has left us," he writes,

> are an invaluable national patrimony, with which no other nation has anything to be compared. Whoever rescues them from the danger of being disfigured by faulty copies, and being thus gradually consigned to oblivion and destruction, erects to the artist an imperishable monument and deserves well of his country; and everyone to whom the honor of the German name is dear is bound to support such a patriotic undertaking.... I considered it my duty to remind the public of this obligation and to rouse the noble enthusiasm in the breast of every true German...

The patriotic pitch is grating on the ear today, and would have surprised Bach, who assumed he was of Hungarian stock. (His ancestor Veit Bach was in fact from Pressburg, which is today Bratislava in Slovakia, but which in the sixteenth century was the capital of the kingdom of Hungary). In Forkel's defence, we should remember that he was writing at a time when the French Revolution had proved the value of the national state, and Germany was paying a heavy political price for its disunity.*

Forkel's biography did much to put Bach (if not Germany) on the map. In its pages we see the start of Bach's deification, as

---

* Forkel himself experienced the downside of German disunity. In his bid to write a general history of music he painstakingly scored two collections of Masses from the early 1500s; the score had been engraved and was on the brink of being printed when Napoleon's invasion of the German states interfered. The copper plates were melted down by French forces to make bullets.

if his works were flawless, ineffable, and without any mortal competition past, present, or future, putting a halo over his wig that even today can make the cult of Bach deadly dull. Forkel ends his book with the following kicker: "And this man, the greatest musical poet and the greatest musical orator that ever existed, and probably ever will exist, was a German. Let his country be proud of him; let it be proud, but, at the same time, worthy of him!"

The truth is that Bach was not well known in Germany or anywhere else. There were a small number of connoisseurs like Forkel who collected his works, but next to nothing in the way of general public recognition—certainly nothing like the fame Mozart, Beethoven, and Handel enjoyed in their lifetimes. And Bach's music continued to have no popular resonance well into the nineteenth century. Audiences had to await the so-called Bach Revival—a term used by historians to describe his redis- covery—the first time a long-dead composer had been plucked from the private realm of specialists and given a popular audience.

The beginning of the Bach Revival has a specific time and place. The year was 1829, the scene Berlin, and the protagonist a twenty-year-old Felix Mendelssohn. It was Mendelssohn who organized and conducted a historic performance of Bach's *St. Matthew Passion*, the mesmerizing oratorio that tells the story of the last days of Jesus.

As the grandson of the Enlightenment's most famous Jewish philosopher, Moses Mendelssohn, Felix was an unlikely spark plug for Bach's posthumous glory. Although his family had converted to Christianity, Mendelssohn remarked on the irony that it had taken a Jewish musician to introduce Germany to its most impressive Christian music. In fact, Mendelssohn had Bach in the blood. His great-aunt, Sara Levy, studied with Bach's son C. P. E. and knew his eldest son, Wilhelm Friede- mann. Mendelssohn's mother had studied music with one of

Bach's most devoted pupils, and through his music teacher
Carl Friedrich Zelter, Mendelssohn himself was technically a
great-grandpupil of Bach.*

Mendelssohn also took his Jewish roots seriously. His performance of the *St. Matthew Passion* was substantially cut to
reduce its length (the original is about three hours long) but also
in ways that reflected his sensitivity to anti-Judaism.†

On the evening of the famous performance, the stately
Berlin Singakademie concert hall was sold out, with as many
as a thousand people stranded outside without tickets. Among
those filling the seats were the Prussian king, the crown prince,
the poet Heinrich Heine, and the philosopher G. W. F. Hegel.
Mendelssohn, seated at the piano, conducted from memory.

If Bach ever had a concert that hyped his genius and established his reputation, this was it. The box-office triumph led to
rave reviews and repeat performances, and opened the gates of
the composer's music. Yet even this milestone concert was considered a risky proposition at the time. In 1829 Bach's music was
still not seen as fit for the general public. A few years earlier
Mendelssohn wrote to his sister from Paris, lamenting that Bach
was considered a "mere old-fashioned wig stuffed with learning."
Mendelssohn's partner in the *St. Matthew* production, the singer
and actor Eduard Devrient, recalled how Bach "was at that time
generally considered an unintelligible musical arithmetician."
When the plan to perform the *St. Matthew* was proposed,

> . . . it was seriously questioned whether the public would take to
> a work so utterly foreign to this world. In sacred concerts, a

* The generational links were: Wilhelm Friedemann Bach, J. Kirnberger, Sara Levy,
and Zelter.

† "In Mendelssohn's personal and professional history," writes Celia Applegate in
Bach in Berlin, "the cultivation of Bach was always linked to his efforts to realize
the German-Jewish-Christian symbiosis that was his fraught and ambiguous
inheritance."

short movement by Bach might be accepted now and then as a curiosity enjoyed by only a few connoisseurs, but how would it be to have an entire evening with nothing but Sebastian Bach, whom the public conceived as unmelodious, mathematical, dry, and unintelligible? It seemed a rash undertaking.

The truth is that some in the audience found the performance excessively boring (Heine), or just peculiar (Hegel), while others may have felt that the buried Bachian treasure should have stayed buried. The Bach Revival was a slow-going process. It would take decades before Bach's music would gain mainstream acceptance. And the *St. Matthew Passion* was a lush work of operatic proportions, with a double choir numbering no less than 158 singers in the Mendelssohn production, some 70 instrumentalists, and a dramatic storyline chronicling the last days of Jesus.

The Cello Suites—music for one plodding, low-end instrument that was normally left in the background—would take much longer to reach a popular audience.

SARABANDE

It has a particular sincerity and candour, a musical
vulnerability, like that of a person rapt in prayer.

MSTISLAV ROSTROPOVICH

THE MUSIC WAS like a dead language that had been spoken so
long ago nobody really knew how it sounded. And it was
doubtful that anyone would have even wanted to hear music
for solo cello. Before Casals, cellists did not fill concert halls;
the cello itself was not seen as an important solo instrument.
As George Bernard Shaw, writing as a music critic, uncharita-
bly put it in 1890 — the same year Casals discovered the Bach
suites — "I am not fond of the violoncello: ordinarily I had as
soon hear a bee buzzing in a stone jug."

Casals reinvented the cello. As a young student in Barcelona
he felt that much of the instrument's accepted technique was
holding back musicianship. He freed the bowing arm, which
until then was extremely stiff. And he freed the fingers, invent-
ing a method of extension rather than the standard approach of
shifting the entire hand. He also developed what he called
"expressive intonation," which allowed for minute adjustments
to better play in tune with the harmonic flow of the music.

Before Casals there were cello virtuosos who played solo concerts, but as a sideline, not the mainstay of a career. This was in

large part because the cello repertoire was so thin. Compare the
names of the nineteenth century's great cellists who composed
for their instrument—Davidov, Popper, Offenbach, Goltermann,
Romberg—with pianist-composers like Chopin, Lizst, Mendelssohn, and Rachmaninov. It's not much of a contest. Virtuoso
pianists and violinists had their pick of crowd-pleasing material;
cellists, meanwhile, had limited drawing power.

Even Casals, at the outset of his international career, could
not go it alone as a solo cellist, and played a supporting role for
other musicians. For a while after his successful debut with the
Lamoureux orchestra in Paris, he was living in a cheap Mont-
martre hotel, performing at the Café Suez to make ends meet
and occasionally was helped out by a wealthy widowed bene-
factor. But he soon settled into a decent *pension*, soaked up the
salon life of *belle époque* Paris, and made key social and musical
contacts.

His first major tour brought him to America in 1901 as part
of a trio playing behind the singer Emma Nevada. Casals had
only a backing role, but he did win praise, occasionally eclips-
ing the singer from a California mining town who'd made it big
in European grand opera. They played more than sixty concerts and travelled some 6,000 kilometres. Casals was impressed
by the immense country, full of rough energy and democratic
spirit. He played poker with cowboys in a Texas saloon, got
dusty in a Pennsylvania mine shaft, rode horses in the New
Mexico desert, and attended a boxing match in Baltimore. For
Casals the tour was cut short in San Francisco, when a hike on
Mount Tamalpais resulted in a falling boulder that injured his
left hand. Gazing at his crushed fingers, he had a curious reaction: "Thank God, I'll never have to play the cello again!"

He would play the cello again, but not as a backing musician. After his hand healed, he returned to Europe and
embarked on joint concerts with the British pianist Harold
Bauer in France, Spain, Switzerland, Holland, and Brazil. The

two meshed well together, but it was Casals who mesmerized his listeners. No longer could the cello be dismissed as the warbling of an insect in a stone jug.

In some ways Pablo Casals was an unlikely superstar. On stage he appeared "so unassuming in his appearance and dress," said a review in the San Francisco *Chronicle* of one of his early appearances, "that his masterful playing comes as a surprise." Two years later, during an American tour that included a recital before President Theodore Roosevelt at the White House, he was advised by promoters to start wearing a wig to put some flair into his stage presence. He ignored the advice. Standing a maximum of five foot three in shoes, and rapidly going bald, Casals didn't exactly look the part of a flamboyant European virtuoso. But his command of the cello led to rapturous reviews:

> It is unnecessary to speak of the technical skill of Mr. Casals; he is undoubtedly the greatest violoncellist of all time in his absolute command of the instrument...(*Philadelphia Public Ledger*, 1904)

> The first touch of his bow on his strings proclaims him the master of his instrument, the prophet who delivers his inspired message with single-minded fidelity and unfailing effect... (*Liverpool Daily Post*, 1905)

> As a second solo Casals played something very uncommon. Just fancy one single 'cello playing solo without accompaniment in the large [concert hall]! It looked odd at first sight, but when one heard him play the C major Suite for 'Cello by J. S. Bach one was really charmed. ("Music in Hamburg," *The Strad*, 1909)

The precise moment when Casals first played a cello suite in public is a conspicuously missing piece of information in an otherwise highly documented public career. Casals used to say that he waited twelve years before he mustered the courage to play one of the suites in concert. Given that he found the music in 1890, this would mean the first public performance of the suites was in roughly 1901–02.

In the autumn of 1901 Casals was on a joint concert tour of Spain with Bauer. At the Catalan National Archives, where many Casals papers are stored, there are bundles of concert reviews from those early performances. The earliest review of a cello suite performance can be found in the newspaper *Diario de Barcelona*, which noted that on October 17, 1901, Casals played "the 'Suite' of Bach." His performance was lauded for its diction and dignity; the prelude and sarabande were praised for sounding robust and *belleza*. The following day, another Barcelona paper reviewed the Casals–Bauer concert at the Teatro Principal, praising the "Suite for solo violoncello by that most celebrated member of the musical Bach family." Ten days later, Madrid's *El Liberal* reported that "a Bach suite earned Señor Casals a prolonged ovation."

The cello music that had lain dormant for nearly two centuries was finally going public.

BETWEEN THE DAWN of the century and 1904, Casals managed to play complete cello suites in cities such as London, Paris, Rotterdam, Utrecht, New York, Montevideo, and Rio de Janeiro. Everywhere he went he had to overcome prejudice that the suites were dry exercises composed by a "wig stuffed with learning," better suited for the practice studio than the concert hall. When it was played at all in the nineteenth century, Bach's instrumental music was played mechanically, like a sewing machine. By contrast, Casals charged the suites with emotion.*

....

* It is difficult to find comparisons, as nobody recorded the suites prior to Casals. But there is a recording of the leading German cellist Julius Klengel in which he plays the sarabande of the sixth suite. The recording—made in the late 1920s, long after Casals had been playing entire suites in public—sounds syrupy, with

"How could anybody think of Bach as 'cold' when these suites seem to shine with the most glittering kind of poetry," Casals said. "As I got on with the study I discovered a new world of space and beauty . . . the feelings I experienced were among the purest and most intense of my artistic life!"

He was able to channel those feelings into the music like no one else. Dutch pianist Julius Röntgen wrote to the composer Edvard Grieg in Norway: "To hear him play one of the Cello Suites of Bach is an indescribable delight." After Casals played the fifth suite to Grieg one day, the composer exulted, "This man does not perform, he resurrects!" The promoter and music aficionado Edward Speyer described his playing of the third suite in a London concert:

> The excitement grew from movement to movement until at the end there was a demonstration the like of which can seldom have been heard at a London concert-room. . . . The Bach suite carried away his hearers, because it was Bach played with the strictest regard for classical form and yet with complete spontaneity of feeling, instead of the dry unimpulsive manner which the pundits had tried to persuade us was the right way to play Bach.

Harold Bauer, who witnessed the very first performances, recalled one occasion in Spain when Casals was playing a cello suite. A stagehand approached Bauer with a knowing look:

> "Señor, the composer of that music is Verdi."
> "Of course it is," said I, "doesn't it say so on the program?"
> "I have nothing to do with programs," the man replied, "for I

---

constant sliding, and is missing the raw power and urgency Casals brought to the suites. Klengel's recording also has piano accompaniment, another indication of how revolutionary solo cello was for the nineteenth-century cellists who preceded Casals.

cannot read. But I know it is Verdi's music, for that is the only music that always makes me weep."

The accolades must have kept Casals going, as did the high fees he was now able to charge. But it was a gruelling schedule, averaging about 250 concerts a year. In an era before automobiles or airplanes became routine, Casals carried his own luggage and bulky instrument, rushing to train stations while still drenched with the sweat of performance, eking out a few hours of sleep on the rails from Madrid to Moscow.

Once a year he went on a joint concert tour with Bauer, the mop-haired Englishman with whom he had bonded personally and musically. He made annual solo treks to Russia, first playing the suites in St. Petersburg in 1905, amid the glow of hundreds of flickering candles when the concert hall lost power. He played concertos with orchestras. And he formed what quickly became the most famous chamber trio of the twentieth century with Swiss pianist Alfred Cortot and French violinist Jacques Thibaud. The "Holy Trinity," as the trio was dubbed, toured internationally and made pioneering chamber recordings.

Casals was constantly on the go, leading his mother to write in a letter to her niece that he "travels through Europe, and always I have my heart on a string." But he eventually reduced the length of his tours and settled down. And he attached his own heart to something other than a string.

CASALS FIRST MET the Portuguese cellist Guilhermina Suggia when she was just thirteen years old. She was a promising young cellist who had travelled to a fashionable Portuguese casino to hear performances by Casals, then a twenty-one-year-old rising star. He gave her a few informal lessons and was impressed with her talent. There was a lot to be impressed with. By the time she was twelve, Suggia was first cellist in the

Orpheon Orchestra. A decade later, after studying in Leipzig and garnering praise for performances across Europe, the two reconnected. By early 1907, they were living together in the modest three-level home Casals rented in a quiet neighbourhood of Paris.

Suggia was petite, olive-skinned, with large brown eyes and a prominent nose. Beneath an exuberant—some said volcanic—temperament and a penchant for flowing gowns was an intense work ethic that enabled her to flourish in the masculine world of cello virtuosos. They performed and toured together. On some joint programs they were billed as a married couple; they often referred to each other as husband and wife, apparently because it was more socially acceptable. And although Casals was in a musical league of his own, Suggia would soon be considered by many to be the greatest female cellist of her time. (One area of the cello repertoire, however, was reserved for Casals: the Bach suites. Suggia felt capable of playing only two of the suites, the first and the third, saying that the rest belonged to him alone "until the angels took over.")

A couple of years into his relationship with Suggia, Casals was performing Bach's *St. John Passion* in Switzerland when suddenly, during an especially emotional aria, a foreboding took hold. "At that moment," he later recalled, "I knew with dreadful certainty that my father was dying." He cancelled upcoming shows and raced back to Catalonia, hoping to find his father in the home he'd bought him, in a mountain village where the air was good for his asthma. But the premonition came true. Carlos Casals had already been buried in the small Vendrell cemetery.

In the aftermath of Carlos's death, Doña Pilar urged her son to think about buying a home of his own where he could take time out from his hectic career. He took her advice, and with his ample savings soon bought a small parcel of beachfront property in San Salvador, where his mother used to take him as a child to enjoy the sea. It was the scene of his earliest memory: the shifting play of light reflecting off the Mediterranean and streaming through the window of a guest house as he was emerging from sleep. With his mother's help a villa was constructed on the property; it was expanded over the years to encompass gardens, orchards, a concert hall, and a tennis court.

Casals returned to Paris, where his tempestuous relationship with Suggia did not provide much solace. "There simply was not enough room for two ambitious cellists under one roof," concludes Anita Mercier in a recent biography, "and Suggia was not prepared to sacrifice her art for the sake of life with Casals." Their arrangement seems to have been primarily on Suggia's terms—no formal marriage, no children. In 1912 the romance finally unravelled when the two were vacationing in San Salvador, along with Casals' complicated friend Donald Tovey. The details are unknown, but Casals' jealous nature was triggered. "Guilhermina Suggia was then a young woman at the height of her beauty, if not yet at the height of her powers as an artist," wrote Tovey's biographer Mary Grierson. "Maybe she played with fire—maybe the hot Mediterranean summer had a disturbing effect on the finely balanced emotional poise of these ultra-sensitive people."

A dramatic account of the fiery breakup can be found in the liner notes by music writer Tully Potter for a two-volume recording of historic cello performances. Male visitors to the Casals villa learned quickly not to shower too much attention on Suggia for fear of incurring her partner's wrath. Things came to a head, according to Potter, in slapstick circumstances: "While Tovey was taking a bath, Casals burst in on him, flourishing a pistol and causing him to leap out of the window—luckily on the ground floor—with only a sponge to preserve his modesty."

However the drama transpired, it ended a six-year relationship. One of the last notes between the two was a telegram sent by Casals on December 31, 1912. "At the moment the clock strikes midnight I shall be alone, and thinking of you with all my heart," he wrote. "Perhaps you will think of me too." It was the one piece of correspondence that survived—Suggia had stipulated that all her letters to and from Casals be destroyed after her death.

Casals threw himself into his concerts, playing in England, Russia, Italy, Budapest, and Bucharest. Around him the walls of Europe seemed to be closing in. Paris was no longer a haven, not without Suggia by his side, and it would not for long remain a convenient base for the concerts he'd been playing—the First World War was about to break out. In early 1914 Casals sailed to the United States for the first time in a decade, aiming to put what he called the "most cruelly unhappy episode" of his life behind him.

MINUET

*Symbolizes more than any other dance the ideals
of nonchalance, elegance, subtlety, and nobility of
the French court.*

OXFORD COMPOSER COMPANIONS: J. S. BACH

WITHIN A MONTH of his arrival in New York, an exclusive story
in the weekly *Musical America* solved "the mystery surrounding the sudden visit of Pablo Casals to America." He was
getting married. It was a shock to virtually everyone close to
Casals. The woman he hastily wed was Susan Metcalfe, a thirty-
five-year-old American singer and socialite.

Not long after Casals split with Suggia, Metcalfe had suddenly appeared backstage after one of his Berlin concerts. It
was not the first time they had met; the two had appeared on
the same program in New York a decade earlier, when Casals
played a cello suite and she sang a few soprano numbers.
Although she was born in Italy, Metcalfe's father was an American
physician; her mother was from a family that for generations
had staffed the post of secretary to the Grand Dukes of Tuscany.
"Susie" Metcalfe was refined, somewhat reserved, and possessed
a respectable singing voice. She was attractive and petite (two
inches shorter than Casals), with dark hair and delicate features.
Gentler in demeanour than the hard-edged Suggia, Metcalfe

was more than likely a rebound romance for Casals; they had apparently decided to marry by the end of their brief Berlin encounter. A few months later, in April 1914, they tied the knot at a low-key wedding in New Rochelle, a suburb of New York City, where the Metcalfe family lived.

The couple planned to set up base in London, and ended up spending summers at the villa in San Salvador. Metcalfe was especially out of her element at the villa, where Casals was surrounded by his extended family, the conversation was in Catalan, and the setting highly provincial for a member of New York high society. The relationship degenerated quickly.

In May 1915 Metcalfe wrote a letter in French to Casals about how upset she was over his reproaches that she was naïve, lacking understanding of the world, and "terribly spoiled." She countered that "all the scenes of jealousy" that he staged, "the lack of confidence that you make me feel constantly . . . hurt me, and not only emotionally but physically."

Both Metcalfe and her mother were soon dispatching letters to Casals' mother in Spain about how badly the relationship had deteriorated. Metcalfe's mother wrote in elegant French to Doña Pilar about "how Pablo tormented his wife with the violence and injustice of his reproaches." He doesn't love her for who she truly is, wrote Helene Metcalfe, but instead wants to mould her. She did not couch her words in diplomacy, describing Casals' character as "jealous, egotistical, and autocratic."

Spain remained neutral in the First World War, which enabled Casals to go back and forth to the United States. But he was sickened by warfare, and contributed to the Red Cross and other humanitarian organizations. He also formed a Beethoven Society in New York with Bauer and others to defend Bach, Beethoven, and Mozart at a time when jingoist attitudes were out to ban German music. Yet early on in the war Casals had clearly taken sides. In a letter written in 1914 by one of his wife's friends, Lydia Field Emmet, she relates Casals' views that while he admired the organizational efficiency of Germany over France or Russia, the difference was that "Germany covets the earth, and becomes a menace through the very organization one admires."

As warfare was tearing Europe apart, his own marriage was suffering. "I regret with all my heart," Casals wrote in French to his wife in 1917, "all the chagrin [grief] that has come to us and that you feel you no longer love me and are no longer able to live with me." The turbulence did not take a toll on his cello playing, however. A few weeks before writing the letter to Metcalfe he captivated a Chicago audience with the third cello suite, performing it, according to one review, "with ravishing beauty of tone and with technical impeccability."

But as he and Susie drifted apart, Casals started spending more and more time in Catalonia. After the war he turned his energies to conducting and formed the Pau Casals Orchestra in Barcelona. Conducting was a natural progression for Casals, and it freed him from what had been two decades of whirlwind touring. Stirred by Catalan patriotism, it was also his way of giving something back to his homeland and putting Barcelona on the musical map. He built the orchestra from scratch with modest resources, doubling the standard pay of musicians who joined his orchestra and keeping the enterprise financially afloat with his own earnings as a cellist.

Catalonia once again became Casals' home. Every summer he left Barcelona for two or three months to spend time in San Salvador. Each day began at dawn with playing Bach on piano, usually from The Well-Tempered Clavier, as the villa's pet canaries chirped harmony from their cages. From the triple-arched veranda it was a few steps onto the hot sand of the beach. Along the shore he rode Florian, a jet-black Andalusian Arab steed, or took a stroll with Follet, his German shepherd. Tennis, chess, and music rounded out the idyllic picture.

Inside the villa, a music room could seat an audience of several hundred; in an adjoining chamber that he dubbed La Salle du Sentiment hung photos of family and friends and cherished mementoes. Another room, containing crystal chandeliers and painted wall panels depicting allegorical scenes, had been transported intact from the eighteenth-century palace of a Catalan nobleman.

Outside, from the raised promenade in his back garden, Casals could survey the luminous waves of the Mediterranean. Or, facing the front of the villa, he could contemplate the neat rows of olive trees, their silver-green leaves shimmering in the light. He could have been mistaken for some eighteenth-century duke in his domain, devoted to the cultivation of art and enjoyment of nature.

But it was a time of crushed hopes for the domain of Catalonia. Spain's new captain-general, Miguel Primo de Rivera, declared himself dictator, backed by King Alfonso XIII. Primo, a Catalan himself, in short order banned the Catalan flag, the language, and the national dance. Even the nameplates of Catalan streets, once bilingual, were sliced in half, leaving only the Spanish version.

The economy, after benefiting from the wartime boom that neutrality had brought, was suddenly in a downturn. Class conflict sharpened. And the Spanish army suffered an epic defeat in its Moroccan protectorate, losing more than 15,000 soldiers and civilians to Abd el-Krim and his Rif tribesmen.

Meanwhile, Spain was being ruled by a dictator who would work around the clock for months only to suddenly disappear for a weekend of wine-soaked carousing with gypsy friends. In Madrid, a night spent in the cafés would end at the dictator's home in the small hours of the morning with the issuing of grandiloquent pronouncements, many of which were rescinded after a good night's sleep. But while Primo jailed or exiled his opponents, there were no executions on his watch. And he did rack up one triumph by ending the unrest in Morocco, thanks mainly to French military assistance. Prodded by the king, Primo finally stepped down after learning that he did not have the support of the military, and died a broken man several months later in Paris.

For Casals, the bleak political climate was matched by his own personal isolation. He and Metcalfe had pursued their separate careers, and after fourteen years of marriage that lasted much longer on paper than in practice, they officially separated. In 1929 the Queen of Spain died in her palace. Despite his republicanism, Casals had never hidden the fact that he considered her his "second mother."

But the woman he was closest to in life remained his real mother. In recent years Doña Pilar, a quiet woman with her son's prominent nose jutting out from beneath thick blue spectacles, had become a fixture at the seaside villa. She had selflessly supported his career, even at the cost of her marriage, moving to Barcelona, Madrid, Brussels, Paris, and back to Barcelona as his career dictated. For Casals there was a strange, deep calm about his mother, a firmness and solidity that had gotten him through so much of life's trials.

In March 1931, after a concert in Geneva, Casals was handed a telegram that brought news of his mother's death. A month later, elections ended the monarchy. The Second Spanish Republic, desperately desired by Casals for so long, had come into being.

GIGUE

The more grave impressions produced by the movements
that have gone before are gathered up into a cheerful
and animated form, and the hearer goes away with a
sensation of pleasant excitement. PHILIPP SPITTA

Y PLAN TO take a summer vacation in Europe while research-
ing the Cello Suites brought mixed results. I knew of the
Casals Museum in San Salvador and was lugging around a
doorstopper of a biography on the great cellist, an excellent
book by H. L. Kirk that pointed me in a few directions but was
too weighty for travel. I scribbled down some geographical
leads and mailed it back to Canada. In Spain I hunted around
for the streets and cafés of Casals' early years. I found Calle
Ample, the street where he discovered the suites in a second-
hand music shop. But when I wandered into the street's only
music shop to ask in broken Spanish about Pablo Casals, I might
as well have been asking after Don Quixote.

At the Catalan National Archives in San Cugat, a suburb
north of Barcelona, I was able to go through many of Casals'
papers. I pored over newspaper reviews from his early concerts, and gazed at what initially felt like the Holy Grail of my
search: the edition of the Cello Suites that Casals had found in
1890. But music is more than a series of inky bars and blobs on

paper. How much could I say about the tobacco-hued, dog-eared text held together with tape and paper patches here and there, and riddled with mostly incomprehensible blue pencil markings?

Casals' hometown of Vendrell, an hour south of Barcelona, was dusty and vaguely hostile. On the day I visited, explosive *booms* ricocheted off shuttered buildings that lined empty streets. Small knots of men with moustaches threw menacing glances my way. I slinked through the narrow streets looking for Casals' boyhood home, half fearing that a putsch was in progress. The commotion turned out to be nothing more than a festival for the local patron saint (although that summer actual bombs were going off in Spain, placed by Basque liberation groups). Despite the fierce firecracker activity, nothing celebratory appeared to be going on in Vendrell. As for the Casals sites, there was the requisite museum in the small home where he had lived, the church where he played organ, and not much else. The town was grim, provincial, impervious.

I followed the olive trees down to San Salvador, where at least the Pau Casals Museum, with its user-friendly exhibits, was an uplifting experience. In the magical courtyard I was able to sit in a meditative calm and contemplate my subject. On the beach I swam in the waters the cellist had once delighted in. But overall, Spain offered slim pickings for research.

Before leaving for Europe I'd managed to arrange only one actual interview. The renowned cellist Mischa Maisky had recently released a recording of the Cello Suites, and I noticed in the liner notes that he lived in Belgium. I was going to Brussels to visit an old friend and figured I'd try to snag an interview with a real live famous cellist. I searched on the Web for his coordinates and located an email address, and to my surprise Maisky's personal assistant replied: "Even though Mr. Maisky is incredibly busy at the moment, since the subject of your book is obviously very dear and important to him, he will be happy to do his best to cooperate with you in this matter."

A HEATWAVE HAD enveloped the Belgian village of La Hulpe when I arrived outside the art deco mansion belonging to Maisky. I felt like a detective attempting to pry information out of some wealthy eccentric who had no business talking to me. My reason for being there—that I was writing a book about the Bach Cello Suites—seemed an unlikely story.

I had taken the mid-morning train from Brussels to La Hulpe, about forty kilometres south. From the train station I set out through a maze of village streets and Flemish signs to Avenue de la Corniche, and after a few wrong turns trudged through the intense heat to number 92, the last residence on a dead-end street. The home commanded a vast driveway behind a heavy wrought-iron gate. I took stock of the eye-pleasing building, an immense cream-coloured, boxy structure with decorative pegs lined up beneath the cornice like a giant towel rack.

I buzzed the intercom on the security gate. After I identified myself, an electronic click followed and the gate slowly opensesame'd, clearing the way to the mansion. I passed manicured shrub islands and a silver Lexus suv, stopping at a small portico with a green domed roof. A black door with gold grill-work opened and a maid led me through the residence to a salon.

Mischa Maisky is a small man with a bird's nest of grey hair and a beard that would not look out of place on an Afghan mountain tribesman. He has full lips, a hawkish nose, and an attractiveness that is Slavic, feudal, and a touch melancholic. He was wearing a thick gold dog collar around his neck, blue pajama-type pants, small dark slippers, and a black T-shirt with a caricature of a cellist. The effect was midway between Rasputin and Liberace. He was immediately likeable.

The cellist eased onto a lemon-coloured loveseat made of carved wood, trimmed with gilt, and crowded with embroidered pillows. Behind him stood some Asian vases and a framed photo of Maisky with a cello. Ample windows displayed the verdant Flemish countryside that is his backyard. There was an avant-garde candelabrum, a bronze bas-relief of a nude figure, and a glass table with a centrepiece of dried flowers and several glossy coffee-table books. Among the titles was one about Victor Horta, the father of Belgium's art nouveau architecture movement, who had designed this particular residence as his summer home.

After discussing the heatwave over tall glasses of cold water that the maid brought in, the conversation quickly moved to the Cello Suites. "It is like a great diamond," said Maisky in a thick Russian accent, "with so many different cuts that reflect light in so many different ways.

"It's the most difficult program I ever played and ever will play. It requires an incredible amount of concentration and energy. That's the reason why when I play three suites at a concert I always change three shirts—because I'm soaking wet, not because I'm trying to make some kind of fashion statement."

Maisky was eleven years old when he first laid eyes on the sheet music. It was a gift from his older brother, Valery, who himself became an accomplished organist, harpsichordist, and musicologist. Valery inscribed some words of wisdom on the title page: "Work as hard as you can all your life to be worthy of this great music."* Mischa Maisky took the advice. "I never stopped playing the suites," he recalled, "except for when I was in jail."

At fourteen Maisky moved from Riga to Leningrad to study at the conservatory. By 1968 he'd won a prize at the highly prestigious International Tchaikovsky Competition and begun

---

* Valery Maisky eventually immigrated to Israel, where he recorded with Isaac Stern and founded the Israel Bach Society. He died in a car accident in Germany while touring with an orchestra that was performing the *St. Matthew Passion*.

studies at the Moscow Conservatory with one of the planet's foremost cellists, Mstislav Rostropovich. Soon he found himself entangled in Soviet politics. The fact that Rostropovich, a human-rights activist, was his teacher didn't help matters. In 1969 Rostropovich came to the support of the dissident writer Aleksandr Solzhenitsyn and invited him to live at his dacha. That same year Maisky's older sister emigrated to Israel, another reason for Soviet authorities to clamp down on the young cellist.

Maisky had been recording his lessons with Rostropovich on an old, beat-up reel-to-reel tape recorder that he'd purchased with prize money. He didn't have money in those days for a suit or a half-decent pair of shoes, but Maisky felt that what Rostropovich was teaching him was so important it would have been "criminal to let it disappear in the air." When his tape recorder broke down, he looked for a superior machine, which for the ordinary citizen was all but impossible to find in Soviet Russia. As it happened, he found himself being offered — "it was definitely arranged by the authorities" — certificates that one paid hard currency for and that could be used in specialty shops where luxury goods were reserved for foreigners and elite Communist Party members. "I was arrested on the spot, put away for illegal operations, or whatever it was called."

He was sent to a small village about forty kilometres from Gorky, a place called Pravdinsk. An eight-storey factory there produced paper for *Pravda* ("truth"), the official newspaper of the Soviet Union. Deprived of a cello, Maisky lived in barracks and laboured alongside petty criminals and thieves. His job in this forced-labour camp was shovelling cement, and he was one of two workers responsible for filling eight large trucks. "It was very tough," he recalled, "not just because of the cello. It's one thing not to be able to play for two years and another to be forced to shovel cement. I was shovelling ten tons of cement a day — building Communism. Obviously unsuccessfully!"

By the time he emerged from the camp fourteen months later (not counting time served in a Soviet prison), Maisky was without his coveted diploma from the Moscow Conservatory. He had completed sixty-three of sixty-five exams; missing were cello performance and "scientific socialism."

By January 1972 Maisky wanted out of the Soviet Union, diploma or not. But he was liable for three years' military service, a situation that would have ended his hopes of becoming a cello virtuoso. The way out was via the psych ward. Through friends he got an influential psychiatrist to commit him for two months, thus making the cellist untouchable as far as the Soviet military was concerned. "I didn't have to pretend that I was Napoleon or anything." Upon his release he applied to emigrate, and six months later he was in Israel.

In his first public concert in years he played the tragic strains of the second Bach suite. But good fortune was in the cards for the former Soviet convict. After his debut at Carnegie Hall, an anonymous donor gave him a magnificent eighteenth-century cello. And by the time Bach's 300th birthday rolled around in 1985, Maisky was able to release his own recording of the Cello Suites. It did very well by classical music standards, selling more than 300,000 copies and winning two major prizes. The *Times* of London praised it as a work that "captures the sense of a lone musician responding inquisitively and strongly, with all his mind and technique, to divine dictation."

Maisky, who calls the Bach suites his personal bible, sees all sorts of hidden signs and numerological coincidences in the music. At a small guest house that he converted into a studio and called Sarabande, he had a fence built with all the notes of the fifth sarabande crafted in the metalwork. He gleefully points out that the studio's address is 720, his Montagnana cello was built in 1720, the year he came to the West was 1972 — and the year in which Bach has traditionally been thought to have composed the music is 1720.

But the essential mystery of the suites still eludes his grasp. After realizing how much his interpretation of the suites had changed since 1985, he made another disc in 2000 for the Deutsche Grammophon label. And he doesn't expect that most recent recording to be his last word on the subject.

Maisky's big-toned, expressive style of playing strikes some critics as over-the-top — "Dostoevskyian in emotion," to quote one of his bad reviews. But he feels strongly that "limiting Bach to a baroque composer is an insult to such a genius. Bach was much bigger than this. He happened to be a baroque composer because he lived in that period. He is the greatest Romantic of his time, and the greatest modernist of his time. Listen to the sarabande of the fifth suite. It sounds like it could have been written yesterday!" The greatness of Bach's music, Maisky insisted, is that "it doesn't belong to any time or place."

SUITE NO. 3

(C major)

Suitte 3.

Prelude

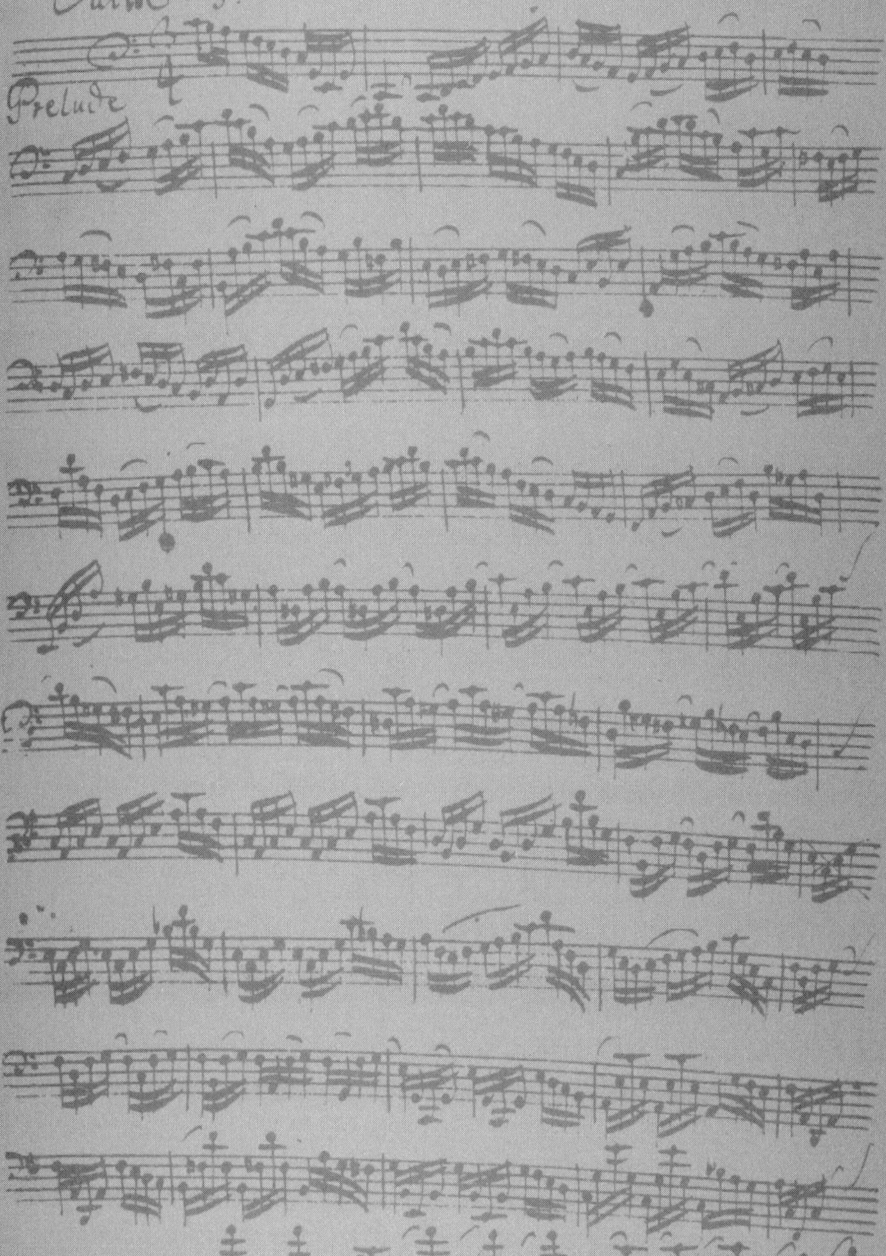

PRELUDE

C major, the richest and most resonant key for the
cello, inspired Bach to veritable cascades of sound ...
his personal key of joy.

HANS VOGT, JOHANN SEBASTIAN BACH'S CHAMBER MUSIC

L OVE IS PROCLAIMED in the downward, swooning scale, an
amorous rush, a falling into someone's arms. The pitch is
romantic. The smitten notes promise everything. Again and
again the lover makes his case, rising from the deep notes of
desire to heavenly rhetoric. There is cajoling, the pulling of
strings, the laws of nature. The world is not to be retired from;
the force of life barrels ahead. It is a pleasurable momentum,
followed by a stretch of tension, the euphoric overlap of single
notes, a coming together, an embrace.

She was the youngest daughter of a court trumpeter from
Weissenfels. An exquisite singing voice. A praiseworthy figure.
Barely twenty years old. The two certainly knew each other by
June 1721, when Anna Magdalena Wilcken was employed as a
court singer at Cöthen and took Communion at St. Agnus
Church in town. Although Bach was not in the habit of taking
Communion (he did it once or twice a year), his name is men-
tioned on the Communion list for the same day as was Anna
Magdalena's—perhaps the young singer had brought him to

the pews. In September the two were named in a baptismal register as godparents to the son of a palace butler.

Precious little is known about how Bach and Anna Magdalena fell for each other. But there is a hint of secret courtship contained in the words of a mysterious aria, usually attributed to Giovannini, that was soon inscribed in a music book for her pleasure:

> To be too free and open / is oft with danger fraught.
> So we must well arrange it, / that they discover naught
> So if thy heart be mine, love, / as mine is truly thine,
> Of this give not a sign, love, / no not the slightest sign.

Bach's one professional trip in August 1721 was to Schleiz, where he performed at court. Midway in the journey, he would have stopped at Weissenfels, quite possibly using the occasion to ask trumpeter Johann Caspar Wilcken for his daughter's hand.

"On December 3, 1721," reports the Cöthen castle church register, "Mr. Johann Sebastian Bach, widower, Capellmeister here to His Highness the Prince, and Mistress Anna Magdalena, legitimate youngest daughter of Mr. Johann Caspar Wülcken, Court and Field Trumpeter of the Music of His Highness the Prince of Saxe-Weissenfels, were married at home, by command of the Prince." Although second weddings were often subdued affairs, the wine bill points to a joyous and even extravagant event. The groom had purchased a major shipment of Rhine wine for the occasion, 264 quarts of it, worth 84 thalers and 16 groschen, representing about one-fifth of his annual salary.

The marriage was a much-needed boost for the thirty-six-year-old widower. Anna Magdalena, at twenty, became stepmother to Bach's four small children, ages six to eleven: Wilhelm Friedemann, Carl Philipp Emanuel, Gottfried Bernhard, and Catharina Dorothea. His household was restored to order. And his finances benefited from the high income Anna Magdalena continued to draw as a court singer in the prince's band.

Aside from instantly becoming a stepmother in charge of a large household, Anna Magdalena was a professional singer, a skilled music copyist, and, one can assume, a muse for the man she called Sebastian. She stole time away from her domestic schedule to copy out his compositions, hurriedly getting parts ready for performances or sale, in a clear, neat hand, her musical calligraphy very soon becoming indistinguishable from that of her husband's. Bach's out-of-town performances at various courts included his wife, who, as he described in a rare letter, "sings a good clear soprano."

But it was no marriage of convenience. The evidence suggests that Bach had fallen for his young bride like a rapid-fire downward scale. Although little is known of Bach's personal life, we do know that he purchased for her a songbird. On another occasion he procured for her half a dozen yellow carnations. A family letter noted that Anna Magdalena "values this unmerited gift more highly than the children do their Christmas presents, and tends them with such care as is generally given to children, lest a single one wither."

They were intimate musical confidants. Not long after the wedding, she started an album in which he entered tunes for her pleasure and education. In her own flowery handwriting she titled it the "Little Keyboard Book for Anna Magdalena Bach." It would be filled in a few years and followed by a second notebook of dyed green parchment with gilded edges, fastened by a red ribbon. "There is no doubt that Bach loved her deeply," writes biographer Percy M. Young, "and the songs of [the 'Little Keyboard Book'], tender and intimate, and combining the impulses of sacred and profane love, are as moving as any of their kind." The music included songs transposed for her voice, harpsichord suites, fashionable light tunes, and early attempts at composition by their children. One could also find love songs in the well-worn pages, such as Giovannini's aria "If you want to give me your heart you must begin so in secret."

ALLEMANDE

*Are allemandes the most mysterious, the most profound
pieces in the suites?* ANNER BYLSMA

THERE WAS ROMANCE in the winter air at Cöthen: the twenty-
seven-year-old bachelor prince was getting married. Just
eight days after Bach's wedding to Anna Magdalena, Prince
Leopold wed his nineteen-year-old cousin Friederica Henrietta,
Princess of Anhalt-Bernburg. Five weeks of celebrations—
balls, masquerades, illuminations—followed the wedding, for
which Bach provided some music, now lost.

The princess modified the atmosphere at court. Bach described her as an *amusa*—someone who had no use for music.
In fact she owned some elegantly packaged sheet music, which
casts doubt on Bach's epithet. But in all likelihood the princess
was jealous of Leopold's special bond with Bach—not to mention Anna Magdalena, another young newlywed who was
drawing a substantial salary from the royal coffers as court
singer. Music was in any case an expensive and time-consuming
interest that took the prince away from his princess.

Changes in priorities were soon evident in the court budget.
During Bach's first two years in Cöthen, music spending had
increased. Now it was declining. The number of musicians in
the prince's orchestra was down by three, including a top

violinist. In their place a dancing master was hired. Spending for music was now about four percent of the court budget, competing with items such as the wine cellar, the princely stables, and the palace gardens. The princess herself was allotted an annual allowance of 2,500 thalers, higher than the entire court budget for music. And Leopold decided to create a ceremonial palace guard of fifty-seven soldiers, a costly faux military move that bolstered royal pretensions more than security.

Bach, once again happy in his home life, saw his career in peril. "I had a gracious Prince, who both loved and knew music, and in his service I intended to spend the rest of my life," he wrote to an old friend years later. "It must happen that the said *Serenissimus* should marry a Princess of Berenburg, and that the impression should arise that the musical interests of the said Prince had become somewhat lukewarm, especially since the new Princess seemed to be an *amusa*."

The budget cuts to music-making at court cannot be attributed solely to the new princess. Leopold was experiencing a cash crunch due to a family dispute that led to loss of feudal revenue. Then there was the question of the prince's fragile health. Everything taken together, Bach sensed which way the wind was blowing. And considering his overtures to Hamburg and Berlin over the previous two years, he had obviously been mulling over his options well before the *amusa* arrived on the scene.

Cöthen at the end of the day was still "Cow-Cöthen," a marginal court in the middle of nowhere. The official religion was the Prince's Calvinism, and the Bachs had to content themselves with a very modest Lutheran church run by a very unimpressive pastor. Another downside was the school system; at least one classroom was crammed with 117 pupils. Bach, a successful professional who himself never made it to university, had hopes of higher education for his sons Friedemann, C. P. E., and Gottfried Bernhard.

Other feelings may have surfaced. In April, Bach received news that his brother Jacob had died. After they were orphaned, the two young boys had relocated to Ohrdruf, where they lived with their older brother, Christoph. Jacob's career had taken him farther afield. After apprenticing in his hometown of Eisenach, he'd left for Poland, where he joined the royal Swedish army under King Charles XII "as oboist in the guards." There is one report of his being in Constantinople. Aside from the fact that his first wife died at about the same time as Maria Barbara and that he also remarried, virtually nothing is known of Jacob Bach. He died in faraway Stockholm, a musician attached to the Swedish court.

Bach's other brothers Jonas and Balthasar had both died very young many years earlier, and his older brother, Christoph, had recently passed away at forty-nine. Jacob's death would naturally have made Bach question his own longevity and consider the best way of securing the future of his own three sons.

Beyond all these concerns was Bach's restless nature, his tendency to become dissatisfied with a job after a spell, to feel constrained by limitations, musical and otherwise, and not to be content with the status quo, but to move forward once he'd mastered the musical possibilities offered by any given situation. So when the job of cantor opened up in Leipzig, a university town that would have offered an excellent education for his sons, a more cosmopolitan lifestyle for his wife, and many musical opportunities for the composer, Bach applied.

It was a respected post that did not lack for candidates. Bach applied only after his friend Georg Philipp Telemann, the music director in Hamburg, won the job but turned it down when the Hamburg authorities upped his salary and improved his working conditions. Even after Bach entered the fray, the Leipzig council next offered the job to Christoph Graupner, the Capellmeister in Hesse-Darmstadt. But Graupner's employer refused to release him. An important page in music history, though nobody realized it at the time, was about to be turned.

Unlike the employers of Telemann and Graupner, and unlike Bach's former employer the Duke of Weimar, who'd tossed him in jail, Prince Leopold graciously agreed to let Bach go. In a letter to the Leipzig town council, the prince released his prized Capellmeister with what must have been a heavy heart. Leopold stated that his court was "at all times satisfied with his conduct...And now, seeing he is minded to seek employment elsewhere, and thereto hath sought our gracious permission to retire, We [sic] do by these presents accord him the same, commending him heartily to others."

It could not have been an easy letter for Leopold to write — only nine days earlier his princess, the *amusa,* had died. But by then Bach had passed the point of no return. Still, it must have been with mixed feelings that, in May 1723, Bach looked over his shoulder at the three rugged towers of the Cöthen castle fading from his view. "At first, indeed, it did not seem at all proper for me to change my position of Capellmeister for that of Cantor," he wrote in a letter. "Wherefore, then, I postponed my decision for a quarter of a year; but this post was described to me in such favorable terms that finally (particularly since my sons seemed inclined toward studies) I cast my lot, in the name of the Lord, and made the journey to Leipzig, took my examination, and then made the change of position."

COURANTE

*The passion or affection which should be performed in a
courante is sweet hopefulness.* JOHANN MATTHESON

PABLO CASALS WAS voting for the first time in his life. In 1931 he
cast his ballot for the Republicans, who swept to power and
ushered in Spain's Second Republic. King Alfonso XIII, who as a
child played toy soldiers with Casals at the royal palace, was
advised to leave Spain to avoid violence. "We are out of fashion," he remarked after the election. With crowds starting to
demonstrate outside the palace, the king promptly departed by
car to the coast, where he boarded a cruiser for exile in France.
"The fall of the monarchy," wrote Alfonso's polo tutor, the
Marqués de Villavieja, "gave me a greater shock than any fall
from a polo pony."

The new republic, which promised to restore Catalonia's
long-awaited autonomy, marked heady days for Casals. The
fifty-four-year-old cellist was named president of the Council
of Music and awarded Catalonia's "medal of the state." He was
made an honorary citizen of Barcelona, and a central avenue in
the city was named after him. He conducted his arrangement
of the Catalan national dance, the *sardana*, for thirty-two cellos.
He was swept up in events, galvanized, for once politically at
one with his surroundings.

There was a cultural flair to the Republic that appealed to Casals. Manuel Azaña, the new prime minister, was an illustrious essayist and translator of Voltaire. His cabinet colleagues included a philosopher and a historian, while the poet Ventura Gassol was minister of culture in the Catalan regional government.

A few days after the creation of the government, Casals conducted the Orquestra Pau Casals at the great palace of Montjuïc, overlooking Barcelona. The music was Beethoven's Ninth Symphony, with its "Ode to Joy" chorus proclaiming universal brotherhood. But the new republic was caught between bitter enemies on the right and difficult friends on the left. The economy was suffering on account of Wall Street's crash, a tumbling peseta, and capital flight. It wasn't long before a military coup was attempted, a national strike broke out, churches were torched, and violence flared between anarchists and police. Within eighteen months new elections were called, this time featuring women voters for the first time in Spain — one of the Republic's constitutional accomplishments.

The centre-right government that resulted from the vote tried to roll back many of the reforms undertaken by the previous regime. Meanwhile, the political extremes became more extreme. The radicalized socialist party, fired up by its own wild rhetoric, decided to launch a general strike to topple the government and restore left-wing purity to the Republic. It failed miserably. The government responded by outlawing the strike and declaring a state of war.

In the north, striking miners were bombed into submission by the air force. In Asturias, an anarchist commune that replaced money with coupons was brutally suppressed by security forces at the cost of a thousand lives. In Catalonia, Lluís Companys, head of the Republican Left of Catalonia party, appeared on the balcony of the regional government building to proclaim "a Catalan state within a Spanish Federal Republic." He was unceremoniously arrested. (So was Casals' brother

Luis, who apparently was connected with a brief battle to defend the Catalan state. He was released after ten weeks.)

Elections were set for February 1936 — the last free election Spain would experience for forty years. Parties of the left and centre-left, adopting a program of agrarian reform and autonomy for Catalonia, banded together to fight the election as the Popular Front. They won, but by the slimmest of margins: less than two percent of the vote.

Despite the moderate complexion of the new Popular Front government, the right reacted as if a Bolshevik revolution were at hand. The ideological barricades had by now gone up across Europe. In 1936 there was no shortage of soldiers, monarchists, landowners, and Catholic activists in Spain who took their cues from Hitler or Mussolini. Confronting them was an alphabet soup of leftist parties and trade unions — anarchists, syndicalists, anti-clerics, Communists, Trotskyites, socialists. Held back from progress for so long, Spain was catapulted into the twentieth century with all its explosive isms. Fascists oiled their guns. Communists awaited instructions from Moscow. Anarchists were never so organized.

On July 18 Casals rehearsed his orchestra in Barcelona, preparing for a concert the next day that would open the Barcelona Olympiad, a political counterpoint to the Olympic Games in Nazi Berlin. During rehearsal at the exuberantly modernist Palace of Catalan Music, Casals received a note from the minister of culture: a fascist military revolt was expected in the city that night. Casals notified the musicians that the concert was cancelled, adding that he did not know when they would be together again. He suggested finishing the symphony "as an adieu and an au revoir for all of us." As he ran the orchestra and choir through the "Ode to Joy," tears clouded the maestro's score.

Outside, on the hot, tense streets of Barcelona, other preparations were underway. Barricades were constructed, gun shops ransacked, cars and trucks requisitioned, and crude grenades fashioned. The working-class organizations were taking matters into their own hands to confront the fascist *coup d'état*. That same day, a pilot with a playing card torn in half flew to the Canary Islands with instructions to pick up a Spanish general who held the other half of the card. The general, a short, pot-bellied man by the name of Francisco Franco, was to take command of the fascist rebels.

Within forty-eight hours, the rebels, bolstered by Junker aircraft provided by Hitler to transport their troops from Spanish Morocco, had taken the south and west of the country. Wherever the army rebels prevailed there followed savage execution of their opponents — real or imagined — from governors loyal to the Republic down to the lowliest of union officials. Socialists and anarchists were hunted down, and Freemasons were summarily shot for good measure. But in cities where worker organizations were able to get their hands on weapons, the military uprising was crushed.

In Barcelona the rebellion began just before dawn the next day, when soldiers from a local garrison were allotted shots of rum and ordered to march up the Diagonal, the main thoroughfare, where Casals happened to be living. But the rebels were met with factory sirens that alerted armed workers, who confronted the soldiers with homemade bombs, sniper fire, and barricades. By the end of the day the military rebellion was routed. In Madrid as well, the plotters failed.

But the Republic was reeling. It quickly became clear that while Nazi Germany and fascist Italy were aiding Franco's rebellion, the European democracies, led by Britain, would not back Spain's legitimate government. And the Republican government soon found itself facing a dual threat. On the one side was a military coup, and on the other, socialists and anarchists setting in motion a power grab of their own. "The rising of the right," observes Antony Beevor in *The Battle for Spain*, "had pushed an unplanned revolution into the eager arms of the left."

Casals retreated to San Salvador, where his villa suddenly looked suspiciously opulent to the anarchists roaming the countryside. "Since I had the big house and gardens in San Salvador," he later recalled, the anarchists "thought this was luxurious and every day in Vendrell, when they had their meetings to decide who they were going to shoot next, my name and that of my brother Luis came up every day in the list, but one or the other would say: no, not Pau Casals. We have to think [about] this very carefully."

He buried papers and burned his letters from the royal family. He was a leftist in conservative eyes, but extreme leftists saw him as a well-connected monarchist. "Later the Anarchists were overcome by the Communists," Casals recounted, "while on the other hand the troops of Franco were approaching Catalonia. Thus we were caught in the middle of two fires, fearing for our lives from both sides."

SARABANDE

Now the music evokes a dreamy sadness.

MSTISLAV ROSTROPOVICH

CASALS BEGAN RECORDING the Cello Suites on a desperate note. With civil war raging in Spain, he couldn't play in his homeland anymore; he refused to perform in Russia under the Bolsheviks; and he had boycotted Germany since Hitler came to power and Italy once fascism took over. "In a period of acute physical danger and emotional turmoil," writes biographer Robert Baldock, "Casals *needed* to play."

Recording the suites in their entirety went against the grain of what the music meant to him—intensely personal masterworks in a constant state of evolution. He was concerned that he wouldn't be able to do justice to the music. And he hated the "steel monster," as he called the microphone, which picked up background noise he wasn't even aware of. But in the autumn of 1936, four months after civil war erupted in Spain, a devastated Casals allowed himself to be convinced by Fred Gaisberg, the legendary head of EMI, to go into the studio in London. He began with the second and third suites.

Casals read the newspaper reports coming out of Spain in those anxious days of November. The epic Battle of Madrid, which has been called one of the most extraordinary in modern warfare, was underway. Attacking Madrid was a well-equipped army loyal to Franco that was made up mostly of Moroccan tribesmen and Foreign Legionnaires (the latter dominated by criminals and fugitives), backed by German and Italian tanks and aircraft. Defending the city was a vast urban mass led by the Republican militia, the International Brigades (volunteers from more than fifty countries, many under Communist control), and Soviet advisers, as well as a grab bag of idealists, anarchists, and battalions of workers organized according to trade, among them separate units for barbers, tailors, schoolmasters, and graphic artists.

The fighting centred on University City, a cluster of faculty buildings that lent the battles some bizarre symbolism. For the Republicans, nothing less than civilization hung in the balance; Madrid was to be the "graveyard of fascism." The army rebels, for their part, could employ the slogan of their Foreign Legion founder: "Down with intelligence, long live death."

Buenaventura Durruti, the legendary anarchist leader, led 3,000 fighters to defend the campus, but they were spooked by Moroccan machine-gunners. The anarchists, still working out their new policy, "the discipline of indiscipline," fled the academic battlefield. The first building to be captured by Franco's forces was the school of architecture. Volumes of the *Encyclopaedia Britannica* were used as makeshift barricades; faculty hallways echoed with the crackle of gunfire and commands shouted in Spanish, Arabic, Catalan, French, German, and Italian.

In the university's Clinical Hospital, a German International Brigades battalion, led by the author of a pacifist novel, placed bombs in elevators timed to explode in the faces of Moroccan soldiers one floor up. Other Moroccan fighters became casualties of their own hunger, eating inoculated animals that were being used for experiments. Durruti himself was killed by what was said to be stray gunfire, but what was also rumoured to have been an anarchist bullet fired in protest against the "discipline of indiscipline" policy. The Institutes of Hygiene and Cancer and the agriculture department fell to the military rebels. Only the Hall of Philosophy and Letters stood between Franco's forces and the rest of Madrid.

When Casals went into the Abbey Road Studios to record the second and third suites, the battle was uppermost in his mind. German and Italian aerial bombing of Madrid had intensified, targeting the Prado and other cultural landmarks, as well as hospitals, to gauge the impact of terror on a civilian population. It was the first time in history that a capital city had come under concerted air bombardment.

On the same day that Casals was in London recording the two Bach suites, British Foreign Secretary Anthony Eden announced that his country would prohibit British ships from delivering arms to Spain (that is, to the Republican government)—this at a time when thousands of German soldiers and air force pilots, as well as Italian Black Shirts, were providing crucial support to Franco.

"It is all very well," Casals remarked, "to say that the people of Spain must settle their own problems, yet how can they do it when Franco has the arms?" He played the tragic second cello suite and the passionate third suite, sending his heartfelt notes into the "steel monster" of modern recording technology.

Madrid, against all expectations, was saved from the fascist attack, but it would not prove the graveyard of fascism. By refusing arms to the Republic, Britain, France, and the United States forced the Spanish government to turn to the Soviet Union for assistance. The net result was increasing control by Moscow, a debilitating Sovietcentric influence that both propped up and poisoned the Republican cause.

On May 31, 1938, fascist Italian forces supporting Franco in Spain (as well as brothels and cabarets in the vicinity) aimed the first of their bombs at Granollers, a town near Barcelona. It was an odd target, given the lack of any military significance.

More than a hundred people, mainly women and children, were killed.

Two days later, in Paris, Casals returned to the recording studio to lay down the optimistic notes of the first cello suite. The bombing of Granollers would not have surprised him — Barcelona had suffered terribly from the fascist bombing campaign. Two months earlier, as Hitler was taking over Austria, a raid by Italian bombers had left a thousand people in the city dead, with twice as many wounded. Casals knew that the areas under Republican control had been steadily shrinking. But Catalonia, still in Republican hands, was holding out.

The day after recording the first Bach suite, Casals was back in the Paris studio recording the powerful, explosive notes of the sixth suite. Surrender was not at hand.

In the autumn of that year, as Franco's troops marched closer to Barcelona, a grim atmosphere hung in the air of the Catalan capital. Severe shortages of food, fuel, and electricity in the bomb-scarred city were compounded by the arrival of a million refugees fleeing the fascist advance, including six hundred thousand children. Casals was in Barcelona rehearsing for a concert at the Gran Teatro del Liceo on behalf of the Children's Aid Society. During one rehearsal a bombing raid shook the venue, and the musicians in the orchestra scrambled to take cover in the auditorium. Casals quickly regained his footing and picked up his cello. He played a Bach suite, hitting notes that would have sounded like courage as well as consolation. The immediate danger passed and the orchestra resumed its rehearsal.

At the concert, which was broadcast on radio, Casals appealed to the democratic countries (which had just let Hitler walk all over them in Czechoslovakia) not to abandon Spain. "Do not commit the crime of letting the Spanish Republic be murdered," he pleaded. "If you allow Hitler to win in Spain, you will be the next victims of his madness. The war will spread to all Europe, to the whole world. Come to the aid of our people."

He embarked upon a hectic touring schedule, from Belgium through southeastern Europe to Greece, Turkey, and Egypt. By Christmas he was back at the villa in San Salvador—now filled with refugees and a sense of dread — as Catalonia steeled itself for Franco's final attack on Republican forces.

A rushed ceremony took place at the University of Barcelona in which Casals was awarded an honorary doctorate; under the circumstances—Fascist forces were on the outskirts of the city—the diploma was handwritten. Thoughts of exile were on the minds of most people attending the ceremony. The same day, the Republican government abandoned Barcelona for Gerona. A few days later, Casals shut the door of his villa and headed north.

All of Catalonia seemed to make a last dash for the French border. When France finally opened the frontier in the final days of January, the first massive wave of half a million Republican refugees poured into the country. Shivering from cold, wrapped in blankets, clinging to paltry belongings (in some cases clumps of earth from their villages), and serving as target practice for Nazi planes, the Spaniards were placed in squalid internment camps patrolled by Senegalese guards.

Barcelona fell quickly, almost without a fight. Franco rescinded Catalan autonomy overnight; the *sardana*, Catalonia's national dance, was outlawed; and the Catalan language was banned.

Casals was by then on the French side of the Pyrenean border, in the dusty village of Prades. His room at the Hôtel Grand became the unofficial headquarters for a refugee relief operation. The world's most famous cellist began sending out appeals for international aid; when supplies arrived, he rented trucks to get the food, clothing, and money to his compatriots. At the camps he witnessed scenes of suffering that brought Dante's *Inferno* to mind. And though he himself was infinitely better off than the refugees, his situation was grim. Many of the refugees would be able to return to Spain, but Casals could not—Franco's chief of propaganda, General Queipo de Llano, had vowed that once Casals was captured, both of his arms would be cut off at the elbow. After a war that had killed more than half a million Spaniards, Franco's forces began liquidating what would be an estimated 200,000 more people considered to be enemies of the new fascist regime.

Visiting his friends the Eisenbergs in Paris, Casals fell into a deep depression. He did not leave his room for more than two weeks, oblivious to the view from his seventh-floor window, overlooking the Place de la Porte Champerret. "I was overwhelmed by the disaster that had befallen my homeland," he later wrote in a memoir. "I knew of Franco's reprisals in Barcelona and other cities. I knew that thousands of men and women were being imprisoned or executed. Tyrants and brutes had turned my beloved country into a monstrous prison. I did not know at first what had happened to my brothers and their families—word reached me that fascist troops had occupied my house at San Salvador. These things were too horrible to think about, but I could not drive them from my mind. They surged up in me—I felt I would drown in them. I shut myself up in a room with all the blinds drawn and sat staring into the dark...I remained in that room for days, unable to move. I could not bear to see or speak with anyone. I was perhaps near to madness or to death. I did not really want to live."

Friends eventually persuaded him to return to Prades, where he frantically began writing letters, appealing for help, and getting supplies to the camps. He played the occasional benefit concert in Paris to raise funds for refugee relief. To his dismay, Britain and France—now with bigger problems to worry about in Europe—recognized the Franco government. He suffered from headaches and dizzy spells. A friend, the poet Joan Alavareda, who lived in an adjoining room at the hotel, gave Casals a walking stick so that he could knock on the wall at night if he needed help.

The evacuation of German and Italian military forces from Spain was completed by June 1939. In Berlin, Hitler reviewed 14,000 members of the Luftwaffe's Condor Legion, which had played a key role in supporting Franco. Italian soldiers fresh from the Catalonian battlefields were received in Rome by Mussolini. The fascist troops would be needed elsewhere.

On June 13, Casals went into the Paris studio one last time to complete the cycle of Bach's Cello Suites. He recorded the fourth and fifth suites, connecting the wrenching notes of despair and loss.

Three months later, the nightmare scenario he'd been dreading came to pass. No longer was he safely in exile. Hitler had invaded Poland, setting in motion the Second World War.

BOURRÉE

Intonation is a matter of conscience.
PABLO CASALS

CASALS' RECORDINGS OF the Cello Suites were the first-ever complete studio accounts of the music, and destined to be the most famous and far and away the most influential. They were a long time in gestation: the records were released in the early 1940s, more than half a century after he had first discovered the suites.* The recording experience itself, forged in the crucible of the Spanish Civil War, took its toll on Casals. A week before going into the studio to record suites four and five in 1939, he wrote to the Gramophone Company that the "two Bach Suites are for me the most terrible thing to record." A month later he lamented that the studio effort "has cost me, besides several months' work and the exhausting effort of the recordings, a full week in bed as always."

However painful the process, the results were spectacular. Critic Norman Lebrecht, ranking it one of the best classical recordings ever made, praised Casals for having brought "grandeur, dignity and, above all, hope" to the Bach suites. "This is

---

* The 12-inch 78 rpm records were released on the Victor label in three instalments, beginning with suites two and three in 1940, one and six the following year, and four and five in 1950.

as much a testament as a performance, a blueprint for the cello future." The discs put the Cello Suites into general circulation and led to a dizzying number of recordings. At New York City's Virgin Megastore on East 14th Street, to take one example, no less than twenty-four different versions were recently for sale. The Casals was among them; despite the intense competition, it has never gone out of print.

Like Casals, other cellists have anguished over their versions, approaching Bach's masterpiece with reverence and fear. Even the great Mstislav Rostropovich was reluctant to record the music. Late in his career, when he finally plucked up the courage to record all six suites, he explained on the performance video how cautious he'd come to feel. "I am now sixty-three years old," he says gravely. "Only twice in my life have I recorded a Bach suite. Forty years ago I recorded the second suite in Moscow...and in 1960 I recorded the fifth suite in New York. In both cases I cannot forgive myself. I acted rashly."

Matt Haimovitz, the ponytailed cellist who at age thirteen substituted for his teacher in a Carnegie Hall concert—alongside Rostropovich and Isaac Stern—has fearlessly played the Bach suites in rock bars and pizza joints. (He has also found the courage to perform on cello Jimi Hendrix's version of "The Star-Spangled Banner" and Led Zeppelin's "Kashmir.") Yet when it came to recording the Bach suites, he confessed to "some trepidation at creating a fixed expression of these beloved works."

Other cellists record the Bach suites again and again to keep up with their own changing interpretations. "For many years," writes the Hungarian cellist Janos Starker, "I thought of asking J. S. Bach how he wanted his Violoncello Suites played. It made the hereafter seem palatable and even desirable." With five recordings under his octogenarian belt, Starker seems to be the record holder.

For the time being, anyway. Pieter Wispelwey, the Dutch cellist whose rendition is wonderfully smooth and sneaky, says he plans to record the suites every seven years as a "barometer" of his playing. Mischa Maisky, meanwhile, strolled into a Zurich stereo shop one day when the third suite from his 1985 recording happened to be serenading customers. His interpretation of the music had changed so much in fifteen years that he no longer recognized his own version. He quickly lugged his cello back into the studio.

The desire to rerecord is so strong because interpretations can vary so wildly, even within the same cellist's career. Deprived of Bach's original manuscript, cellists are forced to make more decisions than usual. They have no "indications" from the composer, the notation that usually guides musical characteristics such as tempo, dynamics, bowing, styles of play and various sonic curlicues. The Cello Suites are a blank slate, a Rorschach test that allows cellists to put their own stamp on Bach and interpret the music as they see fit—or as they think Bach would have wanted his music played.

The question of being true to Bach and his era—known as "authenticity"—has become a musicological battle fought with strings and vibrato. The purists aim to play Bach as his music is thought to have sounded circa 1720. This affects everything from the type of strings on the cello (gut) and the instrument itself (period instruments are favoured) to the size of the concert hall (small, preferably), the tuning (lower), and the use of vibrato (none).

The period police are not impressed with Casals, pioneer though he may have been. These hard-liners dismiss him as more Romantic than authentic, playing it fast and loose with the baroque facts, taking liberties with Bach's score, and indulging in syrupy emotions. But a major problem facing "authentic" players is the unavailability of an authentic eighteenth-century audience. Listeners these days have all sorts of music and ideas in their heads that did not exist in Bach's time. Can listening to a piece of music on an iPod in an air-conditioned room, with a knowledge of rock, jazz, and salsa, ever really be the same as hearing it during the eighteenth century in the candlelit castle of one's Most Serene Highness?

Or what about the beautiful spot about twenty seconds into the gigue of this suite that sounds like a riff in the hands of a rock guitarist? It is a bold, churning phrase that would not be out of place on a Gibson Les Paul wielded by, say, Jimmy Page of Led Zeppelin. Bach's audience, two centuries before the electric guitar was invented, could not have heard the notes in remotely the same way. Historical faithfulness has its limits.

But the popular notion that Bach's genius is so indestructible it can survive any style doesn't hold water with authenticity-minded cellists such as Wispelwey, who has made the suites his trademark. After a Montreal recital, Wispelwey told me that an overly Romantic approach to the suites—like that of Casals—detracts from the music's "inner beauty." In Wispelwey's view, Casals may have been trailblazing, but his recording of the suites is nonetheless "a historical schmaltzy document. I hear more Casals than Bach. Of course, I always want to hear a cellist making a statement or coming up with his interpretation, but there's not enough Bach."

Bach, however, is in the ear of the beholder. I find Wispelwey's recording to be among the most seductive of accounts, but there are other opinions. In a 2003 review of his marathon performance of all six suites at Alice Tully Hall in New York, *New York Times* critic Jeremy Eichler suggested that Wispelwey's version "sounded like a familiar language strangely rendered with its own private syntax." Eichler continues:

> The most striking aspect was his phrasing, which ranged from appealingly unconventional to simply odd....Mr. Wispelwey took broad liberties in tempo and pacing, often grouping clusters of notes against the grain and dispatching musical ideas with an impressionistic blur. (The Allemande of the Second

Suite drifted free of Bach altogether as the cellist, performing
from memory, seemed for a few perilous moments to have lost
his place.)

There is an entertaining story about how far the music can
be stretched beyond recognition. The famous Russian cellist
Gregor Piatigorsky was once giving a recital in a small French
town when he launched into Suite No. 2, hitting the first note,
a D, and suddenly experienced a total blackout. He had no idea
what the second note was. So Piatigorsky held the D and proceeded to improvise his way through the entire prelude. When
he reached the allemande, he regained his footing and resumed
playing the actual Bach suite. Unfortunately, the only cellist in
town was sitting in the front row with his students, all of whom
were clutching scores of the music. After the recital they
trooped backstage, seeking autographs from Piatigorsky and
wanting to know, "Maestro, what edition did you use?"

In truth, there are as many good versions as there are good
cellists. Comparing recordings of the Suite No. 3 prelude
recently, I found the sound of Steven Isserlis super-smooth;
Anner Bylsma, dry and eccentric; Pierre Fournier, elegantly
relaxed; Pieter Wispelwey, gorgeously magical; Mischa Maisky,
grandiose; Matt Haimovitz, lyrical and playful, stretching the
phrases like elastic bands. Everyone will have their preferences
(Isserlis won the taste test for me that day), but never do I want
to hit the Stop button once any of these excellent cellists is
bowing Bach.

These musicians, and legions of others, make a compelling
case for their own interpretations. If nothing else, the lack of a
manuscript in Bach's hand has ruled out any definitive claims
to authenticity. And beyond that, there is an inner logic and
beauty to the suites that flourishes with so many approaches.

Listen to Casals in the prelude of the third suite: it begins as
a glorious collapse, picks up the pieces, gathers momentum,

and plunges into a maelstrom, straining, nearly breaking apart, only to emerge with bouquets of chords and a declaration of love. Every listen brings fresh discoveries. Isolate the lowest notes from the high ones and they speak with a separate voice that is fascinating. Or consider the prelude's midpoint cacophony, which comes shockingly close to noise, yet with a full orchestra bottled up somewhere inside the cello, clamouring to be heard. The dance movements that follow are a succession of jauntiness and raw energy, heroism and devastation, tunefulness and timelessness.

Casals sounds authentic, and not because of the hiss and squeaks and crackle of the vintage mono recording. Even though his mindset was Romantic, his use of vibrato exaggerated, his knowledge of baroque history limited, and the recording technology of his time primitive, Casals played the suites the only correct way—by breathing life into them.

GIGUE

No cheap nonsense, absolute clean and nice intonation,
and let's dance the dances — it's as simple as that —
da-dee-da-da-da-da... WALTER JOACHIM

THERE WAS AN old man whom I would often see shuffling along
the sidewalks near where I live in Montreal. He moved with
a cane, gingerly negotiating the street corners like so many
landmines strewn between his high-rise apartment building
and a café he favoured. He stood out on account of his advanced
age, his air of elegance, and because he soldiered on despite
obvious frailty.

On a sunny autumn day I was eating a sandwich on the *ter-
rasse* of a local café, the Pâtisserie de Nancy. At a nearby table sat
the man with the cane. He was engaged in some small talk with
a stranger seated at another table. I picked up shards of their
conversation: Germany... Singapore... Shanghai... orchestra...
cello. *Cello?* I finished my sandwich, introduced myself, and
took a seat at his table.

Walter Joachim had a shock of white hair, an aquiline nose,
soft blue eyes, and eighty-nine and a half years' of lines on his
face. His hands trembled with Parkinson's, but his memory
was as sharp as it was long. Yes, he was a cellist — the former
first cellist of the Montreal Symphony Orchestra, no less. I

mentioned my interest in the Cello Suites and Pablo Casals. Walter said he remembered him well.

In 1927 Walter was a fifteen-year-old German cello student in Düsseldorf. He was somewhat familiar with the Bach suites and had started to learn a few of the movements in no particular order a year or two earlier. But the notion of playing an entire suite from beginning to end—a generation after Casals' first performances—was still virtually unheard of. "I learned it as exercises," he told me. "Movement by movement, and never played them together... That's what we learned when we were young. Who dared to play a whole suite alone?"

That year Casals performed a concerto with the Düsseldorf Symphony Orchestra, and also played an entire Bach cello suite. In the audience that night was Walter. The performance of Suite No. 2 transformed him. "It was like having a nervous breakdown," he told me. "I started really practising on the Bach suites when I went home. I didn't want to forget what I had heard."

Walter absolutely needed to hear more, so he followed the Catalan cellist by train to nearby cities such as Essen, Dortmund, and Cologne. "I toured with him, ran after him, and heard everything." At every stop along the way Walter had his eyes fixed firmly on Casals' fingering and bowing. "I tried to copy what he did, bowings for instance, methods, ideas...I didn't take notes, I didn't need notes—ah, how we remembered! The details! We all wanted to learn it!"

Walter and his circle of friends "knew it was great music, but we also never thought that the public would accept" the performance of an entire cello suite in concert. "A man with the name of Pablo Casals could afford to do it. If any one of us would have liked to have done it—maybe it wouldn't have been any good, I don't know—the public would have been offended. Of course, there was this aura around him too, you know—the great master plays a whole suite by Bach. He was a god. Couldn't do wrong."

After following Casals around, Walter went back to his cello studies. He was a gifted sight-reader and earned much-needed money by playing in the coffee houses and theatres of Cologne. In 1931, not yet twenty years old, he was hired to join a small orchestra that played across Europe and ventured as far as India, where he spent the better part of a year.

"I travelled all around," he recalled. "Kashmir. Darjeeling. We were a sensation in India. We were asked to play the festivities of the viceroy [in Calcutta]. It was the King's Club; no Indians were allowed in this club; service was with white gloves. We always had so much champagne that nobody could finish it. We worked seventeen hours per week; we did not know what to do. We started a symphony orchestra with an architect who told us he could conduct. The military band supplied the brass and the flutes and oboes and clarinets, and the strings were all from the restaurants and hotels around Calcutta. It was a disaster. It was horrible. I had a good time, but musically the orchestra was a catastrophe. Everybody played his own intonation, the second trumpet always three times as loud as the first trumpet—oh, terrible.

"I learned a little Urdu. We all had personal servants. And the servant I had was old enough to be my grandfather. So I could not call him 'boy' or by his first name. He was very nice and patient with me. I went to religious services with him, and he explained to me many things about religion and philosophy. He was a very bright man. Ali—I don't know what his second name was. And I bought a monkey with which I amused myself. We played. He was sitting on my shoulders for hours when I was practising."

Throughout, Walter played the Bach suites, sometimes with the monkey on his shoulders. "Every day. At least one or two movements. All the way through, never missed a day. I started my day usually with Bach or a scale, played a bit of Bach, then worked on the technical things that I had to play. You had to be on your toes."

In a subsequent interview at his modest apartment in a west-end high-rise, Joachim continued his story. By 1934 he was back in Germany—Nazi Germany—visiting his parents and performing some concerts, including what would be his last one in the country. It was in Leipzig. He was suddenly faced with imminent arrest for being a Jew in Germany, compounded by the fact that he had a history with the wife of an influential Nazi.

"I tell you also why I would have been arrested immediately. A former girlfriend of mine, German girl, had married a very important Nazi, and he had found out that I had a thing going with his wife before he was married. *Ja*, she loved me. He wanted to kill me with his hands, naturally. Nice woman, very nice lady.

"I had to leave immediately; I knew that someone was going to go after me. Somebody, a German musician, told me, 'See the guys there in the leather coats? They're here to arrest you.' He came to see me where I was performing and said, 'Don't go home.' My colleagues brought my things. Luck's not the right word. I would have been arrested; somebody would have informed. I got out illegally with a congress of Catholic priests, to Marienbad [in Czechoslovakia], by bus—a congress for preachers."

Friends dressed Walter up as a priest, giving him a collar, insisting that the clerical disguise was the best way to escape from Germany. His passport dangerously identified him as Jewish, but it was hidden away in his baggage. From Leipzig the bus crossed the Czech border en route to the spa town of Marienbad, then to Prague.

"In Prague I sort of arranged the music for a hotel. I played myself the classical stuff and played in a nightclub in the same hotel. I had a wonderful pianist, John Turner, a blues singer and pianist, a violinist who sang very well, and a black drummer who was born in the Sudan and learned in New York. Characters! It was a hit, this outfit—unbelievable."

Walter remembered playing in Marienbad, a Czech resort town in the Sudetenland—a territory coveted by Nazi Germany—when Hitler visited. "I was in Vienna when it happened," he said, referring to the Nazi annexation of Austria, which was soon followed by the takeover of Czechoslovakia. "I was in the Sudetenland when it happened. I was in Prague when it happened.

"I got out on an English plane. My brother had arranged for me a job in Kuala Lumpur, a hotel. And then the British soldiers—we were, after all, born in Germany, my brother and myself—we had the choice when the war broke out: to go to Australia and be interned or to go to Shanghai, where you give the guy twenty dollars and say, 'I lost my passport.' There's nowhere to deport you from Shanghai, nowhere to go. So I went to Shanghai. And the next day I became first cellist of the Shanghai Symphony."

IT WAS WALTER who suggested that I learn how to play the cello. After our first meeting at the Pâtisserie de Nancy we would often bump into each other. He'd be at the café having lunch and I'd join him, or he'd be walking home at an elegantly glacial pace and I'd take his arm and escort him along Monkland Avenue to his apartment building. He shared gossip about famous cellists, critiqued their style of playing, and spun tales from Düsseldorf to Kuala Lumpur and Shanghai to Montreal. He mentioned that his string quartet had cut an album with Glenn Gould, and I went out and bought the CD.

I'd travelled to Spain, Belgium, France, and eventually Germany in my search for the Cello Suites, but more often than not the trail had gone cold ages ago. Then, out of the blue, popped up this living, breathing link with the past. To stumble upon Walter was to befriend the Cello Suites; he embodied their history, from his days as a cello student in Germany to hearing Casals play to surviving the Second World War. To discover him on Monkland Avenue when I was struggling with the complicated idea of a book about the Cello Suites was, if not a divine sign, a major encouragement.

When I explained to Walter my idea for this book, he listened politely and wished me luck. I got the distinct impression he thought I'd need it. And when I asked him what I should do in order to better understand the Bach suites, he told me to learn how to play the cello. Not that I could ever be any good, he cautioned. I was too old for that to ever happen. But it would give me some insight.

THE AMAZING THING about playing the cello is its deep resonance, how the tones fill your entire body as if it were a sound box of flesh and bone. Every note is a bold statement. I play acoustic guitar, but its single notes vanish soon after they're struck. Compared to the cello they seem ephemeral and thin. (Chords are a different matter, a full-bodied advantage the guitar has over the cello.) Notes on the cello can be sustained for so long because of the bowing; rather than the soft plucking of a guitar string that disappears into thin air, bowing is like a deep-tissue massage. And just holding the instrument—its burnished wood, the baroque scrollwork above the peg box, those iconic f-shaped sound holes, the sheet music written in the bass clef—is enough to transport me to an eighteenth-century aristocratic salon.

I rented a cello at Lutherie Saint-Michel in downtown Montreal and started taking lessons there. There was a spring in my step whenever I entered the shop with my entry-level cello in its canvas bag. The sounds of string players trying out instruments mingled with the hubbub of the atelier, where the raw material of orchestras was being shaved, glued, strung, and tuned in what looked like a medieval workshop. Lessons took place upstairs. I quickly learned how difficult an instrument the cello is to master. Knowing guitar made it somewhat easier, but manipulating the bow of a cello is tough slogging: holding it just right, making the wrist relaxed enough while at the same time sufficiently rigid, pointing the bow in just the right direction, attaining just the right amount of friction on the string, slicing across the strings at just the right spot.

Then there's the absence of frets, those signposts on the fingerboards of plucked string instruments. Having to *hear* where I was on the fingerboard, without being able to see fret markings, was a huge hurdle. Guitars have frets. You can see where your fingertips are meant to be positioned, from the first fret up to the fifteenth. On the cello, there is instead a vague feeling (for me, very vague) that one's finger has found the right place, a visceral sense that the correct note is being played (or "stopped," to use the terminology). Getting it just right is what *intonation* means — not a tad sharp or a bit flat, but right on that sweet spot that produces the desired note.

I started off with the basics, learning how to hold (or rather, slow dance with) the bulky instrument and to wield the bow, which brought archery to mind. I learned the rudiments of reading the bass clef, simple rhythms, and eventually more challenging tunes like "Twinkle, Twinkle, Little Star." To put so much energy into mastering a nursery rhyme with such modest results was sobering. I had to scale down ambitions that had been intoxicated by my constant exposure to the Cello Suites.

To be so close to the cello, even as a limited cellist, was deeply satisfying. As my bow cut across the strings, horsehair against steel, a powerful low tone would be unleashed. It was wonderfully primal, like a bow dispatching a quiverful of notes. The invention of string instruments was in fact closely linked to the bow and arrow. Some inventor banged swords into ploughshares while another, more harmonious soul turned archer's bows into viols. And playing the cello did feel nicely neolithic, or at least a civilized way to process the primitive.

Occasionally I would play one note that I would recognize as the starting tone of one of Bach's preludes, and it would produce a thrill. One lesson came on March 21, and I mentioned to my teacher, Hannah Addario-Berry, that it was Bach's birthday. "I guess I won't live long enough to ever tackle a Bach piece on cello," I said. To my astonishment, she replied that there was an exercise book called *Bach for the 'Cello: Ten Pieces in the First Position* (the spelling *'Cello* seemed charmingly archaic—its original form, short for violoncello).

I found the sheet music and began learning a few pieces. They were a challenge, but much more worth the effort than "Twinkle, Twinkle." There was even a sarabande, a minuet, and a gigue in my new red book, though none were from the Cello Suites. Of the few pieces that I learned to play, one in particular, called "Minuet in C," stuck in my head and entered my dreams. While listening to an old disc I'd found in a second-hand music shop, I was startled to recognize my little song being performed on the harpsichord. Titled "Minuet in G" on the disc, it comes from *The Little Notebook of Anna Magdalena Bach*, the collection of pieces from 1722 that Bach assembled to advance his young wife's keyboard technique. And although the provenance of this tune is uncertain, I had learned two other pieces that were undoubtedly composed by the baroque master.

I was playing Bach on the cello. And as Walter had predicted, it was bringing me closer to the suites.

I HAD BEEN meaning to resume my interview with Walter for the past month, but events got in the way. Whenever I telephoned him he was feeling under the weather and suggested I call back in a few days. He had the flu at one point and was in the hospital for a few days. He hadn't been to the Pâtisserie de Nancy in a month. I aimed to continue our formal interview— we had only reached 1938—sometime in December. I was out of town early in the month, and when I returned I called him twice. Nobody picked up the phone.

Two days later I had a cello lesson set for 1 p.m. I got a call from Lutherie Saint-Michel informing me that the new teacher hadn't come in to work and my lesson was cancelled. I scanned the entertainment section of the *Gazette* over a coffee, and there was the headline:

Walter Joachim Was Montreal Symphony Orchestra Cellist
German-born musician counted many famous players among
his students

A photograph of Walter with a cello accompanied the obituary. He had died two days earlier. Among the observations included in the article was the fact that "His daily routine during the last decade included an afternoon stop at a coffee shop on Monkland Avenue."

I went out for a walk and traced the route to his high-rise apartment through the crisp, cold air and solid sun of late December—along Monkland Avenue, moving unsteadily in some places where ice had formed, unsteadily as Walter would walk, and went to the Pâtisserie de Nancy as private homage to a friend I had come to know late in life, but just in time.

SUITE NO. 4

(E-flat major)

PRELUDE

*These works are nightmares, gripping, dry, rattling
skeletons of compositions, bloodless, fleshless, staring
anatomies.* KAIKHOSRU SORABJI

PLAYING THE CELLO is an arduous effort—the sliding, sawing,
hammering, pulling off, and pressing of steel strings on
wood. Here in this workmanlike prelude the fingers of Casals
are carrying out the instructions of Bach, making big stretches
to join eight difficult notes, as if constructing a weighty, boxy
chordal contraption and hoisting it down and up the fingerboard. It is a vast, churning mechanism, a movement very
much in motion, with shovelling, grinding, and turning. There
is heavy clockwork, the digging of earth. Neither happy nor
sad, but resigned to one's fate.

For a long time I thought this prelude, alone among the
suites, had a humdrum, plodding quality. Yet repeated listening
reveals understated charm. The Dutch cellist Pieter Wispelwey
hears "strange intervals" and "mysterious corners" in the movement. "It's under the surface—all these little secrets," he says.

"There is nothing dashing about this Prelude," writes the
French cellist Paul Tortelier in the liner notes to one of his recordings. "It has beautiful things to say, and it says them simply
and fully, expounding its arguments in the unhurried manner

of a great orator who is absolutely sure of his ground, and who need not harangue his audience to hold their attention."

The oratory does go somewhere. This prelude contains one of the most intriguing payoffs to be found in any of the suites. It comes after about two minutes of that heavy, mechanical opening, when a trap door opens to reveal a swirling cluster of exotic semitones. You can hear a Near Eastern flourish, a lamentation that would sound at home in a foreign house of worship.

Then the movement picks up where it left off, resuming its mechanical drive, but soon veers off track into another rhythmic frolic, wrestling its way to a rhapsodic ending. But wait—it is a false ending; the notes start up yet again, only later reaching the terminus. In the hands of Casals, this sluggish grind starts to feel burdensome (perhaps because he made his recording during the painful summer of 1939). One might have preferred the earlier, false ending as a full stop. Other cellists give the movement more lightness. But who's to say what the composer's intentions were? Or how he felt when he wrote the piece.

Bach left the princely residence of Cöthen in May 1723 to take up employment in the town of Leipzig. Four carts loaded with belongings, followed by two carriages carrying Bach, his young wife, his sister-in-law from his first marriage, and five children,* arrived at their new home in Leipzig. Thanks to the curiously detailed report by a Hamburg newspaper, we even know the time of Bach's arrival: two o'clock in the afternoon.

The contrast between the two places would have been striking. Cöthen, for all the creative contentment it had provided Bach, was insignificant and provincial, out of the way and out of fashion. Leipzig, a town of just under 30,000 people, was,

---

* Anna Magdalena, either pregnant or about to become pregnant, was the mother at this point of only one child, the newborn Christiana Sophia Henrietta, who would survive only three years. The other children, by Bach's first wife, were Catharina Dorothea, Wilhelm Friedemann, Carl Philipp Emanuel, and Johann Gottfried Bernhard.

after Dresden, the second most important city in Saxony. The town that was dubbed "Little Paris" boasted lanterns on its main streets, one of the finest universities in Germany, coffee houses, pleasure gardens, a thriving publishing industry, and three annual trade fairs that drew merchants, printers, publishers, and nobles from across Europe.

One can imagine the impression cosmopolitan Leipzig made on the young family, especially fourteen-year-old Catharina and her younger brothers Friedemann, Emanuel, and Bernhard. The children might have ventured out that first evening to stroll the streets lit by oil lamps on oak posts, and patrolled by four night watchmen who carried rattles to signal the hours. There were grand bourgeois homes taking up entire blocks, public promenades, and cafés filled with tobacco smoke and a trendy new beverage called coffee. "Cow-Cöthen" would have felt far behind.

But as Bach settled into the family's newly renovated apartment in St. Thomas School, he might have questioned the wisdom of his move. Going from Capellmeister to cantor was to move a rung down the ladder in professional status. And whereas he'd been paid to compose freely at the Cöthen court, in Leipzig his responsibilities as cantor came with a raft of nonmusical tasks. "One cannot help feeling a little sadness," writes Albert Schweitzer, "when one reads the agreement that Bach had to sign upon his [hiring]."

The new job required teaching music and other subjects to senior students at St. Thomas School, directing the choirs at the city's two main churches on alternate Sundays, and overseeing the organists and musicians, as well as being responsible for performance material and instruments. There was also music to be directed at weddings and funerals, for which he was very happy to be paid extra. But Bach can only have found it taxing to serve as school inspector every four weeks, which meant making sure the pupils (his three sons among them) were out of bed at 5 a.m. and saying their prayers, supervising their meals, and maintaining overall discipline. After a year he'd had more than enough, and paid a school official to do the inspection job for him. But conflict with superiors over these sorts of mundane issues would continue to plague him.

Despite the sprawling workload, Bach's first years at Leipzig were stunningly creative. After using his time at Cöthen to compose secular instrumental music, he now began producing vocal music designed for Lutheran church services. After just five years or so, Bach had composed more than 200 cantatas, as well as his monumental St. John Passion and St. Matthew Passion, the latter heralded by many (though not in Bach's day) as the greatest piece of music ever written.

At home, Anna Magdalena had her hands full. The couple had moved to Leipzig with five children, including their new-born girl. Within five years there were five more births, though only two of them survived beyond a few years. The Bach residence encompassed three floors in the same building as St. Thomas School, which meant the composer was surrounded by not only his rapidly expanding family but also more than fifty boarding-school pupils in the dorms. Bach's study, which looked out onto a tree-lined promenade, was separated from the junior classrooms by only a thin partition. The back of the building overlooked gardens, the river Pleisse, and a mill, the sounds of its wheel presumably blending with the music coming from the school practice-room. The mill wheel likely brought to mind Bach's ancestor, the "white bread baker" Veit Bach, who in the sixteenth century, according to family lore, would strum his cittern accompanied by the rhythmic grinding of the mill, a sound perhaps not unlike the mechanical turning effect of this prelude.

At least one suite, this one, was probably composed in Leipzig. We do not know whether Bach actually planned the six suites as one cycle or whether they were created individually at different times and only later unified as a collection of six. The uniform structure of the suites suggests a common plan, but that does not mean all of the suites originated in the same period. One sign that they did not is found in the fact that suites four and six "stand apart from the others through their virtuoso runs, frequent chordal stops, and greater length," according to the definitive Bärenreiter edition of the music. Another indication that some suites were composed at different times is the title of this prelude; where all the others are called *prelude*, this one is written in the German as *praeludium*.

There is one other clue in the prelude: that trap door of snaky semitones that warbles out of nowhere to make a nearly Eastern statement. The forces of Islam were pressing against the borders of Austria when Bach was composing the Cello Suites; the foreign-sounding notes might have been inspired by Turkish or Arabic influences. But the phrase sounds heavily Hebraic—is it conceivable that Bach came up with a Jewish reference here? And where might he have come into contact with a Jewish person, if not in cosmopolitan Leipzig?

ALLEMANDE

*In Bach there is too much crude Christianity... He
stands at the threshold of modern European music but
he is always looking back toward the Middle Ages.*
FRIEDRICH NIETZSCHE, 1878

IN LEIPZIG'S MUNICIPAL history museum there is an artifact that
must have exercised dread in the city during the time Bach
lived there. Hanging in a showcase is a steel sword complete
with brass hilt and leather scabbard. From 1721, for more than a
century, it was the weapon brandished by Leipzig's official
town executioner. We know the sword was used. In 1723, the
year Bach arrived in Leipzig, eighteen-year-old Susanna
Pfeifferin was beheaded in public for being a "child-murderess."
In 1727 a thief-murderer was eventually beheaded after a number of unsuccessful attempts. Other executions during Bach's
time included various thieves, another child-murderer, and
three men together, one of whom was broken on the wheel.
And in 1732 the gallows were repaired to dispatch an unnamed
foreigner from Bohemia. By then no one had been hanged
since "a Jew" some years earlier.

Bach in all probability would have witnessed some of the
executions. His pupils at St. Thomas actually sang hymns as
part of the execution ritual. The grim scenario would begin

once the prisoner emerged from detention, surrounded by Saxon soldiers. The students began singing as the condemned was displayed to the gathering crowd and taken along a processional route through the Grimma Gate of the walled city and to the Rabenstein place of execution. The city gates were closed, and a strange quiet shrouded the market square. There the ceremony concluded with military drums, cavalry, foot soldiers, robed officials, and, finally, the fall of the executioner's sword. Once the fatal blow was struck, the gates reopened and the hubbub of life resumed in the city.

In 1723 Bach began composing the *St. John Passion*, the first of his two oratorio-like masterpieces, which told the Passion (or Crucifixion) story of Jesus based on the Gospel of St. John. The powerful work alternates choral numbers with solo vocal numbers, uses freely composed verses and hymns, and taps Italian operatic genres. The unforgettable beginning of the *St. John Passion*—a brewing storm of ominous and eerily beautiful chords—was first performed during Good Friday vespers in 1724 at Leipzig's St. Nicholas Church. "One can only guess what impact that uniquely touching work made," writes Bach biographer Peter Williams. "...the congregation can never have heard anything like its opening bars."

But, musical greatness aside, the work remains problematic. The *St. John Passion* is a composition with a dark side. The thorniest issue is what some perceive as anti-Semitism in the text, and possibly in the music. The main problem boils down to assigning blame for the killing of Jesus. The Gospel of John holds the Jews responsible for forcing the hand of a benevolent governor to kill their imposter king. Ergo, they are eternally damned.

The music historian Richard Taruskin has placed the *St. John Passion* on a list of artworks that possibly reinforce anti-Semitism. In his multi-volume *Oxford History of Western Music*, Taruskin draws a distinction between what the message meant in the eighteenth century and what it means today.

He suggests that in Bach's day the message that the Jews killed Christ was uncontroversial — everyone in Christendom thought as much, and that factoid in a libretto (however disturbing to post-Holocaust ears) was a thoroughly mundane reference back in 1724. But three centuries later the political climate has changed and the message is more dangerous.

I heard a performance of the *St. John Passion* in 2006 by the Montreal Symphony Orchestra, under the baton of its newly hired maestro Kent Nagano. Nagano could be a poster boy for what's new, multicultural, and cool in classical music. He is at the other end of the spectrum from the old-school tyrannical conductor who barked commands in a heavy central European accent as if he were privy to secret instructions from Mozart or Beethoven. Nagano was hired after the MSO's previous maestro, Charles Dutoit, stormed off the podium and quit in a hiring spat after the players' guild accused him of the orchestral equivalent of spousal abuse.

A Californian of Japanese parentage, Nagano has rock-star hair and sculptural cheekbones; he has even modelled for a Gap jeans ad. He has programmed Frank Zappa, has worked with the Icelandic alternative-rock diva Björk, and until not long ago led the onetime hippied-out Berkeley orchestra, which he began with three decades ago. He is the epitome of the New Age sensitive maestro. Yet in a pre-concert talk about the *St. John Passion*, the question of its intolerant dark side never came up.

The concert that evening employed supertitles, opera-style, so that the text of the music was projected above the stage in both English and French. After a shaky start, the performance reached the sublime heights one expects from Bach's vocal music. The music was played with mostly modern instruments in a stripped-down orchestra that also featured a core of period instruments: an archlute, a viola da gamba, a pair of violas d'amore, and a harpsichord. Seated in the acoustically ideal second-tier balcony, I was well placed to enjoy the music and follow the text. I can't say that the words killed the experience for me, but they did add a measure of discomfort. From the first reference to Jesus being taken away by "Jewish police," the drama bluntly hits the listener over the head with the fact that Pilate resists crucifying him. It is the Jewish crowd that clamours for crucifixion, beseeching the Roman governor to do it and rejecting his offer of clemency.

When the chorus belted out a raucous number that consisted solely of the words "Crucify, crucify" and the elderly lady sitting next to me stirred and started swaying to the upbeat rhythm, I wondered whether the text was running through her mind in any emotional way. I also tried to imagine what members of the church congregation of Bach's day felt after hearing such a performance. Perhaps the anti-Semitic component of the story was a commonplace touchstone of faith. But the Passion performance would have been structured as bookends to a sermon that might have touched on questions of sin, betrayal, apostasy. One wonders what would have been the reaction of some Leipzig townsfolk, after hearing the church service and two hours of highly charged Passion music, had they bumped into a couple of Jewish merchants in town for the city's famous trade fair.

One prominent musicologist questions whether the trouble lies in Bach's composition, which dramatically intensifies the text. "I wonder if the St. John Passion readily lends itself to anti-Jewish construal because of the highly expert musical setting of the biblical choruses," writes Michael Marissen. "No matter what the St. John Passion's arias, chorales, and framing choruses may have to offer as commentary, what may still ring too easily in people's ears today are the terrifying repetitions of the biblical text's 'Crucify, crucify!' If Bach's biblical choruses portray with great intensity the way some Jews reacted to Jesus, does this mean that the St. John Passion in part or in toto projects a universal hatred or negative view of the Jewish people?"

Marissen's answer is no. He argues that while Bach's libretto borrows liberally from various contemporary German Passion settings for the arias, its versions of some of these commentary verses "do not contain the egregiously anti-Jewish remarks found in their well-known source." In his probing book *Lutheranism, Anti-Judaism and Bach's St. John Passion*, Marissen concludes that Bach's Passion shows scant interest in the question of who killed Jesus. The focus is more on accountability for the death, and based on the concept of original sin, the view here is that all human beings are personally responsible for Jesus' death. Marissen doesn't deny that there are parts of Bach's *St. John Passion* that cast Judaism in a negative light. But overall he believes the work represents a step forward from previous works of a similar nature, opening the possibility of dialogue between creeds and focusing on the chorus that proclaims, "Be fully at peace."

Might Bach ever have known a Jewish person? Where might that Hebraic musical phrase in the fourth suite's prelude come from? Some scholars say that it's doubtful Bach was ever well acquainted with anyone Jewish. Jews had been driven out of Saxony in the sixteenth century. In Bach's day they were officially barred from living in Leipzig and—like Catholics and Calvinists—forbidden from owning property in the city. But there were some exceptions, such as a Jewish family named Levi that was living in Leipzig early in the century by order of the Saxon king, against the wishes of the city council. By the time of Bach's death there were seven Jewish families in the city. And Jewish merchants were allowed in Leipzig during the thrice-annual trade fairs, each of which lasted two or three weeks. A substantial amount of the commerce flowing during the fair—the pre-eminent trade event in central Europe—was handled by Jews, who were given entry passes, required to wear a piece of yellow cloth, and forced to pay steep taxes and fees. Bach could easily have wandered into the fair to purchase, say, a pipe from a Jewish tobacco merchant.

Or Bach's travels might well have placed him in contact with Jews, perhaps in a city like Hamburg, where a substantial Jewish population existed that was not confined to a ghetto.* There was even a Jewish enclave near Cöthen, in Grobzig, which was given formal status by the Prince of Cöthen in the mid-1720s. It is also possible that some of Bach's Christian acquaintances in Leipzig had Jewish roots, such as Johann Abraham Birnbaum, who would write a famous defence of Bach's music in the 1730s.

But if Bach ever came across Jewish music, it was more than likely while he was living in Leipzig, which would explain the mosaic of notes in the fourth prelude and provide a clue that he was working on the Cello Suites well into the 1720s.

---

* It is noteworthy that possibly the most virulent anti-Jewish polemics from Lutherans in this period came from the pen of Erdmann Neumeister, an orthodox Lutheran pastor in Hamburg. A four-day anti-Jewish riot erupted in Hamburg in 1730, instigated at least in part by a sermon delivered by Neumeister. Marissen points out that Bach set several Neumeister texts to music, though none that mention Jews or Judaism.

COURANTE

*[The key of E-flat] was reserved mostly for moments
of sublime seriousness, appropriate for dying thoughts,
or of love unto death, whether human or divine.*

DANIEL HEARTZ, MUSIC IN EUROPEAN CAPITALS

"VEXATION, ENVY, AND persecution" were the three most personal words ever to emerge from Bach's quill. There may have been others, but these three were the ones that survived the centuries. They were discovered in the late 1800s in the Moscow state archives in the form of a surprisingly candid letter Bach wrote to Georg Erdmann, the schoolmate with whom he made his long trek to Lüneburg at age fourteen. The subject was his working conditions in Leipzig. "I find that the post is by no means so lucrative as it was described to me," Bach complained in the letter, "...and the authorities are odd and little interested in music, so that I must live amid almost continual vexation, envy, and persecution..."

Bach's work as St. Thomas cantor, which encompassed the St. Thomas School, four main churches, and various municipal jurisdictions, made it likely that he would get tangled up in squabbles with officialdom. What made it inevitable was his stubborn, pugnacious character, sensitive to slights and finely tuned to matters of social prerogative. But there was also a political dimension to the disputes. Like much of the eighteenth-century world, Leipzig was caught in a tug-of-war between absolutism (the king) and the so-called estates, the latter being a hodgepodge of municipal interests together with some university and clerical parties that were defending their own rights against royal encroachment.

In this battle Bach appears squarely on the side of absolutism. For his time, Bach was not a modern man. The newfangled Enlightenment views, from Newton to Voltaire, that were spreading across Europe apparently held little attraction for him. He was rooted in the past, his mindset nearly medieval. Still, his professional ambitions were greater than any absolutist sympathies. When, for example, the Duke of Weimar blocked his move to Cöthen, Bach didn't for a second think he should know his place in a divinely ordered society that created dukes to implement the will of the Almighty. He resisted, ending up in the duke's jail, and ultimately overcame the absolutist obstacles to get to Cöthen and his new position of Capellmeister.

In Leipzig Bach was hired as a cantor, but he tried as best he could to continue being a Capellmeister, a preference that placed him on the side of the nobility and royalty. As if to illustrate the point, shortly before moving to Leipzig, Bach had a new personal seal made that superimposed his initials in a mirror image. The design was elegantly topped with a crown.

The Leipzig town council that hired Bach was divided into two factions, reflecting the era's political divisions. The estates faction was looking to hire a cantor in the traditional sense of the job, someone who would focus on teaching and the school as well as being responsible for music at the city's main churches. The absolutist faction, tied to the Saxon king August the Strong, was looking for a brilliant composer whose art would radiate splendour on the royal court in Dresden—that is to say, a Capellmeister in all but name. Bach was hired as the absolutist candidate.

In any case, Bach remained a Capellmeister on paper following his move to Leipzig. He still held the honorary title for Prince Leopold, who had graciously allowed Bach to leave Cöthen. Bach, accompanied by Anna Magdalena, returned to Cöthen at least twice, in 1724 and 1725, to provide music for his former prince. One can imagine Leopold's feelings as he listened to these two musicians, whom he had liked enough to hire separately on their own merits, a couple who had fallen for each other at his court, were married in the princely chapel, and had now moved up in the world. The devotion was on both sides. When in 1726 Bach started to publish his works for the first time, he dedicated the *Six Partitas*,* his set of harpsichord suites, to the newborn son of Leopold.

In Leipzig Bach would continue to value and employ his title of Cöthen Capellmeister for as long as Leopold reigned. When his battles with Leipzig officials developed, the self-described "Capellmeister to His Serene Highness the Prince of Cöthen" took umbrage in letters. He was quick in these minor disputes to assert his prerogatives, petitioning his claim ever upward until it reached the apex of authority, the Saxon king, who must have wondered why he was being pestered with such trifling matters.

A case in point was when Bach learned that another organist in town had taken over the cantor's traditional right to control various services at the university church. These services were a peripheral part of Bach's workload, but they represented the loss of an annual stipend. Bach wasted no time in protesting. The university authorities at first refused to budge, but under pressure from the prickly cantor agreed to restore one of the services and half the salary to him. Still

---

* The first partita is the only one of the set that begins with a *praeludium*. The prelude of this fourth suite is also the only cello suite that Bach apparently titled "Praeludium," which suggests the genesis of this cello suite could possibly have a similar time frame to the first of the *Six Partitas* — the mid-1720s.

dissatisfied, Bach then took his complaint to the highest power in the land, August the Strong.

Bach timed his action well. In the autumn of 1725 he performed an organ recital at a church in Dresden, the base of August the Strong. Bach knew Dresden. It was where in 1717 he had engaged in the organ duel with the Frenchman Marchand, emerging the winner by default when an allegedly fearful Marchand slipped out of town on a pre-dawn coach.

Bach's recital, according to a Hamburg newspaper, was "very well received by the local virtuosos at the court and in the city since he is greatly admired by all of them for his musical adroitness and art." The Leipzig cantor then used the occasion to register his first complaint to the king about the rival organist. Before the year was up there would be two more letters composed by "Your Royal Majesty's and Your Serene Electoral Highness's most humble and obedient servant." In the letters Bach combats the university officials regarding his loss of responsibilities and the twelve thalers at stake. Using language that suggests he would have made a formidable lawyer, he refutes the university's arguments point by point, gives a detailed accounting of the thalers in question, and even includes affidavits signed by the widows of two previous St. Thomas cantors. When the royal dust settled the following year, August the Strong made an even-handed ruling that awarded the twelve thalers to Bach, while allowing the other organist to play for the university church service.

We do not know Bach's reaction to the ruling. But he soon stepped up his efforts to pay homage to the Saxon ruler. In 1727, when the citizens of Leipzig marked their monarch's birthday, Bach was commissioned to compose the music (now lost), which was performed before the king by forty musicians with a backdrop of 300 torch-carrying students in the market square. The text of Bach's birthday cantata — printed on white satin, bound in deep scarlet velvet with gilt tassels and gold fringes — was presented to His Excellency the Chief Cupbearer, who voiced appreciation in the name of the king, who himself was cordoned off by a contingent of Saxon soldiers.

Later that year Bach was again called on to compose music, this time to commemorate the death of the king's wife, Christiane Eberhardine. A noble student commissioned the work, turning to the well-known poet Johann Christoph Gottsched to write the text. More wrangling followed because the ceremony was to take place at the university church, where the organist there was again trying to block Bach's authority. In the end Bach won the turf war and directed his funeral ode from the harpsichord.

Bach's ability to identify himself as a Capellmeister was shaken the following year with the premature death of Prince Leopold at thirty-three. He travelled to Cöthen one last time to provide the funeral music, accompanied by his wife and his eldest son, Friedemann, and several hired musicians. Bach and Anna Magdalena, surrounded by old friends and colleagues in the castle where the couple had made music so often as fledgling lovers, can only have been deeply saddened by this untimely adieu to their late prince. The spring funeral was held in the illuminated cathedral, its walls veiled in black, with Bach's music greeting the horse-drawn hearse that carried the princely casket. The music is now lost, but it borrowed no fewer than nine movements from the *St. Matthew Passion*, which Bach had premiered two years earlier. If seeing this sublime Passion music reworked for a more worldly purpose might perturb some devout listeners, it apparently did not trouble Bach, who must have found the emotional occasion equal to the masterpiece.

The composer must have appreciated the high quality of his *St. Matthew Passion*. Of course he could never imagine that this music, exactly one hundred years later in the hands of the twenty-year-old grandson of a celebrated Jewish philosopher, would launch his popular reputation.* Nor could it have crossed his mind that it would one day be a contender for the greatest music ever composed. Despite the religious halo often placed over Bach's head, he had no problem recycling intensely sacred music for secular purposes. And the court atmosphere of Cöthen, where his art no doubt had a receptive audience, might have been considered by the composer a worthier venue for one of his masterworks.

For his efforts, Bach was paid the handsome sum of 230 thalers by the court of Cöthen. But it would be his last commission for the princely house. With the death of Leopold, so too expired Bach's title of Capellmeister to the Prince of Cöthen. And he was not enthusiastic about being merely the cantor of a Lutheran boarding school.

BACH'S FRUSTRATIONS IN the workplace were soothed by his affection for Anna Magdalena and their close-knit family life. The Bachs had arrived in Leipzig with five children. Over the next couple of decades, Anna Magdalena would give birth to thirteen children, six of whom survived to adulthood. She had put aside her career as a talented soprano to follow her husband to Leipzig. Whereas she was a highly paid court singer in Cöthen, in Leipzig she wouldn't get much opportunity to sing in public. Bach's job was to provide music for church services, where women were banned from performing. Her singing career, as a result, was probably reduced to performances at princely courts and impromptu concerts at home.

Bach clearly appreciated his wife. Although overworked by his responsibilities as cantor and his own creative projects, he

....
* At the time of the March 1729 funeral, in the neighbouring town of Dessau, the mother of Moses Mendelssohn was pregnant with the future philosopher.

managed to find the time to show his affection with a songbird, yellow carnations, and romantic poetry.

He also took obvious pride in the academic accomplishments of his sons, an opportunity he had never had. As the first St. Thomas cantor in recent memory who was not a university graduate, Bach may have felt sensitive about the issue. (His predecessor was the highly educated Johann Kuhnau, a lawyer and linguist who had even written a satirical novel.) His limited scholastic background may have felt like a disadvantage in his many legalistic squabbles with authorities, and he was determined to ensure first-rate schooling for his sons. All of them attended university. Friedemann and Emanuel progressed from St. Thomas School to the reputable University of Leipzig. In their first Christmas in Leipzig, a proud father presented Friedemann with a certificate symbolically marking his registration for eventual matriculation at the university.

Bach had a special relationship with his first-born son. The father–son music lessons, which began seriously when Friedemann was ten, were immortalized by the exercise book Bach wrote out, filled with small preludes, dance settings, and suites, and known to history as the *Little Clavier Book for Wilhelm Friedemann Bach*. "Few glimpses of any composer's life and father's affection are clearer than the one offered here by one little piece of music," writes biographer Peter Williams. The father–son relationship is detected in one small item from the book, an allemande that Bach apparently began and the boy continued, but was unable to return to the tonic key without his father's help. That little book would one day become one of the most influential guides for keyboard instruction.

In Leipzig during the 1720s the boy his father nicknamed "Friede" was old enough to accompany Bach on a number of out-of-town trips, and when he got older, to the opera in Dresden. "Friedemann," Bach is quoted as saying, "shan't we go again to hear the lovely Dresden ditties?" The two presumably had more highbrow musical tastes. Or did they?

By the late 1720s Friedemann was on his way to becoming one of Germany's finest organists—eventually he would be considered *the* finest. To get a well-rounded musical education, he was sent away to take private violin lessons in Merseburg, the only of Bach's sons to be given that opportunity. When Bach and Anna Magdalena travelled to Cöthen at the end of the decade for the funeral of Prince Leopold, Friedemann joined them in the performance. And when Bach got word that Handel was visiting his mother in nearby Halle, he was too ill to travel himself but immediately dispatched his eldest son to personally invite the famous German expat to visit him in Leipzig.*

The number-two son, Emanuel, was not as close to Bach, but his future success hints that he may have benefited from being less emotionally in debt to his father than was Friedemann. Bach, naturally, was his teacher. By the age of eleven it was said that Emanuel could play his father's keyboard music at sight. And by the late 1720s both sons were working as Bach's assistants with private instruction, rehearsals, and copying of music (so was Anna Magdalena, whose handwriting had by this time become indistinguishable from her husband's).

Despite his growing family and ongoing production of spectacular compositions, by the end of the decade Bach felt tied down in his post. His independent temperament did not square with a position that was circumscribed at every turn. He was constitutionally unsuited to the job of cantor.

....

* Handel, either busy or not terribly interested in meeting another local organist, politely declined. It was the second time Bach had attempted to meet up with the celebrated composer. Back in 1719 he travelled to Halle when he heard Handel was visiting, but arrived too late. Although Handel and Bach were born within weeks of each other and in towns not far apart, they would never cross paths.

After the death of Prince Leopold, when his title of Capell-meister expired, Bach wasted no time filling the void on his résumé. He promptly managed to secure the title of Capell-meister to the Duke of Weissenfels. It was purely an honorary title, but he obviously desired it. In a way, Bach even took control of his own *Capelle*. In 1729 he become director of the Collegium Musicum, a chamber music concert series that was held weekly in Zimmermann's café. His combined activities during this period—publishing his harpsichord partitas, becoming titular Capellmeister again, leading the concerts at Zimmermann's—show that Bach was refocusing his creative energies outside the church and away from his day job as cantor.

One wonders if at age forty-five a midlife crisis was at work. Bach was used to being surrounded by death, but one eighteen-month period at the end of the 1720s was heavily marked by loss. Aside from the death of Prince Leopold, Bach lost two children (a newborn and a three-year-old son) as well as his first wife's older sister, Friedelena (who'd been living in his household for two decades), and his last surviving sibling, his older sister, Maria Salome.

As the decade closed, Bach continued to run into troubles with school and city officials. He had composed a stunning body of high-calibre work that numbered some 200 cantatas, each one seemingly better than the next, at least two Passions, and a slew of dazzling instrumental works, including the Cello Suites. His abrupt end to cantata composition around this time may have been because he had put together more than enough material than he would ever need for church services. Meanwhile, the disputes with Leipzig authorities gathered steam. Within a year, the cantor would be at a breaking point.

SARABANDE

Apt to move the Passions and to disturb the tranquility of the Mind. JAMES TALBOT, 1690

WHEN NAZI GERMANY launched its invasion of France, Pablo Casals was living in exile just across the Pyrenees, in Prades. It was as near to Catalonia as he could get without actually being in Franco-ruled Spain. But with the German invasion in June 1940 his situation changed drastically. The Nazis quickly occupied the heart of France. In unoccupied parts of the country, the collaborationist Vichy regime would soon hold sway. Later the Germans would move in directly.

Performing a Bach suite in Holland or Switzerland, as he'd done earlier in the year, was now out of the question. The risks multiplied. Spain might also join the war, in which case Franco's soldiers would pour across the border and deal with Republican irritants like Casals in the way they knew best: a bullet to the head.

For the time being, Casals had adjusted to life in exile. Along with his widowed friend Señora Franchisca ("Frasquita") Capdevila and the Alavedra family, Casals relocated to a quaint two-storey cottage across from the *Hôtel de ville*. With its twisting cobbled streets, whitewashed homes with red-tiled roofs, and acacia trees in bloom, the village of Prades easily conjured up the Catalonia of his youth. There were morning walks with his now slow-moving dog, Follett. He would lift his hat in greeting to Mont Canigou, the majestic peak that since the eleventh century had been a symbol of Catalan identity.

Casals was now sixty-six years old. Money was tight, as his bank account had been frozen by the collaborationist authorities. Food was scarce—he got by on boiled turnips, beans, vegetables, and the occasional potato. He began to suffer from headaches, dizzy spells, and rheumatism in his shoulder. His regular visits to the camps holding Catalan refugees left him feeling deflated; he knew he was living in far better conditions. But he was also a high-profile target if the war came closer to home. In November 1942 the Nazis took control of unoccupied France, and Prades fell into the hands of the Vichy militia and the Gestapo. Casals' cottage was under surveillance. Some townsfolk turned hostile, and rumours swirled about the Catalan cellist: resistance member, Communist, anarchist, assassin. He lived in constant anxiety.

On one particular afternoon his worst fears materialized. An official car pulled up in front of his cottage and three Nazi officers knocked on the door. Casals was writing at his worktable when he heard footsteps coming up the stairs to his room. The Germans entered his room, clicked the heels of their gleaming boots, and gave the *Heil Hitler* salute. They were eerily polite.

"We have come to pay our respects," they informed him. "We are great admirers of your music—we have heard about Casals from our parents, about concerts of yours they attended." They asked if he needed anything, then wondered why he was lodged in such cramped, shabby quarters rather than living in Spain. Casals replied by stating his opposition to Franco. They soon got to the point of the visit: Casals was invited to travel to Germany and play for the German people. He declined the offer, saying that his position regarding Germany was the same as it was for Spain. A strained silence followed.

The senior officer then spoke. "You have the wrong idea about Germany," he said. "Der Führer is greatly interested in the arts and in the welfare of artists. He loves music especially. If you come to Berlin, he himself will attend your performance. You will be welcomed by all the people. And we are authorized to say that a special railroad car will be placed at your disposal..."

Casals had an excuse up his sleeve. He couldn't perform a concert because he was suffering from rheumatism in his shoulder. The Nazi trio then requested an autographed photograph. He reluctantly complied. "And while we are here," continued the lead officer, "perhaps would you do us a personal favour? Would you play some Brahms or Bach for us?" Casals replied that his rheumatism made it impossible. The Nazi officer walked over to the piano and played a Bach aria. Then he asked to see Casals' cello. The older man obliged, removing his instrument from its case and placing it on the bed. "One of them picked it up, and the others touched it," he recounted. "And suddenly I felt deathly ill..."

But that was the end of it. The Germans walked out, sat in their vehicle for a while, then returned to take photographs of Casals standing on the porch before finally leaving.

Had he agreed to play in Nazi Germany Casals would have found the music of Bach to be extremely welcome. Hitler's main musical obsession was Wagner, but the Nazi pantheon of composers included Beethoven, Bruckner, Schumann, Brahms, and Bach. Mendelssohn, by contrast, who did so much to make Bach famous, was denounced as a Jew, his statue in Leipzig toppled, his music banned.

The responses of musicians under Nazi rule were as varied as with other citizens in France and Germany. Casals' former colleagues in the great Cortot-Thibaud-Casals trio, who had replaced him with cellist Pierre Fournier in 1940, were more politically flexible. Alfred Cortot occupied a cultural post in the Vichy regime and performed a number of concerts in Nazi

Germany in 1942. Jacques Thibaud, who lost a son in the Second World War, performed with Cortot at a Mozart festival in Paris organized by the Nazis.*

In 1944 the Allies invaded Normandy, the Nazis pulled out of France, and Casals geared up for his return to the concert hall. Although he'd given a number of local benefit concerts to aid victims of war, he had not performed publicly during the German occupation. "Now that the enemy has been forced to leave," he wrote a friend, "I have resumed my practicing and you will be pleased to know that I am making daily progress."

He was inundated with concert offers. The day before Christmas, a letter was printed in the *New York Times* informing readers that Casals was not in a Spanish concentration camp but "living in seclusion in the south of France." A blank cheque arrived from an American promoter. From Paris alone came fifty-six invitations to stage his first postwar concert. But he chose London. He had spent the war years tuned in to the BBC for news, sometimes huddled beneath a blanket to muffle the incriminating sounds in occupied France. He had looked to Britain as the guarantor of a free Spain. In 1945 Casals boarded a British Airways plane—the airline refused to accept payment—en route to his first concert with an orchestra since before the war.

The performance took place at the Royal Albert Hall. Backed by the BBC Symphony Orchestra under Sir Adrian Boult, he performed the Schumann and Elgar cello concertos, capped by the otherworldly sarabande from the fifth cello suite as an encore. Germany had surrendered only twenty days earlier, and Casals was received as a hero. Twelve thousand people came to hear him, and he required a police escort to get from the

* Cortot was arrested after the war. Upon release, he was banned from performing for one year. Thibaud died in a plane crash in 1953 en route to entertain French troops in Indochina. Casals never forgave Thibaud but later mended fences with Cortot.

dressing room to the car after the concert. He was driven straight to a studio, where he played his arrangement of the Catalan folk melody "The Song of the Birds" and spoke a few words in Catalan, which were broadcast along with the evening's concert by BBC's Foreign Service.

His enthusiasm for England, though, wouldn't last. Four months after this first trip, Casals returned for a concert tour. By then it had become clear to him that London had more pressing concerns than the fate of Catalonia. The Western powers, having just defeated Germany and then Japan, were moving the pieces across a geopolitical chessboard against Soviet Russia. Rolling back Franco's fascist regime in Spain, a regime that in any case had made anti-Communism its calling card, was not a priority. Casals was stunned. He could not understand how the West could make its peace with the Spanish dictator who'd sided with Mussolini and Hitler.

To protest these politics, Casals cut short his British concert tour and left England. France proved equally disappointing. He played some benefit shows in Switzerland, and then he made his decision. By December he had decided not to perform again in any country that recognized Franco's rule. Then he ceased performing anywhere at all.

Casals planted his cello in Prades, in that remote valley where the orange-coloured earth nourished lush vineyards and orchards. He was seventy years old. It may have come as some relief not to have to play, not to have to make compromises with a world that had let him down.

BOURRÉE

The more worn a string, the better it sounds. And do
you know when it sounds best of all? Just before it's
about to break. PABLO CASALS

IN THE LATE 1940s Casals was in self-imposed exile from the
concert stage. In his mid-seventies, he assumed he was heading into his sunset years, and by any reckoning was entitled to
a dignified retirement.

Though Prades was provincial and inaccessible, its land-
scape was very familiar to a displaced Catalan. The Pyrenees
village, which had been conquered by France in the seventeenth century, retained much of its Catalan flavour. Casals felt
almost at home.

His routine was pleasant enough. He began each day by
playing from Bach's *Well-Tempered Clavier* on the piano, then
heading out for a walk with his German shepherd, cocking an
ear for birdsong and saluting the snow-capped peak of Mont
Canigou. He played his cello, which now looked the worse for
wear. He was constantly lighting his curved pipe with matches,
which would occasionally fall into his instrument's sound holes.
He could hear them rolling around inside when he picked up
the cello, which looked as if it hadn't been cleaned since the
Civil War. A piece of paper was lodged under the bridge for

support, and a broken matchstick was wedged under a string on the peg box to keep it taut.

Casals made a little time for composing, took on a few pupils, wrote letters in Spanish, Catalan, and French, and continued to occupy himself with the plight of Catalan refugees. It made for an agreeable, if parochial, end point for the century's greatest cellist.

Yet those who knew Casals, in particular a younger generation of musicians who met him for the first time following the war, saw his retirement as needless isolation that was prematurely wasting a historical figure. They urged him to return to the concert hall. But Casals, like Mont Canigou, the symbol of Catalan patriotism, would not move. If anyone wanted to see him, they would have to go to the mountain.

The man who did eventually move Casals was Alexander Schneider, a Lithuanian-born violinist with an electrified burst of hair and talent and energy to match. Schneider put a promising chamber music career on hold to study with Casals in Prades, focusing on Bach's sonatas and partitas for solo violin. He was determined to ease Casals out of exile. The year 1950 was coming up, marking the bicentennial of Bach's death, and Casals was receiving numerous invitations to play for the occasion. "Managers, officials, and admirers in all places of the world," reported the New York Times, "have pleaded with him to make his great art available for concerts in their countries. They have offered him enormous fees, palatial homes, and honorary titles, but he has persistently declined."

It pained Casals to decline many of the invitations, and most painful was a Bach concert planned at St. Thomas Church in Leipzig. What brought him out of retirement was the idea for a Bach festival in Prades under his own conducting baton. Schneider brought the plan to Casals and worked on him for half a year before Casals finally agreed. He had not changed his politics. "England and America promised us that after the war the Allies, in whom we had all our faith and to whom we gave all our support, both moral and practical, would support us," he told *Life* magazine. "Thousands of Spanish people fought with the Allies against the Germans. I, too, risked my life many times, believing them. They abandoned us. It would not be dignified to go to those countries and earn their money under such circumstances." But the cause was gathering dust. Silence was depriving Casals of his most effective means of protest. Only his cello could bring attention to his politics. He would restring his weapon.

The out-of-the-way mountain town of 4,300 was an unlikely venue for what turned out to be one of the most significant musical events of the postwar period. Townsfolk had grown used to the sight of their small, balding cellist and the handful of pupils who visited his cottage. Now the automobiles rolling into town and the morning train from Perpignan disgorged some of the planet's most accomplished musicians, among them Mieczyslaw Horszowski, Clara Haskil, Rudolf Serkin, and Isaac Stern.

Rehearsals began in the dining hall of the local girls' school, which was occasionally jolted by the sounds of the passing train. Casals welcomed the thirty-piece orchestra, saying that they were there in homage to Bach but would give pleasure to listeners and themselves in the process. "I thank you for coming," he said. "I love you. And now, let us begin." With baton in hand, he set about turning the musicians, half of whom came from America, into a cohesive orchestral unit. The plan was for six chamber music evenings and six orchestral evenings, which would be kicked off with Casals playing one of the Bach cello suites. He would then turn his attention to conducting the orchestra.

Prades adapted to its new persona. Shops in town displayed Casals memorabilia—biographies, records, and photographs. The local bakery showcased a cake shaped like a cello. An ice cream booth was set up. Catalonian flags and banners flew over the main square. Even the local prostitute reported an upswing in business.

The first concert of the Bach Festival took place on June 2. Throngs of locals lined the floodlit cobbled square facing the Church of St. Peter while ticket holders filed past and entered the church with its ornate altar. Among the audience were minor royalty, patrons of the arts, the French president's wife, and the president-in-exile of Republican Spain, Juan Negrín, who was incognito. There was also a group of Catalans who'd walked across the border and down the Pyrenees to attend, despite the Franco government's official closure of the border. The reason given for the closure was that Casals was organizing a guerrilla force in Prades—with violinist Schneider as his chief of staff!—as a prelude to a communist takeover of Spain. Casals chatted with his compatriots before the concert.

The local religious potentate, the Bishop of Saint-Fleur, opened the festival with a long-winded welcome speech in which he requested that no applause be made in the church. He then gestured to Casals, who emerged from the sacristy and matter-of-factly strode up to the simple wooden platform where his musical resurrection was to take place.

Columbia Records had installed microphones, and the festival would yield more than ten discs from the live recording—with one exception: the solo cello suites. The curtain-raiser for the festival was, on Casals' orders, not to be recorded. In fact, nobody really knew what the seventy-three-year-old cellist sounded like anymore. There were rumours that a muscular problem was the real reason he had stopped playing. Had he been accompanied by piano, or if his cello was to be blended into an orchestral work, the pressure would not have been so intense. But the Bach suites are unforgiving; the player has nothing to hide behind.

The audience rose to its feet in silence, respecting the bishop's request. Casals executed a quick bow. And with a brusque wave of his cello bow he motioned the crowd to be seated. Sixty years after first laying eyes on the Bach suites in a Barcelona shop, he again shut out everything from his mind but the music. Half a century after he had dared perform a cello suite in public, he pressed his bow to the G string in that familiar position.

"The stroke of his bow was like heavy silk," reported an account in *The New Yorker*, "his vibrato was strong and rapid as that in the throat of a young man. What Casals gave was the culmination of a life devoted to technique, enriched by recent sad years of seclusion, and freed once more for pleasure."

When he got to the last note of the gigue, the audience once again rose to its feet in eerie silence, barely resisting the urge to applaud. Every doubt had melted away.

GIGUE

The most exuberant virtuoso movement in all six
cello suites is worked out with extreme concentration,
and yet it seems to have been jotted down in a spirit
of great fun. HANS VOGT

THE SOLO CELLO was for me a perfect entrée into the sound
world of Bach. With the Cello Suites the guitarist in me
could easily relate to the fingerboard of an acoustic string
instrument. And with an instrumental work I was able to side-
step an obstacle that comes with Bach's magnificent vocal
music—Lutheran religious content, not always of the most
poetic form, delivered in German.

But you don't get very far in the world of Bach without realizing that his vocal music represents the ultimate for legions of
listeners. Bach composed wagonloads of vocal music—some
200 cantatas, as well as the two Passions, a few oratorios, a Magni-
ficat, and the Mass in B Minor. File almost all of this material
under *Sublime*, whether it's a single voice simply embroidered
with a bass line or a large choir backed by a baroque orchestra
brimming with trumpets and drums. The human voice, in Bach
as in pop, provides wow factor.

When I got wind of a Bach Weekend taking place in the
spring of 2008 at a bucolic music centre north of Montreal, I

took a look at the program and realized I could—in theory—participate. All I would have to do is sing. I couldn't play harpsichord or cello or any of the standard baroque instruments well enough to contemplate performing a Bach cantata, but my vocal cords were presumably functional. So I filled out the registration form for the weekend and ticked off the box next to *choir*. We would be rehearsing and performing a Bach cantata called *Give the Hungry Man Thy Bread* (*Brich dem Hungrigen dein Brot*).

More than once in my Bach journey I bemoaned the fact that my music of choice was so austere—just one cello. The more I became exposed to Bach's richly textured vocal oeuvre, the more my Bachian enthusiasm would achieve liftoff. I figured it was a sign that I had arrived, that I had successfully made the transition from classical neophyte to classical nerd. But I had never strayed too far from the Cello Suites. Now I would be able to inhabit the inner sanctum of the baroque master's most uplifting music, my voice streaming along in Bach's oceanic polyphony.

I went out and purchased a deluxe recording of the cantata in question, with John Eliot Gardiner conducting the Monteverdi Choir and the English Baroque Soloists. The CD was beautifully packaged and featured the highest production values. But *Give the Hungry Man Thy Bread* initially struck me as a mediocre piece in the Bach oeuvre, lacking the punchy trumpets and percussion of his catchiest cantatas. That first impression, happily, faded with repeated listening—the cantata turns out to be spectacular. By continuously listening to the disc before the Bach Weekend, I planned to get a head start on this choir business.

But I didn't know how to sight-read music. I was not a literate musician; I had never read music beyond chord charts or the user-friendly guitar tablature designed for unschooled strummers. Reading traditional music notation was not something I could do without a laborious act of decoding. I learned how to sight-read in the most rudimentary way when I took cello lessons, but that ability faded when my lessons stopped, and it wouldn't be the same as sight-reading vocal lines for a choir. It finally dawned on me that the cantata was so complex vocally—with tenors and basses and altos and sopranos swooping in and out of the music at different times with different lines in wondrous polyphony—that singing Bach would be no walk in the park.

With my anxiety percolating, I called the number of a neighbourhood music school, explained my situation, and fielded a few alarming questions. How much time did I have? One week. The school arranged for two lessons.

On a Saturday afternoon I headed to the music school with my recording of the cantata and a score of the music that the Bach Weekend organizers had helpfully scanned and emailed. My teacher was Adam, a goateed singer and guitarist whose longish hair was kept in check by a beret. He was cool. He liked Bach.

To determine which part I should sing, Adam had me vocalize. He was of the opinion that I was probably a baritone—midway between the bass and tenor ranges. He suggested I sing the bass; it would be easier and more educational harmonically. But nothing about *Give the Hungry Man Thy Bread* was easy.

We dived into the score and it didn't take very long to figure out I was in way over my head. Even Adam was occasionally lost. Vocal parts were coming in and out of the mix as if cut and pasted by some fiendish turntablist. Equally daunting were the tricky German words. Adam showed me how to read the music and how the time signature worked, which helped. We then went over the notes. We played and replayed the disc I had brought to make sense of the score. It was gorgeous—and ridiculously difficult. A discussion about the timing of the music got mathematical, lost me, and depressed me. The Bach Weekend flashed before my eyes as a humiliating debacle.

"I admire you," said Adam, as the lesson wrapped up, "for jumping into this"—he searched for the right word—"spaghetti polyphony."

A few days later I had lesson number two, this time with Charlotte, a more experienced vocal teacher and a professional singer. Charlotte had me sing a bit and came to the same conclusion about my range. We immediately tackled the score. Before I knew it I was singing the notes with Charlotte at the piano and we were motoring through *Give the Hungry Man Thy Bread*. Or to be more accurate, she was motoring and I was hitching a ride on the slow lane of the autobahn of *Brich dem Hungrigen dein Brot*.

"That's it!" Charlotte would shriek when I managed to more or less imitate a snaky bass phrase and land on the right note. She was so musically vivacious, feeling her way through the cantata, explaining the German diction, and showing me the chords, the other vocal parts, the orchestration, the syncopated rhythm that verged on jazz—the fabulous logic of it all.

"That's the beauty of this stuff," she said. "It makes sense where it's going to go. It will surprise you, but it's wonderful. It's so organic. He'll throw you a curveball—Bach is among the most complicated stuff ever—but it's appealing in that it's still really enjoyable."

Still, I had my issues. "I wish Bach had been Italian," I grumbled after one more failed attempt at Teutonic gargling. Besides, linguistic correctness aside, the German words didn't necessarily sit well with my Judaism. As musicologist Richard Taruskin observed in a review of a Bach cantata that featured an aria titled "Shut Up, Stumbling Reason," there is something terrifying, "perhaps more now than in Bach's own time, since we have greater reason than Bach's contemporaries ever had to wince at the end of a high-pitched German voice stridently shouting reason down." The religious text can also be challenging to twenty-first-century ears. One particularly downbeat lyric for another Bach cantata (No. 179) contains these words: "My sins sicken me like pus in my bones; help me, Jesus, lamb of God, for I am sinking in deepest slime."

Giving bread to the hungry, by contrast, was an excellent theme. I was greatly relieved that the words of my cantata, taken mostly from the Old Testament, were more philanthropic than messianic. But when I had to belt out *"Schnell!"* it left a bad aftertaste.

Charlotte, however, didn't share my wish to croon in the sunny language of Verdi. "Oh, I don't, because then it wouldn't have sounded like this. They didn't have the same churches, they didn't have the same sort of aesthetic, that same kind of bleak pain that allows the really beautiful stuff to be really beautiful—you know what I mean?"

I tape-recorded the lesson in order to practise it on my own. Charlotte wished me well. "You get it, maybe more than you know," she said. "It makes sense."

Three days later my car rolled into the Canadian Amateur Music Centre on Lake Macdonald, in Quebec's Laurentian Mountains northwest of Montreal. Inside the rustic three-storey main lodge I picked up the key to my room and a schedule for the jam-packed weekend. Each of the lodge's forty rooms was named after a notable music-maker; I was occupying Hildegard von Bingen, a medieval German composer and visionary. The room couldn't have been more monastic, though it offered a nicely meditative view of the woods and lake, just emerging from winter.

At a general assembly that evening I took a chair alongside the other Bach weekenders and was handed a dog-eared score of the cantata. The crowd mirrored your average classical music concert: elderly white folk, with a handful of young music students. The chit-chat revolved around who was alto and who was soprano. Two women in the row ahead of me were crocheting. I had a sinking feeling that I had just checked myself into a seniors' residence for the sunset years.

The centre's director went over the rules. No going onto the lake, which was only half frozen. Wake up at 7:15 a.m. No practising after 11 p.m. A birdwatching excursion at 6:15 a.m. Ping-pong downstairs. Meanwhile the amateur instrumentalists had trundled in and were setting up their gear at the front of the room; a woman with angular features took out a cello and I felt immensely envious.

I was pointed in the direction of the back chairs, where men of a certain age were bobbing around and saying "Bass?" or "Tenor?" to each other. Identifying myself as a bass, I was directed to a chair in the designated section between Louis and Yves. Yves, tall, serious, ramrod straight, introduced himself as a professional German diction coach and singer. Louis, who had driven in from Quebec City, also seemed to know his stuff. They turned out to be the star male voices in the solo movements of the cantata, Yves blowing away the crowd with his highly polished, booming voice, and Louis much less impressively straining his cords like a karaoke enthusiast with a deathbed wish.

The amateur orchestra sounded alarmingly wobbly to the ears of someone who'd been listening to state-of-the-art Bach by John Eliot Gardiner. My first impression was of an oompah band that needed to pull up its lederhosen. So much for the indestructible beauty of Bach's compositions. But it occurred to me that this is how his music might have sounded in ages past, performed by local-yokel orchestras and choirs without recordings or modern musicology to guide them. Even Bach often struggled with inexpert musicians and little time for rehearsals.

The conductor, Christopher Jackson, put us through our paces. I was happily able to sing the first page or so but then was lost in the woods. The booming cellistic voice of Yves standing next to me helped my cause, and he would occasionally serve as my personal GPS for the score. But, singing next to such a paragon of vocal virtue, I feared that my wayward voice was a personal affront to Bach, Luther, German diction, and the eighteenth century in general.

The next morning I was soothed out of sleep by some harmonizing sopranos going from door to door on wake-up duty. After breakfast it was back to Bach. I was definitely the weak link in the chain of eight bass singers. A smaller workshop followed in which Yves coached the basses and tenors. They sounded quite good. I also used the occasion to highlight in yellow marker my lines in the score. What with the German words, the changing time signatures, and the notation system on four separate staves, I needed the training wheels.

Over lunch I sat with three older women and was comforted to learn that two of them also found the cantata rough going. A violinist, registered in the choir, lamented that "there are so many notes." Afterwards I took a walk outside the lodge, the sun beating down on the lingering snows of winter. People practising Bach seemed to be everywhere. Outside, one of the younger soloists, Anne-Marie, she of the flaming hair and lovely pipes, was sitting in the front seat of a Pontiac Sunfire going over the score. I bumped into an Ontario woman in a dazed state who was looking for a practice shed with a piano that was supposed to be somewhere in the woods, so she could work on her lines. "It's not obvious," she said of her vocal part. From various rooms of the lodge, the violin and flutes and other instruments of the amateur ensemble could be heard, all straining to master the 300-year-old handwriting of Johann Sebastian Bach.

I decided to skip the afternoon session on German diction and instead practise *Brich dem Hungrigen dein Brot*. I took with me a small tape recorder that contained my lesson with

Charlotte. Practice sheds were scattered about the woods, and I scrunched through the snow in sandals looking for a suitable spot. The first shed I came across had a *Telemann* plaque above the door. I kept going. The next one was called *Bach*, so I naturally went inside the small A-frame cabin, flipped the light switch, and at once noticed a large laminated poster of Bach on the wall. I seemed to be in the right place. I turned on my tape player and went through the entire lesson with cheery Charlotte, my yellow-highlighted score on a wooden music stand and sunshine slashing through the windows.

At that evening's rehearsal I was able to follow the score from beginning to end. Reading it, that is. Singing it still required some blurry humming over parts that involved a few too many intricate notes. "It's a difficult cantata, have you noticed?" the conductor quipped to us choristers. He described it as "one-stop shopping" because of all the musical styles and techniques available in the one cantata.

After dinner there was yet another rehearsal, followed by the evening entertainment — folk dancing, which I skipped. I went to bed early, feeling like an athlete who has prepared all he can before the big game and leaves the rest to some higher power.

The next morning the soprano alarm clocks roused me from sleep, starting a day that involved breakfast, one more rehearsal, and then the "performance." After hearing a couple of Bach instrumental pieces by the much-improved amateur orchestra, we launched into our cantata with newfound vigour. It went well, and for a brief moment — as the high voices mingled with the low and all four registers meshed with the scaffolding and embroidery of violas, violins, flutes, cello, and harpsichord — I experienced my voice as a single wave in a blissful polyphonic ocean of Bach.

When we got to the last movement of the cantata — the chorale, which is a simple Lutheran hymn — the choir, acting on

Bach's instructions, put aside its pyrotechnics and polyphony to fuse into something infinitely more humble. I remembered the conductor urging us to sing generously. This was supremely generous music, he said, with nothing triumphalist about it.

It is hard to avoid over-sweetened sentiments in such circumstances. When I was practising alone in my Bach shed, with fifty-odd amateurs doing the same elsewhere, each in their own way trying their best to nail the music, it struck me as amazing how much this one individual has given to posterity. How many children and students, professionals and amateurs, virtuosos and maestros, not to mention listeners, have done what we were doing for three hundred years, trying to master something purely aesthetic, trying to break a code that connects us to something greater, more accomplished, more perfect than ourselves. I'm not sure what that something is. Does it make us better people? As my Bach Weekend wound down, I was tempted to say yes. But one knows better. The Nazis played Bach as well as anyone else. Infinitely changeable, Bach is what you make of him.

SUITE NO. 5
(C minor)

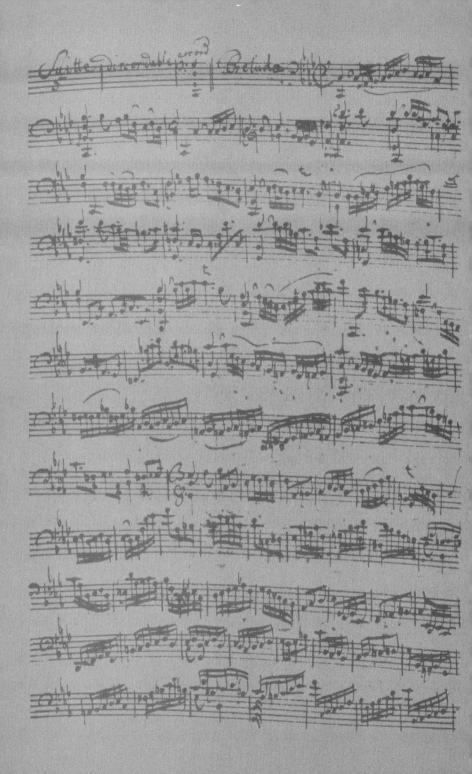

PRELUDE

One feels a colossus in chains, a giant endeavouring to
adjust his powers to the limitations of his medium of
expression. LEOPOLD GODOWSKY

THE NOTE OF foreboding is a C, the lowest string on the cello,
played here as a curtain-raiser that is massive, ominous, and
darkly majestic. The key is minor, and in the first brooding
phrases a weary frame rests in the deepest registers—an old
man telling an old story.

Here is how it came to this. Once upon a time these very
notes were among the most illustrious in Europe. They knew
splendour and extravagance; they were employed at the highest rungs of noble power. But they were surrounded by discord
and difficulties.

A jaunty narrative takes shape. One voice after another
comes in and out. The plot thickens. But is this the full story we
are hearing, or one strand within a greater polyphony? Something feels incomplete.

This is the only suite of the six that calls for altered tuning
of the strings (the technical term is *scordatura*), which means
that the highest string on the cello, the A, is here tuned down
one tone to a G. Why did Bach change the tuning? The experts
are unsure. Quite possibly it's designed to darken the mood.

Mystery surrounds the fifth suite. It is the only suite for which there exists another version composed by Bach, for another instrument—the lute. And the manuscript of this lute suite, in Bach's own hand, has survived. It was dedicated to a mysterious "Monsieur Schouster."

Several questions are raised by the time the cello, off on its clandestine fugal mission, trudges to the end in heavy boots. Why does the fifth cello suite, alone among the set, have a parallel existence as a lute suite? Which version was composed first, the fifth cello suite or the lute suite? And who was Monsieur Schouster?

I FEEL A dizzying sensation when the librarian at the Royal Library of Belgium brings out the Bach autograph manuscript of the lute suite and places it without fuss on an oak desk. Bach's calligraphy jumps out at me in a vertiginous rush of notes, staves, swirls, dots, smudges, stems, and beams with a beautiful, bold, curvaceous purpose.

I'm amazed that I can turn the pages without mandatory plastic gloves or anyone checking over my shoulder. I am touching something Bach touched. The tan paper is thick and sturdy. The title is in courtly French: *Suite pour la Luth par J. S. Bach*. The script is elegantly shaped, the S's resembling the sound hole of a string instrument. The first of the movements is written out on two staves, piano-style, using bass and treble clefs for the high and low strings of the lute.

I turn the pages. There are five of them, written on both sides of the paper by what has been called the most beautiful, flowing hand in the history of music. The paper is browner at the edges, but in remarkably good shape, not creased, not dog-eared, perhaps not even well thumbed. The music looks as if it were written in haste, as if made to fill an order. "*Ja*, Monsieur Schouster, I can have a copy ready for this evening." The penmanship, though, is handsome, with the D's and P's and S's turned out with elaborate flourishes. The key signatures are scrawled with speed, a necessary labour. But the main melodies on the treble clef, with their double swirls and lines, evoke Miró or Kandinsky. One sees waves, moustaches, hieroglyphics.

About twenty-five measures into the prelude there is a time signature and an instruction—"*très viste*" [*sic*] (very fast). It looks like the tempo at which the scribe was working. The calligraphy of the score varies. The prelude is most swirly, becoming hurried and shaky as it proceeds; the allemande, less attractive, is cramped; the courante foreign-looking; the sarabande starkly elegant; the gavotte going from clean to lush and nearly sloppy; the gigue hurriedly precise. It culminates in a "*Fin*" and a flourish that comes across as a weird vertical symbol atop something like a smiley-face emoticon.

I look out the window of the reading room. A courtyard is framed by the Bibliothèque royale, the city hall, a side street, and the square with a statue of King Albert on horseback. The courtyard encompasses a garden dotted with fountains and shade trees. Teenagers have overturned a garbage container and are using it as a skateboard jump. I look again at the title page. It does not look like a dedication for a royal commission. It seems more casual, as if to a friend, or an unimportant business transaction. Another sign of life is in the allemande, where the immortal composer splattered a drop of ink. Or was it brandy?

Later, the two librarians in this department are thrown into a tizzy when I ask about the manuscript's provenance. They scurry off to staff-only areas in search of info for me. For what seems like a very long time I'm left alone in the small reading room with the lute suite sitting idly on the main desk. I contemplate manuscript theft. It seems like a major security lapse that I could so easily exit the library with this Bachian treasure. I would be a more caring custodian, I tell myself. I resist the temptation.

The librarians offer some clues in the way of provenance. Documents at the library suggest that the manuscript was once in the possession of a controversial Belgian music scholar named Fétis. There is also an implication that the lute suite was copied from the cello suite. And the documents identify Monsieur Schouster as a singer at the glittering court of August the Strong in Dresden.

ALLEMANDE

The very measured, almost solemn Allemande seems to many players to be in danger of falling apart structurally; many listeners also lose the thread. HANS VOGT

THE SUPERPOWER EUROPEAN dynasties at the outset of the eighteenth century were the Hapsburgs, based in Austria, and the Bourbons, headquartered in France, who were duking it out for supreme power across the continent. A few lesser dynasties jostled for control in central Europe, among them the Wettins of Saxony, which despite many ups and downs since the tenth century remained the richest state in the Holy Roman Empire.

Saxony's destiny took a radical turn in 1697, when its young ruler, August the Strong, converted from Lutheranism to Catholicism in order to grab the kingship of Poland. For a Saxon prince to rule Poland was not as absurd as it sounds today. European borders were much in flux, and aristocratic dynasties ruled various jigsaw pieces of territory that cut across ethnic, linguistic, and religious lines. Sicily, to take one example, was governed by the Spanish Hapsburgs until their extinction in 1700, after which the island came under the rule of the Bourbon Philip v, the Piedmont prince Victor Amadeus ii, then Charles vi of Austria, followed by the Spanish Bourbons—and all in a period of just thirty-five years.

But with Poland, August the Strong was overreaching. His becoming Polish king was of dubious value to Saxony; for the better part of the next two decades Poland became a bloody theatre for warring Saxon, Russian, and Swedish armies.* As a result, Saxony's power, which could have led all of Germany (perhaps giving Germany a destiny more aesthetic than aggressive), was squandered in a vain quest for kingship.

In the Saxon capital of Dresden, however, court life flourished. August the Strong was a lacklustre military commander but a successful sensualist who lived mainly for the pleasures of the French and Italian courts. The king fathered scores of children with a bevy of mistresses. He transformed Dresden into a resplendent baroque city, a "Florence on the Elbe" embellished with architecture à la Versailles, Italian opera, and a major art collection. The best of everything, from porcelain to portraiture, was on display at court to illustrate that August the Strong was no pint-sized German prince who'd grabbed the throne of Poland, but a king of substance.

Dresden also flaunted the most brilliant musical court in Europe. It was a time when people spoke of the "three H's" of music: Handel, Heinichen, and Hasse, the latter two based in Dresden.† Like Handel and Hasse, Johann David Heinichen had travelled to Italy, where he honed his skills and built a reputation in the opera world. In 1717, the same year that Bach became Capellmeister in Cöthen, Heinichen was hired as Capellmeister in Dresden.

....

* Among those Germans who joined the Swedish forces under Charles XII was Jacob Bach, older brother of Sebastian, who served in Poland as "oboist in the Guards." He popped up later in Constantinople, and died in Stockholm in 1722.

† Part of the reason why Bach never rivalled the three H's in his day was that he never went to Italy and never composed for the opera, which was the springboard for real musical fame. He posthumously overtook that triumvirate, though, as one of the "three B's": Bach, Beethoven, and Brahms.

The crown prince of Saxony, August the Strong's son, had been touring Italy in search of musicians for the Saxon court. He hired not only Heinichen but an entire Italian opera company, which soon began performing in Dresden's new theatre. Built at the huge cost of 150,000 thalers, the fashionable opera house was a horseshoe-shaped structure in which August the Strong occupied a royal box surmounted by a huge crown.

This was the beginning of the glory years of Dresden music-making. Heinichen was in charge of a great constellation of musicians that included Silvius Leopold Weiss, lutenist extra-ordinaire and the highest-paid virtuoso at court; Pantaleon Hebenstreit, inventor of a curious instrument named after him; the brilliant and possibly deranged Italian violinist Francesco Veracini; the Bohemian bassist Jan Dismas Zelenka; violinists Johann Georg Pisendel and Jean-Baptiste Volumier; and Pierre-Gabriel Buffardin, the celebrated flautist who once gave Jacob Bach lessons in Constantinople. A "Monsieur Schouster" would soon join their ranks as a bass singer.

Most of these musicians were colourful characters. Pantaleon Hebenstreit, to take one example, was a novel addition to the Dresden *Capelle*. He was the inventor of a dulcimer-like instrument that spanned five octaves, measured nine feet in length, and required no less than 185 gut and metal strings. He took the instrument on tour in Germany, stopping in Weissenfels, where he was hired as dancing master to the duke. Hebenstreit's instrument had no name until he performed before France's Louis xiv, a big fan who promptly named it after its inventor-practitioner. Thus was born the pantaleon. He played it before the emperor in Vienna, who rewarded him with a gold chain but no position at court. He fared better with August the Strong, who hired Hebenstreit as court chamber musician and "pantaleonist," with extra compensation to cover the cost of his strings.

There was apparently some friction in the Saxon royal court between the central European musicians and the Italians. In his elegant account of music in eighteenth-century European capitals, Daniel Heartz describes a raucous atmosphere among the Dresden musicians in the 1720s. He picks up the story following a brouhaha in which an Italian castrato tore up a score and threw it at the feet of the music's composer.

> Silvius Weiss, the famous lutenist, saw his livelihood threatened when he was attacked by a French violinist named Petit, who attempted to bite off the top joint of his right thumb. On 13 August 1722 Veracini jumped to the ground from a third-storey window, according to Mattheson, who ascribed the incident to a fit of madness brought on by too much immersion in music and alchemy. Veracini hinted darkly in his late treatise that there was threat against his life inspired by jealousy, perhaps implying that this was on the part of Pisendel or Volumier, his supervisors. Veracini's years in Saxon service came to an end. He left and did not return. One other curious bit of information concerning the orchestra is that Pantaleon Hebenstreit became incapacitated by failing eyesight and had to stop playing his dulcimer-like invention, the pantaloon [*sic*].

Unruliness aside, the high quality of music-making in the Saxon capital was unrivalled. The court orchestra of August the Strong would for decades be the gold standard for musicians across Europe. In Leipzig, only two days away by coach, Bach contemplated Dresden with envy.

As the decade wore on, Bach became more and more disgruntled with the authorities in Leipzig. In 1729, when Capellmeister Heinichen died prematurely from tuberculosis, Bach naturally contemplated his own suitability for the post. His lack of experience in Italian opera might have stacked the odds against him, but his desire for some permanent place in

Dresden took hold as his working conditions in Leipzig were becoming unbearable.

Things came to a head in 1730, when the town council heard complaints that Bach was absent from his post without permission, among other transgressions. One councillor charged: "Not only did the Cantor do nothing, but he was not even willing to give an explanation of that fact; he did not hold the singing class, and there were other complaints in addition..." Another councillor called Bach "incorrigible." A vote was held and part of his salary was impounded.

Neither apologies nor explanations were forthcoming. The scrappy cantor instead fired off a lengthy letter under the heading "Short But Most Necessary Draft for a Well-Appointed Church Music, with Certain Modest Reflections on the Decline of the Same." In the memo Bach complains at length about the inadequate singers and instrumentalists at his disposal. He bemoans the fact that the instrumentalists are underpaid and forced to seek work elsewhere to make ends meet. He pointedly mentions the Saxon *Capelle* by way of comparison. "One need only go to Dresden," he writes, "and see how the musicians are relieved of all concern for their living, free from *chagrin*, and obliged each to master but a single instrument; it must be something choice and excellent to hear."

Two months after sending the memorandum, Bach took up his pen to produce a letter that biographers have long been grateful for. It was addressed to his old classmate Georg Erdmann, with whom he'd made the long journey from Ohrdruf to Lüneburg at the age of fourteen. Erdmann had gone on to study law at university; in 1730 he was in Danzig, a Polish city then ruled by August the Strong, employed as a Russian diplomatic agent. The old friends had last met nearly fifteen years earlier, when Erdmann had visited Bach in Weimar. The letter is by far the most personally revealing document by Bach to have survived, and no account of Bach's life is complete without it:

MOST HONORED SIR,

Your Honor will have the goodness to excuse an old and faithful servant for taking the liberty of disturbing you with the present letter. It must be nearly four years since Your Honor favored me with a kind answer to the letter I sent you; I remember that at the time you graciously asked me to give you some news of what had happened to me, and I humbly take this opportunity of providing you with the same. You know the course of my life from my youth up until the change in my fortunes that took me to Cöthen as Capellmeister. There I had a gracious prince, who both loved and knew music, and in his service I intended to spend the rest of my life. It must happen, however, that the said *Serenissimus* should marry a Princess of Berenburg, and that then the impression should arise that the musical interests of the said Prince should become somewhat lukewarm, especially as the new Princess seemed to be unmusical; and it pleased God that I should be called hither to be *Directeur Musices* and Cantor at the St. Thomas School. Though at first, indeed, it did not seem at all proper to me to change my position of Capellmeister for that of Cantor. Wherefore, then I postponed my decision for a quarter of a year, but this post was described to me in such favorable terms that finally (particularly since my sons seemed inclined towards [university] studies) I cast my lot, in the name of the Lord, and made the journey to Leipzig, took my examination, and then made the change of position. Here, by God's will, I am still in service. But since (1) I find that the post is by no means so lucrative as it was described to me; (2) I have failed to obtain many of the fees pertaining to the office; (3) the place is very expensive; and (4) the authorities are odd and little interested in music, so that I must live amid almost continual vexation, envy, and persecution; accordingly I shall be forced, with God's help to seek my fortune elsewhere. Should Your

Honor know or find a suitable post in your city for an old and faithful servant, I beg you most humbly to put in a most gracious word of recommendation for me—I shall not fail to do my best to give satisfaction and justify your most gracious intercession in my behalf. . . .

Danzig seems like an odd choice, a step down for Bach. But perhaps he was in fact thinking of Dresden. August the Strong was at this time also king of Poland, and his court shuttled between Dresden and Warsaw. It looks as if Bach was hoping the well-connected Erdmann could pull strings in Saxon royal circles that would help land him a position in Dresden.

It was during this period that Bach started cranking out pieces designed to flatter the Saxon royal family, composing in a more popular *galant* style, including works that come close to opera. He put his energies into leading the Collegium Musicum, a chamber music outfit staffed by top students and some professional musicians, which performed weekly concerts at Zimmerman's coffee house in the winter and at the proprietor's garden just outside the city in summertime. (The coffee houses of Leipzig, it should be noted, were seen by some citizens as shady places where prostitution and card-playing went on.)

It was at Zimmerman's that Bach likely premiered *Phoebus and Pan* and the *Coffee Cantata*, entertaining vocal works that move in the direction of opera. The former is a satire that pokes fun at new trends in music, with Phoebus and Pan engaged in a singing contest. In the *Coffee Cantata* a young woman, addicted to coffee against her father's wishes, agrees to cut out the habit on condition that she's allowed to marry. These works suggest that Bach was trying his hand at opera to impress Dresden.

If he was, he must have known that he was up against formidable competition. When Bach was writing his letter to Erdmann, Johann Adolph Hasse had just married the Italian opera star Faustina Bordoni, and the couple were slowly and

triumphantly making their way to Dresden at the invitation of
August the Strong. Bordoni had a few years earlier wowed
London with her mezzo-soprano voice in several operas by
Handel. Following a tiff in which she came to blows onstage
with a rival soprano, she returned to Italy, where she met Hasse.
The son of a Lutheran organist, Hasse had found fame in Italy
before embracing both the Catholic faith and the alluring
opera singer. En route to Dresden they performed in Milan,
Venice, and Vienna before making it to the Saxon capital in 1731.
The day after their arrival Bordoni sang for August the Strong,
thrilling the monarch and ushering in a new operatic era for
Dresden. Hasse was named the new Capellmeister at 6,000 thalers a year; Bordoni was also hired by the king, and at twice her
husband's salary (their combined salaries were more than sixteen times that of Bach).

The Dresden premiere of Hasse's opera *Cleofide* was staged
in the autumn of that year. The title page of the libretto noted
that the production was "presented in the royal court theatre by
command of his sacred royal majesty...always great and most
unconquerable." Among those thumbing through the libretto
in the audience that evening was Bach, accompanied by his son
Friedemann. Bach was in fact given a fairly prominent place in
the festivities; the day after the premiere he performed an afternoon recital on the famous organ in St. Sophia's Church, across
the square from the opera house. His recital even got a positive
review in a Dresden newspaper. The item noted that Bach "let
himself be heard on the organ at St. Sophia's Church in the presence of all the Court musicians and virtuosos in a fashion that
compelled the admiration of everyone."*

....
* The newspaper writer then presented a little poem to honour Bach that ended:
 "'Tis said, when Orpheus did his lyre strings awake / All creatures in the forest
 answered to the sound / But sure, 'twere better that such praise of Bach we spake /
 Since he, whene'er he plays, doth each and all astound."

Despite Hasse's appointment, Bach continued to hope for a position or a title at the Dresden court. As it turned out, Friedemann had quicker success there than his father (albeit for a post that was too minor for Bach). The organist of St. Sophia's Church died in 1733, and Friedemann applied for the post. He auditioned before Pantaleon Hebenstreit, who had risen in the ranks of the court hierarchy and was now vice-Capellmeister. (By guarding it so jealously, Hebenstreit had not helped the cause of his namesake instrument; when the famed organ builder Silbermann began mass-producing the pantaleon, its inventor obtained a royal writ blocking manufacture.) Friedemann, an extremely skilled musician, sailed through the trials to best two other candidates on the short list and win the post, receiving high praise from Hebenstreit. Bach's reputation in the Saxon capital had clearly helped, but his own bid for employment would have to wait.

Meanwhile, the sybaritic life of August the Strong came to an end. He bestowed much to posterity, including the music produced at his court; magnificent architecture, which was largely reduced to rubble in the Second World War; and a large percentage of the local population with its share of blue blood on account of his royal lustiness. Despite his heroic sobriquet, August fled the military field repeatedly when threatened, and at one point abandoned his capital to the Russians. More than anything else, his decision to straddle the throne of Poland doomed a leading state to what would soon be marginal status. But for the time being Saxony was still flourishing, and the late king's only legitimate son, Frederick August, succeeded him.

Five months of official mourning followed August's death, during which no public music was allowed. Bach used the time to compose works that would help win him a title or position at court. When the mourning period was over, Bach was able to present the new king with a Kyrie and a Gloria—what would eventually become the Mass in B Minor—along with a petition requesting a royal title. Bach begins with standard deference and then gets to the point:

> To Your Royal Highness I submit in deepest devotion the present small work of that science I have achieved in *musique*, with the more wholly submissive prayer that Your Highness will look upon it with Most Gracious Eyes, according to Your Highness's World-Famous Clemency and not according to the poor *composition*; and thus deign to take me under your mighty protection....
>
> For some years and up to the present moment, I have had the *Directorium* of the Music in the two principal churches in Leipzig, but have innocently had to suffer one injury after another and on one occasion also a diminution of the fees accruing to me in this office; but these injuries would disappear altogether if Your Royal Highness would grant me the favor of conferring upon me a title of Your Highness's Court Capelle, and would let Your High Command for the issuing of such a document go forth to the proper place.

With no title or position forthcoming from Dresden, Bach set about flattering the court with music honouring the new king. In the space of a year, six works were composed by Bach and performed by his Collegium Musicum, marking occasions such as name days, birthdays, and anniversaries of the royal family. The king was sometimes on hand for the performance. On one occasion he paid a visit to Leipzig and the entire population, wearing festive clothing, was required to line both sides of a main street. Another time Frederick August was carried in a sedan chair from the church to the bourse for a reception given by aristocrats. And a memorable performance in the presence of the royal couple took place one evening in the market square. Six hundred students carried torches and four students who were also young counts presented the king with the text for one of Bach's pieces. The four counts "were permitted to kiss the Royal hands," reported the town chronicler, "and afterward his Royal Majesty together with his Royal Consort and the Royal Princes did not leave the window until the music was over, and listened most graciously and liked it well." Bach's principal trumpeter, sixty-seven-year-old Gottfried Reiche, died the next day, overtaxed by a combination of torch smoke and difficult notes.

Bach must have been disappointed that, despite the flurry of works showering praise on the Saxon king, his bid for employment or title seemed to be going nowhere.* In 1736 Bach renewed his petition to Dresden. He sought help from Count Hermann Carl von Keyserlingk, a Russian diplomat and supportive patron. Was there any connection between Bach's old friend Erdmann, the Russian envoy in Danzig, and Count Keyserlingk, the Russian ambassador to Saxony? One can only speculate, but it seems likely.

By 1736 Count Keyserlingk was on friendly terms with Bach; his daughter was a music pupil of Friedemann. A few years later Bach would ensure the diplomat's place in history by composing the *Goldberg Variations* so that the count, who was apparently an insomniac, could be entertained during his sleepless nights. (The music gets its name from Johann Gottlieb Goldberg, the count's young keyboardist, who played the variations while the rest of Dresden was in bed.)

The count must have had influence at the Saxon court, because Bach's petition ultimately bore fruit. Towards the end

....
* Bach compositions during this period, such as the *Italian Concerto*, the B minor overture, and some of his contributions to the Schemelli hymn book show signs of being conspicuously more catchy and modern. The cantata BWV 140 has been likened to one of Hasse's opera arias. And in a work like cantata BWV 30a, writes Bach scholar Peter Williams, the "step from this to opera is not huge, giving admirers now, and perhaps the composer himself, many deep regrets that this was never to be."

of the year, "because of his ability," Bach was finally named royal court composer to the new Saxon king. The official document was initialled by the king, certified by the prime minister, and presented to Bach by Count Keyserlingk. It was an honorific title, not a job, but it was appreciated. Within two weeks Bach was in Dresden giving an organ recital as thanks to the Saxon court.

Bach wasted no time in using his new title, especially when it came to his petty disputes with Leipzig authorities. Now he was the king's composer, and he did not hesitate to pull rank. But his offer in the petition to compose works for the king did not materialize. The royal cantatas were eventually given a new form and recycled with new text as the *Christmas Oratorio*. Bach seems to have reconciled himself to the fact that he was not leaving Leipzig. He started to think more and more about his legacy.

COURANTE

Art does not progress—it transforms itself.
FRANÇOIS-JOSEPH FETIS

WHEN BACH WAS finally granted the title of composer to the Dresden court, his oldest three sons had left home and were starting their own notable careers as musicians. Friedemann was in Dresden as organist at St. Sophia's Church. The position amounted to a part-time job that didn't pay a great deal, but it allowed Bach's oldest and most musically gifted son to find time for composition, teaching, and his studies in mathematics. He was also able to enjoy the cultural perks of the Saxon capital, including the opera and the ballet, and to cultivate friendships with musicians of the Dresden court, such as Hasse, his diva wife Faustina, Pantaleon Hebenstreit, and the flutist Buffardin, who had taught his Uncle Jacob in Constantinople two decades earlier. He also had an entrée to the court via his father's patron Count Keyserlingk. The opulence of the Saxon court would have dazzled him, given the relatively austere lifestyle he was raised in. Did that make him desirous of wealth, status, and luxury? Or was he restless, not unlike his father in younger days, and concerned that as a Protestant organist in a Catholic court he could never really advance his career?

Like his older brother, Carl Philipp Emanuel (C. P. E.) graduated from the University of Leipzig. While studying law he
continued to act as music assistant to his father, and by the age
of twenty had already composed a fair bit of keyboard music. In
1734 he left the family home to enrol in further law studies at the
University of Frankfurt. C. P. E. supported his studies by teaching, directing concerts, and composing music for public events
in a town that had modest musical resources. The study of law,
then as now, was a liberal arts education leading to many possible career paths. It is unclear whether the second-born son of
Bach, who was also Telemann's godson, was aiming for a music
career. In 1738 he was offered a plum assignment, to act as tutor
to a young nobleman embarking on the standard grand tour of
Europe. The young man was the son of the insomniac diplomat
Count Keyserlingk. But as he was to depart, fate swerved for
the young musician: the crown prince of Prussia—who would
one day be known as Frederick the Great—offered him a place
as keyboard player in his entourage.

Bach's third son, Gottfried Bernhard, also left home in the
mid-1730s. His first job was as church organist in the town of
Mühlhausen, where Bach himself had been employed as a
young man. Bach's influence helped him land the post, but it
did not go well. Gottfried Bernhard apparently clashed with
officials there and fell into debt. After a little more than a year,
Bach used his influence again to get him a job in Sangerhausen,
where he fared no better. One year later he disappeared from
the town, leaving behind heavy debts. The town burgomaster
wrote to Bach informing him of what had happened. Bach
replied at length:

> Your Honor, as a loving and caring parent yourself, can judge
> with what pain and sorrow I compose this reply. I have not yet
> set eyes on my unfortunately wayward son since last year,
> when I had the privilege of enjoying Your Honor's many

kindnesses. You will recall that I not only paid his board then but also settled the Mühlhaussen account (which probably caused him to leave that town), and also left a few ducats behind to pay off some debts, thinking that he would now take up a different *genus vitae*. Now I learn, with the deepest dismay, that he has again contracted debts here and there, has not mended his ways in the slightest, but has absconded without giving me the least indication of where he is staying.

What more can I say or do? Since no admonition, not even loving provisions and *assistance*, will any longer suffice, I must bear my cross with patience and simply leave my undisciplined son to God's mercy, not doubting that he will hear my sorrowful prayers and finally, according to His Holy Will, bring him to realize that conversion can only come from Divine Goodness.

Since I have now opened my heart to Your Honor, I have every confidence that you will not impute to me that bad conduct of my son, but will recognize that a devoted father, whose children are dear to him, will do everything he can to help to promote their well-being. Nor do I doubt that Your Honor will try to persuade your Most Noble Council to postpone the threatened mutation until such time as his whereabouts can be ascertained (God being my omniscient witness that I have not seen him since last year), so that we may learn what he intends to do: to remain and alter his ways, or to seek his *fortun* somewhere else. I would not have willingly your Most Noble Council inconvenienced, but I would request only such *patience* until he should turn up, or until it can be discovered where he is....

Within one year of writing this letter Bach would discover the whereabouts and tragic end of his son's life. Gottfried Bernhard had in fact been not very far away, in the town of Jena, where he had registered at the university with the intention of studying law. But in May 1739 he developed an acute fever and died. He was twenty-four years old.

Later that year, Friedemann came from Dresden with a couple of musicians to visit his father. It was August and he stayed for about a month, a visit that would have consoled his father after the death of Gottfried Bernhard. There was music-making at the Bach home. Friedemann's colleagues were both lute players—Johann Kropfgans and the highly renowned Silvius Weiss.

SILVIUS LEOPOLD WEISS was the highest-paid member of the Dresden court orchestra, the hottest lute player of his day and quite possibly the greatest ever. A composer as well, he left behind an unparalleled quantity of some 600 works for lute. He knew Bach fairly well and visited his home several times during his 1739 visit to Leipzig. Had Bach dedicated the lute version of the fifth cello suite to "Monsieur Weiss" it would have been perfectly understandable. But the music's dedicatee, "Monsieur Schouster," long remained a puzzle for Bach scholars. As it turns out, Weiss offers a major clue that helps identify the mysterious Schouster.

Scholars started to notice the lute suite only around the turn of the twentieth century, when the manuscript in Bach's hand turned up at the Royal Library of Belgium. It had once been in the possession of the Belgian scholar and composer François-Joseph Fétis. More than a century before it became fashionable, Fétis arranged "historical concerts" in Paris and Brussels, enjoying mixed success. In his own words, he was aiming to program compositions from yesteryear "with the instrumentation and the system of execution which their authors intended, so that nineteenth-century listeners would have the illusion of attending a sixteenth-century entertainment in the palace of a Florentine nobleman." Unfortunately, Fétis's authenticity credentials were undermined by his habit of counterfeiting his own compositions as the work of old masters. His reputation took a further beating when he absconded with a valuable collection of music and manuscripts from his old job at a Paris library to his new one in Brussels.

It is thought that Fétis acquired the lute suite manuscript from an 1836 auction at the Breitkopf publishing house; after his death it was deposited along with the rest of his papers and scores in the Belgian royal library. Once the manuscript became known to scholars in the early twentieth century, the search for Monsieur Schouster was on. The flowery calligraphy on the cover page of Bach's manuscript reads in French, *"Pièces pour la Luth à Monsieur Schouster."* But the evidentiary trail quickly went cold. There was no record of Bach knowing any Schouster.

There was one Schouster of note in Dresden: Joseph Schouster, a bass singer at the court of August the Strong who was thought to have played the lute as well. Bachian detectives figured they had their *monsieur*, but he was the wrong Schouster. A watermark analysis of the lute suite manuscript showed that the music was penned sometime between 1727 and 1731. The date of birth of Joseph Schouster turned out to be 1721. That would have meant that Bach had dedicated the music to a boy no older than ten, which is highly improbable.

Then, in 1968, musicologists came across a letter that had been mailed more than two centuries earlier. It was written in 1741 by Silvius Weiss and sent to Luise Adelgunde Gottsched, a prolific writer who was considered the most learned woman in Germany. She was also an amateur lute player who took composition lessons from one of Bach's students.

"It is a great presumption," began Weiss's letter to Luise, "for me to be so bold as to avail myself of my pen, since both my handwriting and rough draft are equally weak. However, I have found no other means to unwind myself from a previous anxiety than to pay my respects with the present letter." The anxiety Weiss felt was that a piece of lute music he'd given to Luise was something she already possessed. And Weiss had learned about the lute music she owned through a certain "Monsieur Schuster."

The passing reference suggests a Schuster who was known to Luise in Leipzig but who also had connections in Dresden. A man who either played the lute or was closely associated with the instrument, this Schuster was someone who was within Bach's reach in the period 1727 to 1731. This new evidence led the Bach scholar Hans-Joachim Schulze to discover a Leipzig book dealer and publisher by the name of Jacob Schuster.

Jacob Schuster played a modest role on the Leipzig literary scene in the 1720s and 1730s. He was connected to some faculty members of Leipzig University, among them Johann Christoph Gottsched, husband of Luise, who would become the most celebrated literary critic of his age. (After a disagreement Schuster once derided Gottsched as "an arrogant man who thinks everything he says is oracular.") He also had some success publishing Johann Jacob Mascov, an academic who also sat on the city council. But his attempts at publishing music appear never to have gone beyond the planning stage, Bach's lute suite perhaps being one example. It is not known whether Schuster actually played the lute. It is possible that "he only planned the printing of a collection in which Bach's suite was to be included," writes Schulze. Still, it is conspicuous that Schuster was closely associated with Weiss, Luise, and another musician, Adam Falkenhagen—all of whom were lutenists—suggesting that he was for some reason interested in the instrument.

Might Bach have had some motivation for making a copy of the fifth cello suite for lute and dedicating it to Schuster? There is one intriguing possibility. Schuster and Luise, as well as the influential academic Mascov (teacher of many aristocratic students), were all originally from Danzig. And Danzig was where Bach's old friend Erdmann was working as Russian envoy to the Saxon court. Bach's letter to Erdmann, written at about the same time as the lute suite and with the same calligraphy, also asked his old friend to look into job opportunities.

Danzig may have been a provincial Polish town, but it was ruled by August the Strong in Dresden. By dedicating his lute suite to Schuster, Bach seems to have been working his contacts among influential Danzigers to find work in Dresden. Sadly, if this was the aim of Bach's lute suite, it would fall on deaf ears.

IT JUST so happened that when I visited Leipzig, a recital of the Cello Suites was on the concert calendar. It was an unorthodox performance by a young German cellist named Maria Magdalena Wiesmaier. She was to play the suites in three different settings, with bus transportation provided for an audience on the move. The show was called "6 × Bach."

The first venue was a nondescript warehouse not far from the municipal museum where Bach's portrait hangs. Wiesmaier, fresh-faced and cheerful and with her hair tied back in a ponytail, played suites one and six and played them swiftly, without the so-called repeats, which eliminated duplicate sections but maintained the essence of the piece. It was a refreshing musical architecture stripped down to its essential scaffolding and performed in a bare space without the slightest adornment.

The next venue, where suites four and five were to be performed, was equally unorthodox. The audience was bused from the central Augustplatz to the old trade-fair grounds and deposited in front of a domed neoclassical building. Inside we were offered wine and hors d'oeuvres and then ushered into the central hall. We took our seats beneath the domed ceiling, encircled by fluted columns and shrouded in darkness save for half a dozen small lights beaming from the floor. Shards of light here and there amplified an ankle, an ear, a program. Every sound—footsteps, giggles, a cough, chairs creaking, rumbles of German syntax—reverberated in the eerie acoustics. The venue had the raw materials of a convincing nightmare.

Wiesmaier appeared in the shadows and launched into a prelude. The space resembled an echo chamber; each note was super-sustained and the melodic units were stretched to the breaking point. The overtones washed over the tones and the tones washed over each other. It might have had a certain luxuriant charm for some listeners, but for me the melody was flattened into a New Agey *om*-nificent thrum. The bleeding of lines made for blur. Bach's ruggedly individual notes were force-marched into a collectivity of no distinction (we were in the former East Germany, after all). I soon forgot which suites were being played. As the bus departed the bleak defunct trade-fair grounds, I felt exhausted by the process and decided to skip the final concert.

But all that lush overlapping of notes in an echo chamber raises a question about the fifth cello suite. Is it too sparse as a composition? Is it vastly inferior to the version for lute, which is much more lushly harmonized, with chords fleshing out the bare bones of the cello lines? The lute version is beautiful, and in many places it does sound superior to the fifth cello suite. One does wonder whether Bach might have composed it first, then transcribed the lute music for cello when he decided to bundle together the suites in the standard collection of six. The debate in a way harks back to a key challenge faced by the Cello Suites, that they were considered too dry and difficult—études, really—that needed more harmonic layering. The fifth suite is the most challenging in this respect, and in several places it does sound as if another musical strand is missing.

At the same time, there are places where the minimalism is exquisite, such as in the sarabande, a triumph of musical economy. There are no double stops in the sarabande, never more than one note played at the same time. The empty spaces on the canvas are striking; the effect is of a mystical spaciousness.

It's the favourite movement for many cellists, a piece of music that manages to sound remarkably modern.

The sarabande also sounds conspicuously like another piece of music, an earlier composition by Domenico Gabrielli. Born in 1659, Gabrielli was a virtuoso cellist who by the age of seventeen was a member of the Accademia Filarmonica of Bologna. After becoming president of the orchestra, he was later dismissed for reasons of discipline, then rehired because he was considered indispensable; afterwards he relocated to the court of Modena. He was given the nickname Minghain dal Viulunzel, which in dialect meant "Dominic of the Cello." He died at the age of thirty-one, and his surviving compositions, although barely known, represent the first important step in the development of solo cello music prior to Bach's suites. In his Ricercar No. 7 the first notes bring to mind Bach's dramatic opening of the sarabande in the fifth suite. We have no evidence that Bach had heard the music, which figures in Gabrielli's *Seven Ricercares for Solo Cello*, published back in 1687. But it sounds for all the world as if Bach was quoting from this novel work for cello. And there is one other clue. Gabrielli tuned the highest string on his cello down a tone, the same mystery tuning that Bach uses for this cello suite.

Whether he first heard the sarabande in Gabrielli's composition or in his own head, Bach's imagination was fired by the eloquent austerity. When it came to his version for lute, he resisted the temptation to pile on extra layers of harmony with the fourteen-string instrument. We do not know whether Bach originally wrote the sarabande for the richness of the lute or the ruggedness of the cello. Either way, he was evidently happy to say more with less. The lute version of the fifth sarabande, no less than the cello, is stripped down to its musical core — a meditation that stands outside time and renounces the world.

SARABANDE

*In its darkness of melodic design it is so unusual
that it resembles contemporary music.*

MSTISLAV ROSTROPOVICH

A STRONG SENSE OF Iberian honour was what finally, unexpectedly took Casals back to Spain. During his early years in exile he was often in the company of Frasquita Vidal de Capdevila. Her husband, who had been treasurer of the Casals orchestra in Barcelona, had made a deathbed request that Casals care for his widow. A handsome woman of a certain age, Capdevila became a close friend, although she was sometimes mistaken for his maid. When the Second World War broke out, they, together with other Catalan refugees, stayed in France; after the war, in Prades, she took charge of his domestic affairs. In the words of one visitor, she was a "pleasant, grey-haired housekeeper who fixes his light diet and takes care of his few wants."

In the early 1950s, as the Prades Festival was flourishing, Capdevila's health declined. Suffering from Parkinson's disease, she was bedridden in her last days and unable to bear Casals' absence. A priest was summoned to marry them. "It was a gesture of near-medieval chivalry and grateful affection for the devoted woman," writes H. L. Kirk. She died in 1955.

Capdevila's last wish was for burial in the cemetery of Vendrell, the birthplace of Casals. So for the first time since 1939, he returned to Spain for the funeral. He visited his villa, which had been seized by the Franco regime but turned over to Casals' brother Luis after one million pesetas (Casals called it a ransom) was paid. The world-famous cellist, swarmed by old friends, was overcome with emotion. There were rumours that he'd returned for good, but he was there only to pay his respects to the woman who had been his helpmate for two decades. He returned to France the day after Capdevila's funeral.

Back in Prades, Casals experienced one of those deep depressions that periodically afflicted him. A rare tonic was a young student from Puerto Rico whose presence seemed to lift his spirits. Marta Montañez was just thirteen when her uncle brought her to Prades in 1951. She didn't interact much with Casals, who struck her as "a warm and lovely man," "like a grandfather." She returned five years later to take lessons from the maestro. By this time she was a shade older than eighteen, smart, funny, and beautiful in a way that Casals imagined his mother looked when she was the same age. His mother had also been a young woman from Puerto Rico when she remade her life in Europe. The accent, the face, the dark hair, the colouring—it was all familiar at some visceral level. Soon Martita, as everyone called her, was always by the side of the seventy-eight-year-old maestro. She was fluent in Spanish, English, and French, and was rapidly picking up Catalan; she typed, drove a car, and was as efficient as she was vivacious.

They talked of Puerto Rico. Casals' far-flung tours had taken him close by, but he'd never been to the island. His mother's family, the Defillós, were there. The ocean was there. He wanted to see his ancestral home.

If Puerto Rico had not existed, Casals might have invented it. In geopolitical terms, the country enabled him to experience

Iberia without crossing the border into Franco's Spain, and it gave him proximity to the U.S. without overly compromising his boycott of countries that recognized the Franco regime. It was a delicate moral balancing act, but he had paid his dues for long enough in the dusty French mountain town, and was entitled to some tropical sunshine in the waning days of his life.

The Caribbean island-state was as sweltering as his long-lost homeland, its terrain, vegetation, and beaches reminiscent of Catalonia. His mother, Doña Pilar, had eight brothers and sisters who had remained on the island; he had no shortage of relatives in Puerto Rico, many of whom were waiting dockside when Casals and Martita descended the gangplank of the *Flandre* on December 11, 1955.

Puerto Rico had been well prepared for the visit. The government issued a proclamation of welcome, the newspapers devoted much ink to Casals, and the local Representative delivered an hour-long speech in which he lauded Casals as one of the three pillars of the contemporary world (along with Einstein and Schweitzer). The mayor of San Juan and the wife of the governor were on hand to greet Casals, who was swept away by the emotion of the crowd, repeating "*La tierra de mi madre,*" kissing people, and shedding tears. The maestro and his young associate were whisked away in an official limo with a motorcycle police escort, through the old town to where a welcoming ceremony was held. From there they were taken to an apartment provided by the government.

The following day a more lavish ceremony was held in Casals' honour at La Fortaleza, a sixteenth-century fortress-palace. More moving for Casals was the occasion a week later, when he drove across the island to Mayagüez, visiting the house where his mother was born. In a coincidence that verged on the bizarre, it was the same house that Martita's mother had been born in. A crowd gathered outside the home, and from the balcony Casals played a lullaby that his mother had sung to him, followed by a Bach pastorale.

At the end of the month Casals celebrated his seventy-ninth birthday amid friends from the U.S., a cello-shaped cake, and serenades by university students. In January another gala at La Fortaleza began with a pianist playing Bach's Italian Concerto, after which Casals and Martita played some Handel and Beethoven sonatas. Martita, whose own performance show-cased some Couperin suites, was enthusiastically praised in the local press. By late February Casals was as smitten with Puerto Rico as he was with Martita. "I am in love with this country," he wrote to Alexander Schneider, "... and am so sad to leave it. I feel so much that I am at home here that I have a wonderful idea. What would you say of Prades Festival in Puerto Rico in April 1957?" Casals had decided to make the island his new home.

Casals and Martita returned to France by air at the end of March, but were back in Puerto Rico in November. Casals celebrated his eightieth birthday on the Caribbean island that would be his new home. Plans were fine-tuned for the first Puerto Rico Festival, with Casals conducting and Schneider serving as chief organizer. Casals would open the festival with a performance of the buoyant third cello suite.

In April 1957 the first rehearsal of the orchestra took place at the University Theatre. Casals ran the orchestra through a Mozart symphony as a means of "getting to know each other." He was delighted with the sound. Several hundred people attended the rehearsal. The theatre felt like a sauna—Casals was opposed to air conditioning (he considered it "unnatural") and it had been turned off. His shirt was soaked. He largely ignored the high chair that had been placed on the maestro's podium to ease his efforts. Casals then led the musicians through Schubert's Unfinished Symphony. Suddenly his thoughts went back two decades, to that last rehearsal he had

conducted with his orchestra in Barcelona on the frightening
eve of the Spanish Civil War. Biographer Robert Baldock
describes what transpired:

> Twenty bars into the Allegro moderato first movement he
> made a point about an accent, beating his chest emphatically
> and shouting, "Vroom! Vroom!" to mark the beat in typical
> fashion. He completed the movement and began the second.
> Some minutes later, and quite suddenly, he put down his baton,
> murmured a general apology to the orchestra, and staggered
> from the podium. Clearly in acute pain and his face drained of
> colour, he was helped backstage into a dressing room.

Casals recovered from what would later be diagnosed as a
heart attack. He missed the first Puerto Rico Festival, which
had been tailor-made for him. Schneider took over conducting
duties, but in the capacity of first violinist. An empty chair
stood onstage throughout the festival as a symbolic reminder
of the maestro's absence. After a couple of months' convales-
cence at his apartment, where a hospital bed and oxygen
equipment had been set up (Casals abhorred hospitals and
refused to go), he was practising the cello again and regaining
his technical strength.

His recovery was aided by the doting presence of many
friends and associates, first and foremost Martita. Casals' sister-
in-law asked one of the doctors whether it was healthy for the
maestro to have such "a pretty young girl" around him so
much. It appears that it was very healthy for him. Casals now
looked at the human heart as that most sophisticated of
machines, able to heal itself and gain a new lease on life.

Casals and Martita married in the summer of 1957 in a virtually secret civil ceremony; it took place at his apartment with
just two witnesses. The bridegroom was eighty, the bride
twenty-one. Martita's parents, shocked and unreconciled to

the age gap, did not attend. A religious ceremony, performed by a Passionist father who was a friend of the couple, was held subsequently in a San Juan chapel.

A photograph shows a beaming Casals, looking every inch the proud grandfather in a dark business suit, bald except for a slight fringe of hair on the sides, and with a definite gleam in his pale blue eyes behind rimless glasses. The bride looks prim, happy, and a hell of a lot younger. Attired in bridal white, Martita was a nun-like figure. In fact, her parents were Protestant, and she had converted to Catholicism as a girl. While attending the Marymount School of the Convent of the Sacred Heart of Mary, a high school in New York, she had seriously contemplated devoting her life to a religious order.

Many years after the marriage, Marta said in an interview that "something propelled me that I still don't understand." The decision to marry Casals meant giving up many things in her life, including a cello career. But she was determined to be Casals' partner. "I was very clear I wanted to contribute to his life, and that is what I did."

Casals, for his part, had in a certain sense come full circle. "Here is a strange thing," he told *McCall's* magazine some time later. "There is something of my mother in my wife, in her face, in her way of seeing things. I show the portrait of my mother to people, and the first thing they see is the extraordinary resemblance to my wife. Here is another astonishing thing: The world is a big thing, isn't it? Very well, my mother was born in the same house that my wife's mother was born in. The house is in Mayagüez in Puerto Rico. One hundred and ten years ago my mother was born in that town in that house — and on the same day of the year, November thirteenth. Look at this picture of my mother."

GAVOTTE

*...normally graceful, often gay, and sometimes
also tender and slow.* JEAN-JACQUES ROUSSEAU,
DICTIONNAIRE DE MUSIQUE, 1768

WHEN THE EVENT was broadcast in October 1958, it reached
more listeners than any previous concert in history. The
headliner, the unlikely star of a show that employed the latest
in television technology, was an eighty-one-year-old cellist.

An emissary from the United Nations spent three days in
Puerto Rico trying to persuade Pablo Casals to participate in a
special concert that would honour the world organization.
Casals was interested, but fundamentally opposed to the idea
because it would mean performing in the United States, which
would break his vow not to play in countries that recognized the
Franco dictatorship. Since the Cold War, Franco's Spain, with its
anti-Communist bent, had become a *de facto* partner in the
Western alliance. The U.S. extended military aid to the regime,
and Franco allowed American bases on Spanish territory.

But Casals had grown increasingly alarmed by the threat
nuclear weapons posed to a world in the grip of the Cold War.
He was very much in agreement with intellectuals he knew,
such as Albert Schweitzer, another trailblazer for Bach's music,

who broadcast a series of radio appeals earlier in the year titled "Peace or Atomic War?" Close as Catalonia remained to Casals' heart, the world was not the same place it had been during the old fight against fascism. All political struggles were now overshadowed, he felt, by the nuclear danger.

Finally he agreed to play, convincing himself that the U.N. headquarters in Manhattan were in a politically neutral extraterritorial enclave. Also, he would not play his most personal music — his spiritual signature, the Bach Cello Suites. That too was a way of sustaining his political boycott. But he would play Bach. With Mieczyslaw Horszowski on piano, the two old friends would perform Bach's Sonata No. 2 in D Major. The United Nations Day concert was a two-hour program that aired in forty-eight countries. It included performances piped in from Paris by Yehudi Menuhin and David Oistrakh, who played Bach's double violin concerto; the Boston Symphony Orchestra; Ravi Shankar on sitar; and the last movement of Beethoven's Ninth, from Geneva.

Thirty years had passed since Casals last performed in the United States. His return came on the afternoon of October 24, 1958, after the Political Committee of the General Assembly hosted a caustic debate between East and West national representatives on the question of disarmament. Wearing a dark grey business suit and carrying his cello, Casals strode stiffly into the great hall of the General Assembly, where an overflow audience of 3,000 U.N. delegates greeted him with a standing ovation.

Bent over his eighteenth-century instrument, his eyes closed in customary concentration, the elderly cellist was a small, lone figure in the vast hall of nations. "But his face was a vision of strength and determination," wrote a reporter in the TV section of the *New York Times*, "the firm jaw, the darting eyes, and the obvious command of the crowded hall when he silenced the cheers of the representatives of the nations of the world." Even his hands were captured by cameras in what was a novel high-definition broadcast; it enabled music critics to analyze his broad palms and fingers: pudgy on the right hand, slim on the left from decades of stretching. The sonic result was an enormous tone that reached into the upper balcony with purity and purpose.

"It was a beautiful performance," wrote the eminent critic Harold C. Schonberg. "Señor Casals' bow arm seemed to be as strong as ever. He took the long phrases without any tremor. The breadth of his phrasing, the rhythmic bite of the last movement, and the warm conception all were testimony of a musical heritage and a musical mind that many have called unsurpassed in this century."

After the Bach sonata Casals offered an encore, his arrangement of a tune he pointedly introduced as a Catalan folk song, "Song of the Birds." When he was done, the hall rose to its feet with explosive applause. He was not able to address the audience in the General Assembly chamber (permitted only to delegates of member states), so a recorded statement was broadcast during the intermission of the concert. In his remarks—broadcast on CBS and carried on more than seventy-six radio stations across the world (he did versions in English, French, Spanish, and Italian)—Casals maintained that his performance was not to be taken as a shift in political position. He was motivated by "the anguish of the world caused by the continuation of nuclear danger."

"Confusion and fear have invaded the whole world," he said. "Misunderstood nationalism, fanaticism, political dogmas, and lack of liberty and justice are feeding mistrust and hostility that make the collective danger greater every day, yet the desire for peace is felt by every human being…"

His performance made the front page of the *New York Times*, accompanied by a photograph of the cellist under the headline

"Throng at UN Hails Performance by Casals." His appearance at the United Nations, wrote biographer Robert Baldock, "transformed him, virtually instantaneously, into a globally recognized symbol of peace and, in the uncomfortable but accurate phrase, a 'geriatric superstar.'"

GIGUE

Produces an almost satanic effect with its repetitions of similar motifs. DIMITRI MARKEVITCH

BACH'S INSTRUMENTS OFTEN feel beside the point, as if he composed ideal music, music that transcends instruments, music that was invented to reinvent itself. It's often assumed that a piece of music by Bach is so musically indestructible that it can be played with excellent results on, say, kazoo, pennywhistle, banjo, marimba, saxophone—you name it. Such is Bach's street cred.

His peers in the classical pantheon, Mozart and Beethoven, aren't tampered with nearly as much; they aren't transposed, transcribed, and transmogrified to anywhere near the same degree. Perhaps it has something to do with the steady beat of baroque music, the overlapping voices of counterpoint, or the possibility that Bach's reportedly great skill at improvisation is somehow embedded in the music itself. There was also a rich baroque tradition of borrowing existing music for inspiration. More likely it is due to something unique about Bach's music. From the start, his works have undergone radical transformation.

Bach himself blazed the trail by rearranging his own compositions, and those of others such as Vivaldi, for various instruments and purposes. Violin concertos were turned into harpsichord concertos; cantata movements became organ solos. He didn't hesitate to rearrange a large-scale piece like the *St. Matthew Passion* for Prince Leopold's funeral, he repackaged a grab bag of secular cantatas into the *Christmas Oratorio*, and he transcribed innumerable other works, such as the fifth cello suite (or lute suite, whichever came first).

The tendency to transform Bach grew as his music became known to more and more musicians. It began with his sons Friedemann and C. P. E., who each staged performances of his music with add-ons of their own. Later, Mozart notably arranged in string quartet form some fugues from *The Well-Tempered Clavier*. In the nineteenth century, Romantic composers tended to adapt Bach's works for piano, starting with Mendelssohn and Schumann, who added piano accompaniment to the violin solo works and, in the ill-fated case of Schumann, to the Cello Suites.

One of the most famous examples of reinventing Bach was carried out by French composer Charles Gounod, who in the 1850s took the first prelude from *The Well-Tempered Clavier*, added a soprano melody, and created a kitsch classic, "Ave Maria," using the words of the Latin prayer. Other composers would pluck small bits out of Bach's works and turn them into simpler, catchier items, a practice that resulted in popular tunes such as "Air on the G String" and "Sheep May Safely Graze."

The twentieth century saw more adventurous and larger-scale reworkings. In the 1920s conductor Leopold Stokowski created the first of his many orchestral transcriptions of Bach — lush, brash, and larger than life. They were denounced by Bach purists as sacrilegious, but they boasted a majestic grandeur that broadened his appeal. And they still sell. The 1940 Disney film *Fantasia* included Stokowski's rendering of the Toccata and Fugue in D Minor, which pioneered the use of stereo, showed the conductor shaking hands with Mickey Mouse, and introduced Bach to a more popular audience.

But controversy often surrounded any unorthodox attempts at tampering with the almighty music. Jazz was a major culprit. As early as 1938, the U.S. Federal Communications Commission (FCC) heard a complaint about the "swinging" of music by Bach on the radio. A letter written by none other than the president of the Bach Society of New Jersey to the chairman of the FCC raised the issue in no uncertain terms:

As you are doubtless aware, the country is being swept by a rage of playing classical and traditional songs over the radio in swing tempo. This is causing genuine distress to lovers of fine music. Recently, on two occasions, we heard a jazz orchestra giving a rendition of Bach's "Toccata in D minor." All the beautiful fugue effects were destroyed by the savage slurring of the saxophone and the jungled discords of the clarinet. By no stretch of the imagination could such performances be tolerated except by a people of no discrimination.

The Bach Society president urged the FCC to suspend or revoke the licences of offending radio stations. But efforts to ban imaginative spins on Bach were in vain. The New Jersey Bach Society would have been disturbed by Benny Goodman's rendition of "Bach Goes to Town," or perhaps by the 1937 swing version of Bach's double violin concerto by violinists Stephane Grappelli and Eddie South playing alongside guitar-great Django Rheinhardt. And more jazzified Bach was to come. In the 1950s French pianist Jacques Loussier formed a trio called Play Bach, which toured extensively and released several albums that gave the eighteenth-century composer a brilliant swing makeover.

In the early 1960s an unlikely breakout act was the Swingle Singers, an eight-voice chorus that specialized in swing-singing Bach. Their first two albums, *Bach's Greatest Hits* and *Going Baroque*, sold big and snagged a Grammy award for best new recording artists in 1964. Not all serious Bach players were scandalized. Canadian pianist Glenn Gould, whose idiosyncratic account of the *Goldberg Variations* had made waves a decade earlier, praised the group: "When I first heard them I felt like lying on the floor and kicking my heels, that's how good I thought they were." (The Swingles, like Loussier, have also recorded movements from the Cello Suites).

Rock music would also assimilate Bach, one memorable example being Procol Harum's worldwide megahit of 1967, "A Whiter Shade of Pale," which made it to number one on the British charts, sold six million copies, and was recently pegged at number fifty-seven on *Rolling Stone*'s list of the greatest songs of all time. A progressive-rock item featuring a catchy organ riff, the song was in fact stolen from Bach's "Air on a G String" (more precisely, it was stolen from an advertisement for Hamlet Cigars that had stolen it from Bach). Four decades later, a royalties dispute over the song broke out between two former members of the band and landed in court. One commentator, Rod Liddle of *The Spectator*, suggested that it was "Bach who really should be sitting in the high court looking embittered and grizzled and surrounded by a phalanx of carnivorous lawyers."

In 1968 Walter Carlos released *Switched-On Bach,* an album of electronic transcriptions of some of Bach's best-known works played on a synthesizer. The record rocketed up the pop and classical music charts, selling a million copies and becoming classical music's first gold record in a decade. *Switched-On Bach* went a long way towards popularizing electronic music and the Moog synthesizer, as well as making J. S. Bach groovy in the sixties. And the album may have popularized something else: after its release Walter Carlos decided to resolve a long-standing identity crisis by undergoing a sex-change operation, thenceforth becoming known as Wendy Carlos.

Its gender credentials aside, *Switched-On Bach* was shocking to the old-fashioned baroque fan base. "I played it a few weeks ago and promptly went into deep culture shock," confessed

Harold C. Schonberg in the *New York Times*. "After transfusions, cold compresses, hysteria, and intravenous feeding, I played it again. The reaction was less severe, though there was a mild attack of the shakes and giggles."

Schonberg called it a breakthrough for electronic music, "breathtaking" in its own way. But at the end of the day he didn't like "Bach-Carlos" any more than he did "Bach-Stokowski." Why did modern composers see the need to hyphenate Bach? he wondered. Why should there be, he asked, a new approach to Bach? But the genre genie had long been out of the bottle. As *Time* magazine once put it, Bach has been through "more modern translations than *The Iliad*."

Transcribing the Cello Suites for other instruments goes with the Bachian territory. Robert Schumann, a major booster of Bach in the nineteenth century, was the first to write a piano accompaniment for the suites. He got the idea of adding piano to the cello from Mendelssohn's similar treatment of Bach's solo works for violin. In Schumann's view, adding piano was a way of providing "harmonic braces." The aim was to flesh out the music, making it more vivid for a public unaccustomed to solo string music.

Schumann completed what he called his "Bachiana" project in 1853. But for reasons unknown the pieces were not accepted for publication; the music remained in his head. On New Year's Eve 1853, either Schumann or his pianist wife Clara played the first three suites with a Düsseldorf cellist. The next day they played the last three. The following month, Schumann descended into psychological illness and attempted suicide. The Cello Suites were among his last musical experiences before his decline. He was committed to a sanatorium in March 1854, and died two years later.*

....

* In 1981, "thanks to a stroke of fortune," music scholar Joachim Draheim discovered in a library in the West German town of Speyer a copy of Schumann's work for Suite No. 3. The music finally saw the light of day in 2003 with the release of a disc on the Hanssler label. Performed by cellist Peter Bruns and pianist Roglit Ishay, it

A bolder flight of imagination on the piano was made by the legendary Leopold Godowsky in the 1920s. Godowsky, a maverick musician with unequalled technique, was considered a pianist's pianist; his small hands were insured for $1 million. In the early 1920s, suffering from a sort of existential despair, Godowsky found solace in exotic travel and the works of Bach.

He set out on a concert tour of the Far East, visiting Singapore, Shanghai, Java, Manila, and Honolulu, among other places. During the lengthy journey he fell under the spell of Indonesian music and began transcribing three of the Cello Suites for piano. He wrote that while Bach's "mighty genius" is everywhere apparent in the Cello Suites, the limitations of the cello were an unavoidable obstacle that limited "the master's supreme powers in contrapuntal style and emotional polyphony." By writing the Cello Suites for the cello, Bach had forced himself into the position of a "colossus in chains." Godowsky endeavoured to unchain that genius.

Working in locales as varied as Osaka, Shanghai, and aboard a ship travelling between Java and Hong Kong, Godowsky completed his transcriptions of Suites No. 2, 3, and 5. The arrangement was titled as three Bach suites "very freely transcribed and adapted for piano." They are exquisite, sounding as fleshed out as a Bach keyboard concerto while managing to be as darkly majestic as the cello when required. But the transcriptions, completed in New York in 1923, were mostly ignored, leading Godowsky to further doubt his achievements and question his place in the cosmos.

The 1920s were early going in the recording history of the Cello Suites; it would be a couple of decades before even Casals would release his pioneering discs. But as time went on, other

....

is a lovely work. The piano part is respectful, hugging the coastline of the cello; the result, while anathema to many Bach purists and cellists, is highly likeable. For those unaccustomed to baroque music or solo cello, it could also serve as a sort of Bach for Beginners, a cello suite with training wheels.

instruments entered the fray. My own collection of discs includes the suites performed on viola (Bach's preferred instrument while conducting an orchestra), piano, double bass, lute, guitar, flute, saxophone, marimba, and the twenty-string theorbo.

It all works splendidly well, as does the Swingle Singers doing a gigue with eight voices. Ditto for a gorgeous version of a sarabande that I have featuring no less than thirty-two cellos. Among my current favourites are an obscure piano and bass duo, Kalman Olah and Mini Schulz, who give the Cello Suites a jazz/pop makeover, and a terrific disc called *Lambarena: Bach to Africa*, which employs drums and a xylophone to combine a cello suite gigue with a melody from Gabon.

All these reworkings would have the president of the New Jersey Bach Society spinning in his grave. But it may represent the future of "classical" music. At a 2003 symposium in New York City called "Re-Imagining Bach for the Twenty-First Century," there was much talk of rearranging Bach. A curator played his favourite Bach arrangements, from Stokowski to the Swingles, and speculated whether smell or colours would be enlisted in future recordings of the Leipzig cantor. There were talks on Bach and dance, as well as Bach and jazz.

As it happened, the seminar held at the Lincoln Center focused on the Cello Suites to illustrate Bach's creative possibilities. A pianist and a cellist performed three different arrangements of Suite No. 3 with piano accompaniment, including Schumann's version. I enjoyed all of them. But the highlight for me was a mind-blowing rendition of the same suite on marimba, a deep-toned xylophone played with soft-headed beaters. She-e Wu was the performer, and she gave the suite a wonderful velvety, percussive quality. That evening the cellist Pieter Wispelwey capped the conference by performing all six suites. One had to wonder whether Bach ever meant for the suites to be played in such a completist way, or whether it is a conceit adopted by cellists too eager to flex their muscles. It seemed like overkill. Give me a suite here or there, maybe two or at most three in a row. More than that feels excessive. (It took Wispelwey approximately two hours and twenty minutes to play all six.)

But the search for possibilities inherent in the music goes on. When I hear violinist Lara St. John play the solo violin works to the rhythms of the tabla, I can't help but want to hear the Cello Suites in a similar setting. "MarimBach," *Bach to Africa*, and Jacques Loussier all turn my crank a great deal. The notion of playing Bach precisely as it was played in Prince Leopold's castle also intrigues me, but it shouldn't be the only way of playing it. Casals would never have resurrected the music had that been the case. The tired but true conclusion is that every age reimagines Bach on its own terms. And this power to be reimagined goes a long way towards understanding Bach's longevity.

A recent example is Bach's so-called "Little Fugue" in G minor. Stokowski gave the work his trademark monumentality, cushioned with plush violins and powered by an army division of horns. The arrangement is outdated maybe, arguably excessive, but completely convincing. The same piece of music in 2006 was the subject of a DJ competition held in Eugene, Oregon. The Bach Remix Competition, sponsored by the renowned Bach Oregon Festival, was held to broaden the festival's appeal. DJs worked with a vinyl copy of Stokowski's arrangement with the Philadelphia Orchestra. Bach's little organ fugue was mixed with hip-hop beats and spoken word by competing turntablists. The winner was twenty-year-old Danny Straton, a.k.a. DV8, whose impressive mix earned him $500 and a gig at the festival.

The acid test of a great performance is whether it produces a feeling that there is absolutely no other way for that music to be performed. Casals channelled that feeling in a tremendous way, so tremendous that he was said to have "ruined" the music for a generation of cellists who couldn't free themselves from his mighty imprimatur. But on a good day it is also to be found in Wispelwey, in Stokowski, in Godowsky, in Loussier, and in Danny "DV8" Straton.

ON A GOOD day I can play the prelude of the first cello suite on my guitar. Once I realized how many light-years I was from becoming a cellist with any degree of mastery, I did the logical thing and started learning a Bach suite on the only instrument I can play competently, albeit without so much as one classical tune in my repertoire. Besides, the guitar is not so far removed from the lute, which was good enough for Bach—and for Monsieur Schouster.

I bought an instructional book that contained the prelude of Suite No. 1 written in guitar tablature format. "Guitar tab," as it's known to grateful guitarists who have never done time in a conservatory, illustrates in an easily graspable way how to read music. I set to work, measure by measure, on the first Bach prelude.

There are nearly 2,000 measures in the Cello Suites. In the first prelude, which is the shortest in the set, there are forty-one measures, each containing sixteen notes. Figuring out how to play just a single measure—approximately three seconds of music—could require weeks of sporadic practice until I managed it with authority. Some of the measures were fairly doable, while others forced me to pretzel the fingers of my left hand into odd shapes on the fretboard.

Connecting the various measures in a seamless musical statement was even more daunting. "Each note is like a link in a chain," Casals once intoned, "important in itself and also as a connection between what has been and what will be." I could get stuck on a few links in the chain for an extended period of time.

The first four measures exercised a hypnotic effect on me. To get them down, I repeated them in a twelve-second loop,

playing what felt like a perfectly good song by pop music standards. As an island detached from the rest of the prelude, the
phrase has a circular beauty that works. That phrase, *motiv*, riff,
whatever you want to call it, keeps coming back in the suites,
especially in the first, third, and sixth. At heart it is a "broken"
chord, spelling out—implying—the individual notes of a chord
in piecemeal fashion. Depending on when I'm listening, it
sounds like a cradle being rocked, a gentle wave, the start of a
journey, or a string player warming up with a basic exercise.

There were other measures that stuck in my head, snippets
of the prelude that when played over and over again started to
sound like, to take one example, a powerhouse jazz-funk riff.
Isolate measures fifteen and sixteen and loop them, and you've
got a stand-alone groove that would work wonders in the rock
world. That's part of what makes Bach so rich a font. And I
don't think it's explained solely by the greater complexity of
classical music. For example, blues guitarist Robert Johnson,
who recorded his seminal work in the 1930s, though working
in a much simpler genre, also has phrases in his tunes that last
all of three seconds, but which on their own could power a
perfectly good rock anthem. Bach's Zeppelinesque riff in the
third gigue is a similar example. But the riff that for most listeners powers the idea of the Cello Suites is that simple
sequence of broken chords in the opening measures, the signature of the suites.

Bach also left some very personal signatures. On at least
one occasion he inscribed his own name—B-A-C-H—in the
Cello Suites. He was able to do this because in German usage
the letter B stands for B-flat, while the letter H represents B. By
sequencing the notes B-flat, A, C, and B he was in fact spelling
out his name. This musical signature happens in the soulful
sarabande of the third suite.

Finding number symbolism in Bach's compositions is a
favourite pastime of Bach scholars. It appears that the composer

did occasionally encode numbers in his music, using a Jewish kabbalistic method known as gematria, whereby A=1, B=2, C=3, and so on. The letters of *J. S. Bach*, for example, add up to forty-one, while the letters of *Bach* total fourteen, and many musicologists see those numbers popping up in various ways in Bach compositions. While learning the prelude of the first cello suite, I counted up the number of measures and was stunned by the result: forty-one. It could very well be a meaningless coincidence, but deep into Bach research as I was, it seemed like a gloriously personal sign from the composer, visible only to those initiates immersed in the arcana of his music.

After about six months of practising the prelude of Suite No. 1, I could more or less get through all forty-one measures. Not terribly well, but I could connect the dots. The trouble, as far as I could tell, was that I played it mechanically, like a sewing machine, the way Bach's instrumental music was allegedly (and badly) played through much of the nineteenth century. How was I to properly string the notes together? In a small way I could appreciate the challenge Casals faced when he first tried to figure out the Cello Suites without any cellist or recording to guide him. After getting down the basics—the technical ability to play each of the individual measures that form the prelude—I was faced with the challenge of connecting all the dots in a meaningful way.

I had to somehow shake the feeling that I was a metronome. Eventually I realized that the only way to give eloquence to notes in lockstep with a time signature is to shave off thin slices of time value from some of the notes and let a tiny extra bit of time linger on other notes. Was this taking liberties with the score? If so, it seemed to be working.

As time went on, as Bach's notes passed into my bloodstream, my performance improved. I was better able to put myself in the cello mindset, trying to express the phrasing of the great cellists, first and foremost Casals, who reverberated in my head.

The timbre of the guitar was a different soundscape, softer and smoother and evanescent, its waves disappearing into thin air, where the cello leaves rumbling aftershocks. But learning this small but crucial bit of the music on the guitar has changed the way I hear the Cello Suites. Many measures embody certain ideas, even if the ideas are abstract and hard to put into words, ideas that have to do with finger shapes, abstract sound, my recollection of how the technical hurdles first felt on my fingers—or the idea of a jazz-funk groove embedded in the baroque rhetoric.

In a way, when it comes to the prelude I can now play on guitar, I became like a car mechanic who hears a transmission shift gears on an engine he's worked on, repaired, and maintained. The technical underpinnings are often what's heard when I now listen to the first cello suite. But I can still shut it off. I'm a latecomer to the musicianship of it all. And it's only one prelude, forty-one measures in an ocean of Bach.

As a listener I'm also influenced by the storylines I've read into the music. The first prelude has always brought to mind a boy cellist out walking with his father by the old port of Barcelona in 1890, on the brink of discovering sheet music in a musty second-hand music shop. While Bach may not have written a teenage Catalan cellist into the first cello suite, he did write youth and innocence and the feeling that everything is possible. The second suite will forever remain for me a suite of tragedy; the third, love; the fourth, struggle; and the fifth, mystery. And each suite has its own fine print. The mysteries of Suite No. 5 are of a strange tuning, an elusive Monsieur Schouster, lute players, the glittering court life of the eighteenth century, and characters ranging from August the Strong to Luise Gottsched.

The sixth suite is one of transcendence.

SUITE NO. 6

(D major)

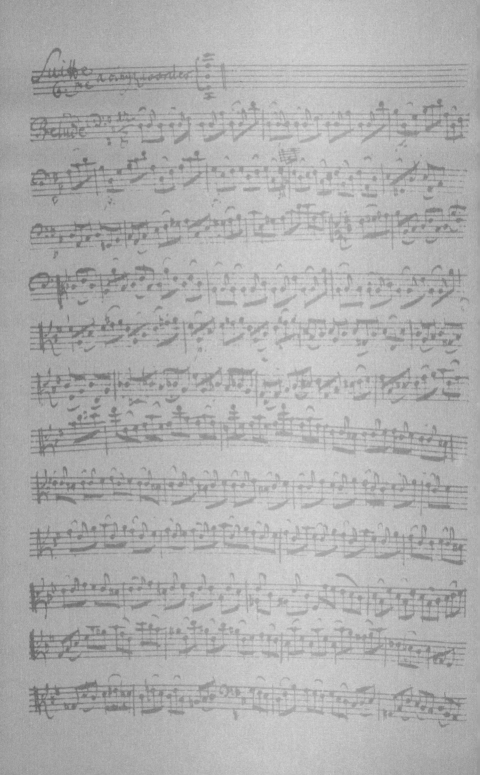

PRELUDE

At bottom he conceived everything for an ideal
instrument. ALBERT SCHWEITZER

THE FINAL PRELUDE is a bolt of lightning — searing, rhapsodic,
and electrified with ecstasy. It harks back to the first suite
with its undulating current, but five suites later is bursting its
bounds with pyrotechnical energy. Here Bach is working with
a large canvas. The trumpets blare, strings soar, drums roll.
The composer pulls off the symphonic effect of a full orchestra
with one bow and a handful of strings.

One more string than usual, it should be noted. The sixth
suite was written for an unspecified five-stringed instrument, an
instrument that seems to have disappeared from history as completely as did the Cello Suites after Bach's death. What was this
instrument? And why did Bach, after writing five highly symmetrical suites for a normal cello, suddenly change the pattern
and tailor this suite for an instrument with an additional string?

He may have been holed up in the confines of his own
imagination, with little care for the logistics of performance.
Or perhaps he picked up a five-stringed instrument that happened to be lying around and proceeded to crank out another
virtuosic suite. Another possibility is that he actually invented
an instrument for the occasion.

The Promethean intro quickly takes on human dimensions, adjusting the volume from thunder to whisper, then back again. It is a prelude of celebration and nostalgia—a sublime summing up that eventually moves higher, ever reaching, venturing so far that an additional string is required, finally achieving its summit in a frenzied dance of notes that is ultimately a journey back home. To get there Bach takes us down a rollicking hill, thrashing chords to pull on the reins, and the final stop is a decorative spin on the melody that began the first suite in the first place. If the six suites ended here and now it would be a perfectly convincing close.

In 1747 Bach experienced his only brush with history: an event that recorded his presence, if only as a footnote, on the world stage. The occasion was a meeting with Frederick the Great, the iron-fisted flute-playing ruler of Prussia who embodied both Enlightenment philosophy and German militarism. By the time Bach visited Frederick's court, Prussia had been transformed into a military powerhouse and a bona fide European power. Bach would have wanted to visit C. P. E., a keyboard player in Frederick's *Capelle*, by then married and the father of Bach's first grandson.

It is not known who arranged for Bach to perform before the Prussian king, but the political timing was right. Six months earlier Austria had been forced to accept Prussia's seizure of Silesia, and Prussian troops ended their occupation of Leipzig.

In early May Bach and his son Friedemann had barely arrived in Berlin when he was summoned to Frederick the Great's palace in nearby Potsdam. The closest thing to an eyewitness account, based on Friedemann's recollection, is found in Forkel's biography:

> The king used to have every evening a private concert, in which he himself generally performed some concertos on the flute. One evening, just as he was getting his flute ready and his musicians were assembled, an officer brought him the written list of the

strangers who had arrived. With his flute in his hand, he ran over the list, but immediately turned to the assembled musicians and said, with a kind of agitation: "Gentlemen, old Bach is come." The flute was now laid aside; and old Bach, who had alighted at his son's lodgings, was immediately summoned to the Palace.

Frederick the Great invited Bach to try out his various forte-pianos (an early version of the piano), located in several rooms of his palace. After a time Bach asked the king to give him a subject for a fugue that he could then improvise on, which the king did. Bach's playing of this "royal theme" amazed the king's entourage and court musicians who clustered around the keyboard. The king then asked Bach to improvise on the theme in a six-part fugue, which he was unable to do on the spot, but he did perform a six-part fugue on a theme of his own, again impressing the palace crowd.

Four days later, a report of Bach's visit appeared in a Berlin newspaper. "One hears from Potsdam," it began, "that last Sunday, the famous Capellmeister from Leipzig, Herr Bach, arrived with the intention to have the pleasure of hearing the excellent Royal music at that place." The newspaper reported that Bach's improvisation on the king's theme "was done so happily by the aforementioned Capellmeister that not only was His Majesty pleased to show his satisfaction thereat, but also all those present were seized with astonishment." Bach, the report added, found the royal theme to be "so exceedingly beautiful that he intends to set it down on paper as a regular fugue and have it engraved on copper."

True to the news item, Bach had his elaborate composition, the *Musical Offering*, ready for the printer only two months later. Two hundred copies were printed at Bach's own expense, including one special presentation copy that was sent to the king who had inspired its royal theme. The music arrived at Frederick's newly completed Sans Souci palace a few days later, complete with Bach's dedication to a "Monarch whose great-ness and power, as in all the sciences of war and peace, so especially in music, everyone must admire and revere."

Given that Prussia had recently defeated Saxony on the battlefield and occupied Leipzig, some observers have sug-gested that Bach met Frederick the Great in the capacity of a peace messenger. Another interpretation is that Bach took a dim view of the king who was a bitter enemy of his own royal patron, the Saxon king. There also may have been conflict on musical grounds. The thirty-five-year-old king's "modern" tastes fa-voured the simpler *gallant* style of music over Bach's old-fashioned polyphony. And it's also conceivable that Bach, as was his wont, might have been seeking a title, a commission, or a job.

It's impossible to know whether Frederick held Bach in great esteem or looked down on him as a fusty fugue-master. Probably he felt a mixture of both. The two were about as dif-ferent as two Germans could be in the eighteenth century. In a gripping history of the encounter, James R. Gaines writes that the "King and the composer faced each other as the embodi-ments of warring values."

Bach was a Lutheran family man who had fathered twenty children. Frederick was proudly atheistic, either a repressed homosexual, inactively bisexual, or asexual, and stuck in an arranged marriage that was never consummated. Bach spoke German; Frederick preferred literary French. Bach had a spirit-ual, nearly medieval frame of mind; Frederick's outlook was ultra-rational, befitting a man of the Enlightenment. And they each stood for different styles of music. Gaines argues that Frederick's request that Bach improvise on the spot a six-part fugue on the "royal theme" was designed to embarrass the older musician because the challenge was all but impossible.*

* Succeeding at Frederick's challenge would have been like "the playing of sixty simultaneous blindfold games of chess, and winning them all," writes Douglas R. Hofstadter in the cult classic *Gödel, Escher, Bach: An Eternal Golden Braid*.

But it is doubtful that Bach possessed much in the way of political loyalty to Saxony and its king. He held the title of royal Saxon court composer, but he was a Thuringian by background and always kept his Eisenach citizenship. His son C. P. E. was an employee of the Prussian king. Friedemann, too, had recently come under Frederick's jurisdiction by moving from Dresden to Halle. Bach's older brother Jacob had joined the Swedish army when that country was at war with Saxony. One also thinks of how the famous composer Hasse comported himself when Frederick occupied Dresden a few years earlier. Even though Hasse was the Saxon king's highly paid Capellmeister, he obliged the Prussian invader's desire to have his most recent opera performed. Hasse later dedicated a new flute sonata to Frederick and accompanied the Prussian king's flute-playing on the harpsichord. Frederick gave him a diamond ring for his efforts.

Warfare, however destructive for most people, was a commonplace activity of princes and kings. The borders shifted, blood spilled, dynasties ebbed and flowed.

The Prussian court did not compensate Bach for the *Musical Offering*, as would have been standard practice. There is no record that Frederick even took notice of the monumental composition that he inspired. It was a piece of music that he probably would have considered convoluted and old hat, but it would outlive the hundreds and hundreds of entirely fashionable and supposedly superior concertos that he championed as king.

By this time Bach had little in the way of expectations from those in power, whether they were town councillors, church authorities, university rectors, or enlightened monarchs. He had made his peace with the fact that Leipzig was disappointing in many professional respects. His career had stalled in Dresden after he finally won the ceremonial title of Saxon court composer. No new job offers were forthcoming.

At home, Anna Magdalena had given birth in 1742 to Bach's twentieth child, Regina Susanna.* His two youngest sons, both born in the 1730s, were rapidly becoming skilled musicians: Johann Christoph Friedrich, who would become known as the Bückeburg Bach, and Johann Christian, who would gain fame as a composer in London. Both C. P. E. and Wilhelm Friedemann were already enjoying impressive reputations as musicians.

Bach carefully maintained the Old Bach Archive, a collection of compositions by forebears passed down from generation to generation, dating back to Johann Bach, who was born in 1604. He also kept a genealogy and family tree that provided capsule biographies of each accomplished musician—including his youngest sons, not yet musicians of any note but whose future occupation was obvious to their father. Bach was looking back to his forebears and casting forward to his children, all of whom represented links in a greater musical and spiritual chain.

During the 1740s Bach grew more and more inward, focusing on his legacy and his art rather than creating music to suit the needs of his patrons. After 1746 he rarely performed outside his own home. In works such as *The Art of the Fugue* and the *Musical Offering*, writes biographer Malcolm Boyd, he was directing his creativity to a small circle of connoisseurs, "works in which Bach, the composer-philosopher, is alone with the impenetrable mysteries of his art." For a composer who had been a craftsman in a nearly medieval sense, creating for specific commissions and occasions, Bach appeared more and more concerned with posterity and shaping his musical legacy.

In 1749 his health deteriorated. The Saxon prime minister, Heinrich von Brühl, sent a letter to the Leipzig burgomaster in which he recommended a candidate to fill the post of cantor at

....

* Bach had seven children with his first wife, Maria Barbara, four of whom survived. Anna Magdalena gave birth to thirteen children, six of whom lived to adulthood. The only one of Bach's four daughters who married was Lieschen, who wed one of her father's best students.

St. Thomas "upon the eventual...decease of Mr. Bach." It is not known what the sixty-four-year-old composer was suffering from, though it appears to have been diabetes. Bach's eyesight had degenerated and his handwriting had weakened. Still, he managed to recover.

The following year, a famous British eye doctor by the name of John Taylor arrived in Leipzig to give lectures on ophthalmology and to demonstrate his surgical skills. Taylor, accompanied by ten servants, travelled in two coaches emblazoned with painted eyes. Bach decided to undergo surgery for his failing and painful eyesight.

The surgery was considered a success, but about a week later a second operation was performed. Bach then took a turn for the worse. "Not only could he no longer use his eyes," wrote C. P. E. Bach, "but his whole system, which was otherwise thoroughly healthy, was completely overwhelmed by the operation and by the addition of harmful medicaments and other things, so that, therefore he was almost continually ill for half a year."

One of the last compositions Bach worked on was *The Art of the Fugue*, which contains fourteen fugues based on a single theme. Fourteen, it will be remembered, was the numerical value of the letters of Bach's name. In his manuscript, the last fugue, the fourteenth, trails off into incompleteness, unfinished. According to C. P. E., who arranged to have the work printed after his father's death, Bach died while trying to finish the fourteenth fugue. And the place where the music comes to a stop is where Bach was writing his own name into the music, composing a musical phrase based on the letters B-A-C-H. It was as if the composer were trying to inscribe his mortal being into the eternal music.

Compelling as the story is, it is unlikely that Bach literally died while trying to finish the fugue. As blindness set in during his last days, he would have been incapable of writing. A few months after the second operation, however, Bach's vision suddenly improved and he was able to see again and tolerate light. "But a few hours later," wrote C. P. E., "he suffered a stroke; and this was followed by a raging fever, as victim of which, despite every possible care given him by two of the most skillful physicians of Leipzig, on July 28, 1750, a little after a quarter past eight in the evening, in the sixty-sixth year of his life, he quietly and peacefully, by the merit of his Redeemer, departed this life."

BACH WAS BURIED in the graveyard of St. John's Church. The Leipzig town council lost no time in hiring his successor as cantor, choosing the musician who had been urged on them by the Saxon prime minister. One city councillor commented that while Bach had been a great musician, he hadn't been a very good schoolteacher.

Bach left no will, so in keeping with Saxon law, his estate was divided between his widow, Anna Magdalena, who received one-third, and his nine surviving children, who received the rest. The estate's inventory has survived—it included, among other items, assets in the form of gold, silver, and medals; one stock share in a Silesian mine; clothing, such as eleven linen shirts; household furnishings; and eighty volumes of theological books. There were also nineteen instruments, among them five harpsichords, three violas, three violins, a lute, and two cellos.

But the most valuable part of Bach's estate was not listed: his music. There was no reference to any of his manuscripts. Whether these were manuscripts of other composers' music, manuals about music, or Bach's own compositions, these items had an "ideal" value—for musicians—which far outweighed their actual value. For Bach, the natural recipients of these works would be his wife and sons, all of whom were musicians. And among the manuscripts, presumably, was the composer's original "autograph" manuscript of the Cello Suites.

Bach's death threw his household into disarray, scattering its remaining members. Anna Magdalena was forty-eight years old, with five children still living at home—an unmarried stepdaughter, two younger daughters, and two sons. There wasn't much in the way of money to go around; rather than accumulate savings, Bach had spent the bulk of his extra income on professional interests such as concerts, instruments, books, and publishing. After various debts and expenses were paid, Anna Magdalena received an estimated 335 thalers, which represented roughly half of her late husband's annual salary. The inheritance couldn't have lasted long, and once it ran out she would have received some income from the welfare department of the city council. She gave some of Bach's cantatas to St. Thomas School in order to retain her home for another six months; she also received the customary half of her husband's annual salary during this grace period. Later she was paid 40 thalers by the city council in exchange for some copies of *The Art of the Fugue.*

The two sons living at home—young Johann Christian and intellectually challenged Gottfried Heinrich—went to live with other siblings, as was customary family practice under the circumstances. Anna Magdalena moved with her three daughters into an apartment in the home of a close family friend, the judge Friedrich Heinrich Graff. Next to nothing is known about her last years. It seems that Bach's eldest sons felt no obligation to help their stepmother. When she died in 1760 at age fifty-nine, she was listed in the burial registry as an "almswoman" supported by charity.

ALLEMANDE

It is annoying that my late father's things drift to and fro like this. C. P. E. BACH

BACH'S MANUSCRIPT OF the Cello Suites disappeared. He most likely left it to one of his sons, who between them received virtually all of his music. At his death, five of Bach's sons were living and all were musically accomplished. In fact, two would rapidly become famous, outstripping the provincial reputation of their father and making the Bach name their own.

The son who has understandably drawn the least amount of attention is Gottfried Heinrich, Anna Magdalena's eldest child, who suffered from some learning disability or mental disorder. He was a skilled keyboard player, described by his brother C. P. E. as "a great genius who didn't fully develop." After Bach's death he went to live with his married sister Lieschen and brother-in-law Christoph Altnikol in Naumberg. He died there in 1763 and is not known to have inherited any of his father's manuscripts.

Johann (John) Christian Bach, the youngest of Bach's sons, achieved a fame his father could only dream of. Known as the "London Bach," he travelled to Italy, converted to Roman Catholicism, and enjoyed celebrity status in England, going by the name John Bach. Only fourteen years old when Bach died,

Johann Christian apparently occupied a special place in his
father's heart. Bach left a generous inheritance to the son he
called "Christel," giving him three keyboards instruments and
in all probability a number of manuscripts. He also received a
modest amount of cash and a third of his father's linen shirts.

A few months after Bach's death, Johann Christian moved
to the Berlin household of his brother C. P. E., who gave him
keyboard lessons and exposed him to the city's leading musicians. Before the outbreak of the Seven Years' War he was
independent enough to leave Berlin, apparently smitten with a
number of Italian singers and possibly travelling with one of
them. He gravitated to Italy, where he continued his studies,
found the patronage of a young nobleman, converted to Roman
Catholicism, and soon established himself as a successful composer of opera.*

By 1762 Johann Christian was in London, where he was
commissioned to compose two operas for the King's Theatre,
the main opera house in the city. From that point on "Mr. John
Bach" was an English composer. His career was aided by the
attention of the British monarchs; he became "music master"
to Queen Charlotte, who'd been a German princess and a
music pupil of C. P. E. before ascending the throne.

Unlike the biography of his father, history has left more in
the way of personal details about John Bach's life. Not long
after his arrival in England, he teamed up with another German
composer from Saxony, Carl Friedrich Abel, and launched a
concert series that lasted nearly twenty years. The two, who
may have known each other in Leipzig, shared a taste for the

....

* He also found time for romantic pursuits, notably with a ballerina in Naples that
earned him a formal rebuke from a government official. On another occasion he
was reprimanded for "joining female singers in the box reserved for them." The
incident brings to mind an episode fifty years earlier, when a young Johann
Sebastian Bach was scolded by authorities in Arnstadt for spending time with a
"stranger maiden" in a church loft.

finer things in life; they became fast friends and lodged together in the newly fashionable Soho district.

Abel was born in 1723 in Cöthen, that small duchy where J. S. Bach composed a fair amount of the suites while in the service of Prince Leopold. Abel's father was Christian Ferdinand Abel, the cellist and viola da gamba player in Leopold's orchestra, which was led by Bach. The elder Abel and Bach were evidently close; Bach stood as godfather to Abel's daughter Sophia Charlotta in 1720. It is even possible that Bach wrote some of the Cello Suites for Christian Ferdinand, who was an outstanding cello virtuoso.

Abel the son became a viola da gamba virtuoso and may have studied under Bach in Leipzig. By the late 1740s he was employed as a gambist in the Dresden orchestra, where he would also have known Friedemann. A decade later he was in London with John Bach. It is not difficult to imagine that he might have come in contact with the Cello Suites at various stages of his career, or that he might have owned a manuscript copy of the music.

In fact, the essential groove of the first cello suite's prelude can be heard in Abel's music for solo viola da gamba.* It is as if the Bach prelude has been surreptitiously enclosed in the music, an undergarment that only intimates might ascertain. Most likely it was Abel borrowing some old ideas to fashion something new. It may even have been an unconscious replication, but it is there.

John Bach and Abel continued to stage their concert series and play together in the Queen's Band, much as their fathers played together many years earlier in Prince Leopold's orchestra. But John Bach far outshone his colleague with his prodigious output of high-quality compositions. "Bach's very best sym-

---

* Most strikingly in the pieces WKO 205 (arpeggio), WKO 208 (moderato), and WKO 198 (allegro), available on the Hyperion disc *Mr. Abel's Fine Airs*, featuring Susanne Heinrich.

phonies," writes music historian Daniel Heartz, "put him alongside Haydn and Mozart at the highest level of symphonic practitioners the age could boast."

John Bach's fortunes declined in his later years. More fashionable musicians appeared on the scene, he was the target of financial fraud by his cleaning lady, and his health suddenly declined. In 1782 he died at age forty-six. Abel fell on hard times, apparently devastated by the loss of his friend, and though his gamba playing remained without peer, his final years were clouded by drink. As the instrument's last great virtuoso, his death also marked the demise of the viola da gamba's popularity, further paving the way for the cello's ascent.

That Abel knew of the Cello Suites seems probable. But he may have simply remembered them from his time in Germany. It is unlikely that John Bach ever possessed the original manuscript of the suites. And whatever manuscripts he did inherit from his father are thought to have been left behind in Berlin, with his brother C. P. E.

CARL PHILIPP EMANUEL Bach, known as C. P. E., was a careful custodian of his father's manuscripts. Although he was first and foremost taken up with his own career — which made him the most famous Bach in Europe during the eighteenth century — and though his vision of music was notably different from that of his father, C. P. E. far more than any of Bach's other offspring safeguarded his father's musical legacy.

When young John Christian left Berlin for Italy, C. P. E. likely purchased whatever manuscripts he had inherited from their father. Added to his own sizeable chunk of his father's musical estate, this left C. P. E. as the major guardian of his father's legacy. His lifestyle and career were more stable than those of his brothers; with his even-keeled temperament, C. P. E.'s storehouse of Bachiana stood a strong chance of survival.

As court harpsichordist to Frederick the Great for nearly three decades, C. P. E. was a key figure in building his father's reputation in Berlin. A few years after his father's death a lengthy obituary was written by C. P. E. and his father's student J. F. Agricola. As well as the musical manuscripts, he possessed a portrait of his father and a copy of the Bach family genealogy. And he conducted some pieces of his father's music, including a performance of the epic Mass in B Minor.

An active member of the European Enlightenment, C. P. E. mixed in intellectual and middle-class circles, befriending philosophers and poets as much as musicians. He was acquainted with the Itzig and Mendelssohn families, leading members of Berlin's Jewish community, which played a pivotal role in transmitting J. S. Bach's legacy. He was also in close touch with Bach's first biographer, Forkel, furnishing valuable information for the pioneering biography that would be published in 1802.

The story of C. P. E. selling off the copper engraving plates used to print his father's monumental *The Art of the Fugue* is often cited to show him in a bad light. But only thirty copies of the posthumously published masterwork had been printed by 1756, and it was likely a burdensome item for C. P. E. to hold on to. This was the case especially during the Seven Years' War, which at one point had C. P. E. serving in the Berlin militia and later forced him to leave Berlin for the safety of Saxony.

Despite his supreme competence and growing fame, C. P. E. had his share of woes. He was chronically underpaid and unappreciated by Frederick the Great. The monarch had narrow musical tastes, which did not include C. P. E.'s adventurous compositions. He was treated as a mere accompanist, and unlike other musicians in the royal *Capelle*, who deferentially tolerated the king's musical faults, C. P. E. could not hide his professional distaste regarding "the royal incapacity for precision in time-keeping."

When the Seven Years' War ended, the Prussian king's zeal for music waned. C. P. E. looked for employment elsewhere, and in 1768 was hired in the city-state of Hamburg, succeeding his godfather, Telemann. By this time C.P.E. was the most famous keyboard player and teacher in Europe. His music was quirky and experimental for the times. But though he embodied (as did John Bach) the *gallant* style that displaced the baroque and would lead directly to the classical style of Mozart and Haydn, his father's influence is at times audible.

For enthusiasts of the Bach Cello Suites there are at least two striking examples in C. P. E.'s work. His Sonata in G Minor for viola da gamba and keyboard obbligato contains a middle movement, the larghetto, which echoes the heart-stopping sarabande of the fifth cello suite. And his effervescent Sonata in C Major for viola da gamba and continuo bass is reminiscent of the first cello suite. The prelude of that cello suite seems to be forever bubbling to the surface in C. P. E.'s second movement, the allegretto.

It is estimated that more than a third of Bach's musical estate was given to C. P. E., which together with other items he acquired amounted to the major component of his father's music. His care went a long way towards ensuring that Bach's music and other family treasures survived. But it wasn't easy. "It is annoying," he wrote in a letter to Forkel, "that my late father's things drift to and fro like this; I am too old and too occupied to hold them together."

C. P. E. died at seventy-four of an acute chest ailment. After his death in 1788, his widow* put his estate on sale to the general public. Included were a portrait in oils of his father and

---

* C. P. E.'s wife was the daughter of a successful wine merchant; they had three children, a daughter and two sons—a lawyer and a very gifted painter who was given the name of his grandfather. Johann Sebastian Bach the younger went to Italy in the 1770s to advance his art, but his health declined prematurely and C. P. E. was forced to send him funds for "three of the most frightful life-and-death operations." A painter of great promise, he died before reaching the age of thirty.

many of his manuscripts, among them major works such as the *St. Matthew Passion*, the *St. John Passion*, the Mass in B Minor, and *The Art of the Fugue*. Most of the estate was acquired by the private scholar and Bach manuscript-hunter Georg Poelchau, who in turn sold his estate to the Prussian Royal Library in Berlin in 1841.

One assumes that if C. P. E. had been given Bach's manuscript of the Cello Suites he would have held on to it and preserved it for the future. But even in the case of C. P. E.'s stock, things went missing.

C. P. E.'s collection—which included some items of his father's music and other composers—was in Berlin's Prussian Royal Library during the Second World War. As Allied bombs were falling on Berlin in the 1940s, German authorities shipped thousands of cultural treasures out of the capital for safekeeping. Much of C. P. E.'s estate was hidden in a castle called Ullersdorf in Silesia (now Poland). As Soviet brigades combed the area in 1945, a tank driver discovered the archive. The KGB had the manuscripts relocated to a music conservatory in Kiev. In 1973 the material was transferred to the Ukrainian state archives, and another quarter-century passed before the Harvard musicologist and Bach expert Christoph Wolff discovered the long-lost musical estate.

No manuscript of the Cello Suites turned up. If C. P. E. ever had them in his possession—and he might have—they had disappeared somewhere along the way from eighteenth-century Prussia to the Ukrainian state archives.

VARIOUS PRESSURES COME with being the son of a great man. Most of Bach's sons seem to have made their psychological peace with his formidable character and gone on to lead highly productive musical careers and responsible lives. This wasn't the case with Bach's first-born son, who apparently carried more of his father's talent than did his brothers. "The burden," writes Percy Young, "of being a son of Johann Sebastian Bach, so it would seem, weighed more heavily on Wilhelm Friedemann than on his brothers." Like other observers of Bach's eldest son, Young reels off a list of character flaws that have tarnished Friedemann's reputation: psychological instability, coarseness, an argumentative nature, and an obstinate artist's pride. Drunkenness is usually thrown into the mix as well.

The emotional trigger for Friedemann's downward slide appears to have been his father's death. Until then his career had been more or less stellar. Favoured by his father, young Friedemann had received a more comprehensive musical grounding than his siblings. He also graduated in law at Leipzig University. By age twenty-two he had been hired (with his father drafting the letter of application) as church organist in glittering Dresden. He was industrious and well connected and managed to pursue a sideline interest in mathematics. But Dresden turned out to offer little in the way of advancement for Friedemann, and he eventually moved to Halle when he secured the prominent post of organist and music director. As in Dreden, his application again benefited from his father's influence. Friedemann was sheltered by Bach's name and dependent on his advice, but he was a tremendously accomplished musician—considered the best organist in Germany, with a particular flair for improvisation.

His father's death seems to have hit Friedemann hard. He went immediately to Leipzig after receiving the news. After the funeral and the estate proceedings, he took his young half-brother Johann (John) Christian to Berlin, where the boy would live with C. P. E. When Friedemann finally made it back to Halle, he was reprimanded for a lengthy absence. Presumably he'd been doing some thinking in the meantime; he soon married for the first time, at the age of forty-one.

The Seven Years' War understandably slowed his career, as did rocky relations with his superiors, but his luck seemed to turn with an advantageous job offer in Darmstadt. Friedemann applied and was hired, but the job slipped through his fingers; apparently there was some issue of inappropriate behaviour. By 1764 he had had his fill of professional disappointments, and out of the blue resigned his post in Halle. It was the last regular job he would ever hold down. Four years later the fifty-seven-year-old composer and his wife and daughter moved to Brunswig and he started looking for work. His behaviour began to look eccentric; for no apparent reason he picked up and moved to Berlin.* Among the things he left behind was his precious collection of his father's manuscripts, which were deposited with an acquaintance to be auctioned off. Much of what was sold has never been found.

"Hardened now in his aloofness," writes Eugene Helm in his account of Friedemann's life, "his unwillingness to see through the eyes of others, and his inability to pursue a task to its end, the aging composer remained in Berlin for ten years, in poverty and ill health, gradually retreating from reality." Bach's eldest son died of a pulmonary disease in 1784, leaving his widow and daughter in total poverty. He also left behind a large body of compositions, many of them brilliant and bold, with dense low-end textures. But if Friedemann did inherit his father's manuscript of the Cello Suites, they—along with most everything else he inherited—had been scattered to the winds.

There is an intriguing footnote to Friedemann's life story. His two sons did not survive adulthood, but his daughter, Frederica Sophia Bach, led an unconventional life. After the deaths of both her parents, at thirty-five she married a professional soldier in the Prussian army by the name of Johann

* Friedemann took on a very small number of pupils in Berlin, among them Sara Levy, great-aunt of Felix Mendelssohn. And he initially enjoyed the good graces of the music-loving sister of Frederick the Great, Princess Amalia, to whom he dedicated a set of fugues. In return he received a silver coffee service and some cash, but quickly managed to fall into disrepute at her palace for trying to displace her court composer.

Schmidt. She had two daughters with Schmidt, one of whom was born shortly before they were wed. But from 1802 onwards Frederica disappears from the records, which led historians to assume that she had died. In the 1980s, however, Bach scholars discovered that Frederica had not died in her early forties; instead she had left her musketeer husband for a textile designer from Silesia by the name of Schwartzschulz. Frederica gave birth to a daughter named Karoline sometime around 1798; no further details about her life are known.

Karoline Schwartzschulz married a cloth-maker with the coincidental name of Johann Gustav Friedemann and had three sons with him. One of those sons, Gustav Wilhelm Friedemann, moved to a German part of Ukraine, then part of the Russian empire, before emigrating with his extended family to the United States in 1892. This American branch of Friedemann Bach's descendants was based in Oklahoma.

Bach's eldest son had apparently entrusted a number of heirlooms and keepsakes to his unconventional daughter, which in turn were passed along through his descendants to the American Midwest. Lydia Paul du Château, a sixth-generation descendant of Johann Sebastian Bach, had inherited a small old wooden trunk containing Friedemann Bach memorabilia. Unfortunately we'll never know if the Cello Suites were among its contents. When Christoph Wolff was put in touch with Lydia in the late 1970s, she regretfully informed the Harvard scholar that the trunk had been lost in 1950 or thereabouts, during a family move to Highland Park, Illinois.

OF BACH'S FOUR sons who achieved musical distinction, the one who has received the least amount of attention is his second youngest, Johann Christoph Friedrich. J. C. F. Bach was a law student who gave up his studies in Leipzig the year his father's health declined. He began work as a chamber musician for a count at Bückeburg, never left the post, and became known as the Bückeburg Bach. His career, at least compared to those of his brothers, appears deadly dull, and that has generally been the estimation of his music. The Bückeburg Bach's share of his father's estate is another disappointing story of treasures gone missing. After his death in 1795, his widow auctioned off whatever manuscripts he had acquired. Not much of his father's legacy seems to have ended up in his hands, but there is one notable exception: the manuscript of the violin sonatas and partitas in Bach's hand was given to J. C. F. Bach. They survived the ravages of time. And if the Bückeburg Bach received the solo violin works—which were like a sister composition to the Cello Suites—it seems logical that he might have equally been given the Cello Suites manuscript.

J. C. F. Bach is noteworthy for one other reason. He had a son, with the sleep-inducing name of Wilhelm Friedrich Ernst Bach, who turned out to be the only grandson of J. S. Bach to achieve any degree of musical eminence. When W. F. E. Bach was eighteen years old, his father took him to Hamburg to visit his famous uncle, C. P. E. Then they travelled to London, where they soaked up the glory that Uncle John, then at the height of his fame, was enjoying. W. F. E. stayed in London, living with his uncle and working as a teacher and piano virtuoso. He left England after John's death and embarked on a concert tour of Europe. He was eventually appointed court Capellmeister and harpsichordist to the Prussian queen in Berlin.

In 1843, when the first monument to J. S. Bach was finally erected in Leipzig, Felix Mendelssohn was happily surprised to meet a surviving grandson of the great Bach. W. F. E., who had travelled from Berlin to Leipzig to attend the event, was by then eighty-two years old. He was the only one of Bach's grandchildren to become a musician. When he died two years later, it marked the end of the Bach family's long musical line.

Meanwhile, Bach's manuscript of the Cello Suites had apparently turned up in Berlin.

COURANTE

The transformations of the courante might be compared to the frolicking of a fish who plunges, disappears, and returns again to the surface of the water.
JULES ECORCHEVILLE

NEARLY TWO CENTURIES after her death, Bach's widow made the news on two occasions. The year 1925 saw the anonymous publication in London of a surprising book touted as the genuine work of Bach's second wife. "Poor as I am, and forgotten," read one passage in *The Little Chronicle of Magdalena Bach*, "living on the charity of the town of Leipzig, and old—I was yesterday fifty-seven years old, only eight years younger than he was when he died—I would not be other than I am now, if it was at the cost of never having known him, never having been his wife." It painted a poignant, historically faithful, and highly romantic view of the Bach household. The book was very successful, going into multiple printings and translations. It was also a fake. The author turned out to be an English writer by the name of Esther Meynell. But even today the book can be found in libraries, is occasionally cited as an authentic work, and remains the stuff of gossip on Bach Internet chat sites.

Then, in April 2006, Bach's widow reappeared. Newspapers around the world carried a story that propelled Anna Magdalena into the headlines. "Bach Works Were Written by His Second Wife, Claims Academic," reported *The Telegraph* of London.

A study by an academic who has spent more than thirty years looking at Bach's work claims that Anna Magdalena Bach, traditionally believed to be Bach's musical copyist, actually wrote some of his best-loved works, including his Six Cello Suites. Martin Jarvis, a professor at Charles Darwin University School of Music in Darwin and the conductor of the city's symphony orchestra, said that "a number of books would need to be rewritten" after presenting his findings to a Bach symposium last week. The findings have been described as "highly important" by Bach scholars and will be published in a doctorate, later this year. Professor Jarvis, who is originally from Wales, used police forensic science techniques to scrutinize manuscripts he believed to be written by Anna Magdalena.

Jarvis told the press that ever since he had first studied the Cello Suites at the Royal Academy of Music in London, he had found something amiss about the music. "It doesn't sound musically mature," he said. "It sounds like an exercise, and you have to work incredibly hard to make it sound like a piece of music." Jarvis theorized that Anna Magdalena wrote them when she was a music student, adding that a woman's work as a composer would never have been acknowledged in Bach's time.

Jarvis's theory has not met with a tremendous amount of support from mainstream Bach scholars. But as British cellist Steven Isserlis pointed out, "We can't say that it is definitely not true, in the same way that we can't prove that Anne Hathaway did not write some of Shakespeare's work, but I don't believe this to be a serious theory."

It is thanks to Anna Magdalena, however, that the Cello Suites survived. Sometime between 1727 and 1731 she made a copy of Bach's original manuscript for a violinist, Georg

Heinrich Ludwig Schwanenberger. Nearly three centuries later, what is known as the Anna Magdalena manuscript remains the closest thing we have to Bach's original.

Schwanenberger, who became a chamber musician at the court of Brunswick-Wolfenbüttel, was a pupil of Bach's in the late 1720s. He also acted as a sales agent for Bach's keyboard partitas and stood as godfather to Bach's daughter Regina Johanna. It was Schwanenberger who penned the manuscript's dust cover; his meticulous reference to Bach and his wife further indicates that he was close to the Bachs. The dust cover of the manuscript refers in French to the violin solo works in "pars 1" and, in pars 2, "Violoncello Solo Senza Basso composée par Sr. J. S. Bach, Maître de la Chapelle et Directeur de la Musique a Leipsic / écrite par Madame Bachen Son Epouse."*

After Schwanenberger's death in 1774, the Cello Suites manuscript somehow became separated from the violin works contained in the same volume; it passed through various indeterminate owners until it reached Johann Nikolaus Forkel, Bach's first biographer. Sometime after Forkel's death in 1818, the manuscript found its way to a major collector, Georg Poelchau. After his death, Poelchau left his collection, including the Anna Magdalena manuscript, to the Prussian Royal Library in Berlin. The manuscript entered the library holdings in 1841, where it seems to have been for the most part ignored.

Anna Magdalena's calligraphy, with its undulating lines and harmonious shapes, its elegant stemming and beaming, had so much come to resemble her husband's that scholars long assumed that the manuscript was in Bach's hand. It was only in 1873 that the great Bach biographer Philipp Spitta discovered that the manuscript was the work of Anna Magdalena. (The

* This translates roughly as "solo violoncello without bass accompaniment composed by Mr. J. S. Bach, Capellmeister and music director in Leipzig / written by his wife, Mrs. Bach."

music notation used to illustrate the chapters in this book is taken from the Anna Magdalena manuscript.)

WHAT PABLO CASALS found in 1890 in Barcelona, forever changing the history of the Cello Suites, was based on Anna Magdalena's manuscript. The edition of the suites that he found was in fact the Anna Magdalena manuscript, edited and published by one Friedrich Wilhelm Ludwig Grützmacher.

A heavily bearded German cellist with a stern demeanour, Grützmacher saw it as his mission to edit great music as if he were operating on secret instructions from long-dead composers. He took liberties with Anna Magdalena's text and in some cases embellished Bach's music with chords, ornaments, and virtuosic flourishes thrown in for good measure. On one occasion a major publishing house rejected one of his other arrangements because of the embellishments, and a livid Grützmacher retorted in a letter:

> Some great masters like Schumann and Mendelssohn have never taken the time to notate all the indications and nuances necessary....My main purpose has been to determine what these masters might have been thinking, and to set down all that they, themselves, could have indicated....I feel I have more right than all the others to do this work.

In a sense, Grützmacher *was* operating on Bach's secret instructions. There is an enduring tradition in classical music of a musician's having been the student of someone who was the student of someone who was the student of, say, Beethoven or Lizst. In the case of Grützmacher, his cello teacher had been Dreschler, who had been taught by Dotzauer, who had been a student of Ruttinger, who was taught by Johann Christian Kittel, a student of Bach's — one of his very last ones, from 1748 to 1750.

But Kittel was an organist, not a cellist, and music practices had changed a great deal by the time of Grützmacher's edition of 1866. Yet Grützmacher's approach, for all its excesses, had a powerful impact on one cellist. A recent Ph.D. dissertation submitted to Florida State University wonders: "Might Casals' thirteen-year-old eyes have been influenced in their outlook by the expressive dynamics and other anachronistic editorial markings by Grützmacher?" Might history, speculates Bradley James Knobel, have turned out differently if the edition Casals found had been less of a gussied-up, subjective version? "Casals' performances and Grützmacher's markings show that they were of one mind in at least one respect: they conceived of the Suites as expressive music capable of having a direct musical appeal to the listeners of their time," writes Knobel. "Grützmacher's edition represents a clear step toward the presentation of the Suites to the listening public, and Casals represents the fulfillment of that vision."

Anna Magdalena also shares some of that credit. Her manuscript contains a number of bowing errors—she was not a cellist and therefore not in a position to correct flaws or to be overly vigilant about string technique. The errors have led many observers over the years to attack her manuscript as being unworthy of her husband. Others have defended her efforts as being closer to Bach's original manuscript than might be immediately obvious. What cannot be denied is that her manuscript was relaxed and inconsistent in various musical details. The happy result is an ink-blot test that has forced cellists from Grützmacher to Casals to put their own personal stamp on the music. By faithfully copying the Cello Suites from her husband's own manuscript—the manuscript lost to history—Anna Magdalena assembled a time capsule of thirty-six movements, giving listeners far in the future a deep-toned masterpiece of Western music.

SARABANDE

He invented and caused to be made an instrument to
supply a particular need he felt lacking in his strings —
an instrument that he christened the "viola pomposa,"
which had five strings and was something between
a violin and a violoncello: he wrote a Suite for it.
ESTHER MEYNELL, THE LITTLE CHRONICLE OF
MAGDALENA BACH

WITH THE ANNA Magdalena manuscript we know what notes
Bach wanted played. What we don't know is what instrument he necessarily wanted the music played *on*. Scandalous as
it may sound, it is even possible that the world's greatest cello
music was not in fact written for a cello.

The mystery centres on the sixth cello suite, which in Anna
Magdalena's manuscript clearly calls for an instrument with five
strings, one more than usual for the cello. The shadowy identity
of this instrument, according to the authoritative Bärenreiter
edition of the Cello Suites, is "a question that has remained one
of the unsolved riddles of scholarship to the present day."

The riddle was supposedly solved by Bach biographers early
on, with a theory that the composer had in fact invented an
instrument for the sixth suite, something called a viola pomposa. But that notion seems far-fetched; Bach was many things

but he was not, so far as we know, an instrument-maker. He might have collaborated with a violin-maker to dream up a five-string cello, but it seems unlikely, especially because one already existed—the violoncello piccolo.

A violin-sized instrument tuned like a cello, the violoncello piccolo in Bach's day was held horizontally, slung from a strap over the shoulder like a guitar. Bach composed a handful of cantatas that specifically called for this instrument, which was played by a violinist, not a cellist.*

The history of stringed instruments circa 1700 is a complicated one: they varied a lot, with many dropping out of existence and new inventions becoming popular along the way. Even within the cello family, sizes, number of strings, and tunings varied wildly. Some cello-type instruments were played *da spalla*, that is, on the shoulder, others *da gamba*—held between the legs like the modern cello. To cite one piece of evidence, Mozart's father, Leopold, noted in his book about violin method in the 1750s that the viola da gamba was played between the legs, adding that "today even the cello is played that way"— suggesting that previously it had not been. That supports the idea that the cello can with historical validity be played on the shoulder, as is the case with the violoncello piccolo.

A handful of violoncellos piccolo have survived from the eighteenth century, but the instrument became extinct in the years following Bach's death. Some ended up being refashioned with smaller necks to make children's instruments. There is one in a Brussels museum; another instrument, built by Bach's friend Hoffman, went missing during the Second World War; and one recently turned up in South Africa.

One contemporary violin-maker is trying to revive the lost instrument. Dmitry Badiarov, a Russian émigré who plays and

---

* The cantatas are lovely pieces of music; most were written in 1724 and 1725 in Leipzig, which suggests a similar time frame for composition of the sixth cello suite—well after 1720, the traditionally assumed date of composition for all the cello suites.

builds violoncellos piccolo, made a compelling case for the instrument when I visited him in his small high-rise apartment on the outskirts of Brussels. An intense-looking man of thirty-five, Badiarov has striking blue-grey eyes that would work well on a wolf, high cheekbones, thin sideburns that descend along his jaw, and black hair pulled back in a ponytail. His features are drawn and angular, his movements slow and gentle, his eyes blazing with conviction—the overall effect is that of a political prisoner on a hunger strike.

Badiarov was anxious to argue his point: that Bach had the violoncello piccolo in mind not just for the sixth suite but for *all* the cello suites—a five-stringed violoncello piccolo for the sixth suite and a four-stringed violoncello piccolo for all the other suites (the instrument existed in both four- and five-stringed versions during the early eighteenth century). From Badiarov's point of view, the Cello Suites, as played by most cellists, lack some subtle, intimate quality. "I felt I was missing something from the music," he told me, "something that I know there is in Bach." He found that missing element in the violoncello piccolo.

A graduate of the St. Petersburg State Conservatory and the Brussels Royal Conservatory, Badiarov stumbled onto his string theory. One of his teachers in Brussels was the renowned baroque violinist Sigiswald Kuijken, a pioneer of the early music movement, who a few years ago asked Badiarov to build him a violoncello piccolo. The more Badiarov researched the instrument, the more convinced he became that the Bach Cello Suites are in fact violoncello piccolo suites. He has one uncontested fact on his side: the Anna Magdalena manuscript does not identify the instrument that the suites were intended for.* In the sixth suite, above the prelude, Anna Magdalena does not call for a different instrument but simply specifies five strings ("*à cinq cordes*").

---

* The dust cover of the Anna Magdalena manuscript does refer to a cello—"*violoncello solo*"—but it is believed to have been written by Schwanenberger, the musician for whom the copy was made.

"I find it strange," Badiarov said, "that Bach would write the last suite for a different instrument, because he did not, and his contemporaries did not, write a cycle of pieces for a given instrument with the last suite for a different instrument." This argument makes a certain amount of sense. Why would Bach suddenly shift gears and write the last suite in his cycle for a different instrument?

One explanation might be that he wanted to use a fuller palette of sound—having one more string gave him more possibilities—to do justice to the last suite, which does blow the others away in terms of finger-sprinting technique. But for Badiarov, his smaller instrument has a more subtle dynamic range, especially when the volume comes down, with a delicate timbre and a quicker response than the cello. "It's amazing," he says, "how well this music fits the instrument for which it was written."

To illustrate his point, Badiarov strapped the violoncello piccolo over his shoulder with a cord looped around the end piece. He tilted the head of the amber-coloured instrument towards the ground at a forty-five-degree angle. And as he played those introductory waves of the first suite's prelude, it sounded refreshingly light, with small, precise etchings of notes—not as shrill as a violin, not as oomphy as a cello.

Whether or not Bach intended the Cello Suites to be played by this instrument, I am struck by a novel idea: that this was the instrument Bach himself used to play the suites. It is known that Bach had a personal preference for the viola. The violoncello piccolo is about the size of a viola and approximates its range. If it was tuned like a cello, Bach would have been able to play the Cello Suites—or whatever he called them—on the violoncello piccolo. The master composer was not merely devising music in his mind as if it were an arcane mathematical formula, but actually playing the suites on an instrument he could feel. I imagine that he would have loved the visceral

sound, the flesh and blood of the notation, working out difficult passages by putting down his quill and trying his hand at
the instrument. And when one of the suites was finished, he
could have picked up the violoncello piccolo, strapped it over
his shoulder like a guitar, and played the music.

GAVOTTE

*It has a tune so powerfully memorable that it has
almost acquired the status of a pop number.*

WILFRED MELLERS, *BACH AND THE DANCE OF GOD*

BACH MAY HAVE written ideal music that transcends the particular sonorities of any given instrument, but the Cello
Suites became famous because they work so well on the cello.
It is hard to imagine a lute player making the Cello Suites one
of history's most successful pieces of music, charming as they
sound on the lute. Or the marimba, guitar, or saxophone, all of
which do the suites justice but lack the cello's unique timbre,
its powerful voice of thunder and prayer.

This is dramatic music, and a dramatic instrument helped
its cause. And for music that was considered dry, cold, and
mathematical, the human factor provided by Pablo Casals
made a dramatic difference. Had Casals become a carpenter, as
his father had wanted, what would have been the fate of the
Cello Suites? It is unlikely we would be hearing them the same
way today.

In his old age Casals transcended the particular sonorities
of his famous instrument, turning to conducting, composing,
and crusading for world peace. But the Cello Suites remained
his daily meditation and musical offering. He had given the

music a platform in concert halls across the globe. The music in turn gave him a political platform.

On November 13, 1961, Casals was granted a private forty-five-minute conversation with the president of the United States. Casals had admired John F. Kennedy since the 1960 election, when he backed the Democrats as the party best equipped to free the world from the forces of dictatorship. After Kennedy's victory there was a polite exchange of letters, with Casals urging the Kennedy administration to end its comfortable relations with Franco's Spain.

The following year a letter from the White House arrived proposing that Casals be honoured at a state dinner at the White House. It triggered some political ambivalence in Casals. By agreeing to play in the U.S. he would be seen as softening his opposition to the Franco regime. In the end, a compromise was worked out whereby the White House event would be held to honour the governor of Puerto Rico. Casals was to perform along with his friends Schneider and Horszowski.

On the day of the White House concert, Casals had his private talk with President Kennedy. They discussed a range of topics, including Casals' previous White House performance, fifty-seven years earlier before Theodore Roosevelt. On the Spanish question, Kennedy made a point of saying that a president inherits a number of policies that he might not personally like, adding that he was committed to the expansion of world-wide freedoms. "You are right," Casals recalled Kennedy telling him, "but you know that a president cannot always do what he would like to do." He was impressed with the frankness and idealism of the young leader.

Before the concert that evening Kennedy spoke a few words to the gathering of some two hundred diplomats, leading conductors, music critics, and Washington insiders. "The work of all artists," he said, "stands as a symbol of human freedom and no one has enriched that freedom more signally than Pablo

Casals." The recital took place in the mirrored East Room, centred on an ornate Steinway piano that reminded Casals of the Cadillac convertible he'd recently purchased for his wife. The musicians then launched into an uneven performance of Mendelssohn, Schumann, and Couperin, followed by Casals' "Song of the Birds."

It was an evening reminiscent of the eighteenth century, reported *Time* magazine, bringing to mind a performance by Haydn or C. P. E. Bach commanded by one of their sovereigns. But Casals in the 1960s had wider currency than any court musician. The concert was broadcast on NBC and ABC, received massive press coverage, and was recorded by Columbia.

The geriatric superstar was everywhere. A few years later the *New York Times* ran a profile under the headline "Casals, 89, Is a Dashing Figure with Busy 2-Continent Schedule." The piece described how his recent "crusade for peace" had taken him from Puerto Rico to Buffalo, from the Pyrenees to Perugia, from a music festival shed in rural Vermont to a ninth-century monastery in the south of France.

Some critics routinely dismissed Casals' "romantic distortions" when recordings such as the *Brandenburg Concertos* he conducted were released in the mid-sixties. He was unruffled by the attacks. He would vigorously defend himself, wagging his forefinger in a signature Spanish gesture and saying, "I was the first to battle the purists of the German school who wanted an abstract, intellectual Bach. I shall not be afraid now that a few critics don't want music to be human anymore."

At age ninety he was unflagging. During rehearsals for the 1967 Casals Festival of Puerto Rico, he "coaxed the orchestra with vigorous beats and occasional shouting." He demanded "more tone, more intensity and faster tempos." And he exhorted the young musicians to "move more." Henry Raymont of the *New York Times* wrote that at one point, while marching the orchestra through its paces in music from Wagner's *Tristan und*

Isolde, Casals walked off the stage, his eyes filled with tears, apparently overcome by the intensity of the powerful music evoking death.

Naturally there had been rumours about his health. He had recently had prostate surgery. Casals suffered from periodic angina, diverticulitis, and arthritis in his hands and feet. But he remained tremendously energetic, conducting three-hour bouts of rehearsal like the one in Puerto Rico. He travelled with a portable oxygen tank, though it was regularly used not for the aging maestro but for elderly ladies overcome by emotion at his concerts.

Casals' health seemed to hinge on his music. His days began at about 8 a.m., with Marta helping him to dress, after which he would make his way into the living room. His breathing seemed laboured and he shuffled with difficulty, badly stooped, head pitched forward. But he went straight to the piano. "He arranged himself with some difficulty on the piano bench," recounted the writer and peace activist Norman Cousins, "then with discernible effort raised his swollen and clenched fingers above the keyboard."

What followed was something of a miracle: "his fingers slowly unlocked and reached toward the keys like the buds of a plant reaching toward the sunlight. His back straightened. He seemed to breathe more freely." The music he played, as he did every morning, was from *The Well-Tempered Clavier*. He explained to Cousins that Bach touched him "here" — placing his hand over his heart. After playing, he appeared straighter and taller, and the shuffle was gone.

Breakfast was followed by a walk on the beach. After lunch and a siesta, the same physical flowering through music took place as he played one of the Bach suites on his cello. Each day was reserved for a particular suite — Monday began the cycle with the first, Tuesday the second, and so on, until he played the difficult sixth suite on Saturday and again on Sunday. The final suite always made him think of a vast cathedral on a bright Sunday morning with all the bells ringing.

He still had that copy of the Cello Suites that he had found long ago in Barcelona. It was cracked and frayed, browning at the bottom of the pages, shored up by paper and tape, its threadbare binding coming apart. He would occasionally hold it up to his face and smell the paper, which he insisted still contained the mingled scents of Barcelona's harbour and the musty music shop on that afternoon in 1890.

IN SEPTEMBER 1973 Casals was in Israel conducting the Festival Youth Orchestra in a Mozart symphony. Despite the intense heat, an uncomfortably long car ride, and occasional use of a wheelchair, he showed terrific vitality. In rehearsals with the orchestra, the ninety-six-year-old maestro went over one particular phrase about a dozen times, arguing for greater expression. "It is not marked in the score—that doesn't matter," he lectured the young musicians. "There are one thousand things that are not marked! Don't give notes—give the meaning of the notes!"

All his professional life, Casals was in the habit of listening to young cellists of promise who were brought to his hotel room while he was on tour. In Jerusalem he was urged to listen to a young Russian émigré named Mischa Maisky. The Russian played Bach's second suite. Casals was "extremely lively and full of energy and we talked for a long time afterward," Maisky fondly remembers. But the maestro had strong opinions on Maisky's playing. Pausing every few words, he said, "Of course, I don't think that what you do has anything to do with Bach."

"I was ready to shoot myself," Maisky recalled. On a brighter note, Casals added, "However, you play it with such conviction that it sounds very convincing in your own way."

Before leaving the country Casals was invited to an informal luncheon with Prime Minister Golda Meir, whose son he had once taught. After lunch he announced that he felt like playing the cello. He took out his instrument and conjured up the sarabande of the fifth cello suite, that sublime movement that uses an empty canvas as much as colour to create ageless music. When it was over, a teary-eyed prime minister hugged him, too overwhelmed for words. It was the last time Casals played a cello suite in public.

Later that month Casals was back in Puerto Rico, applying his fiercely competitive spirit to a game of dominoes. He had taken up the pastime in earnest after moving to the island; it had become a favourite way of unwinding in the company of friends. He and his companions would amuse themselves by periodically awarding each other honorary doctorates in "domino studies." But Casals took the game seriously—he gave no quarter and greatly preferred winning to losing.

Casals was at the home of his friends Luis and Rosa Cueto Coll one evening when partway through the after-dinner round of dominoes he began to feel ill. "I don't think I'll play another game," he said. "Maybe I ate too much." A doctor was summoned. Casals, it turned out, had suffered a heart attack. But rather than go to the hospital he spent several days recuperating at the home of his friends. "He hated hospitals," recalled Marta. "No, no, no—he wanted to be at home."

When he returned home he was well enough to play the cello and take his morning walks on the beach. But not long afterward he awakened in the middle of the night with troubled breathing, and Marta called an ambulance. It was a bumpy journey, with the ninety-six-year-old patient sitting in the front seat to spare his back and complaining to Marta that the "maniac" behind the wheel would kill them all.

In hospital his condition seemed to stabilize; he was chatting with visitors and keeping up with news of the war breaking out in the Middle East. But after ten days he suffered a serious lung embolism. The light of consciousness, that sunshine that he remembered first dawning on him by the sea in San Salvador, was fading away.

"Perhaps I am not religious in the way that many would think," he once told a magazine writer. "But I think if you have the awareness of what you are, you will find God. I find him when I awake. I go immediately to the sea, and everywhere I see God, in the smallest and largest things. I see him in colours and designs and forms."

Friends brought a tape machine and headphones so he could hear some Bach, the first Brandenburg concerto. Not long after losing consciousness, as Egypt and Israel accepted a truce called by the United Nations, he died.

CASALS' BODY LAY in state in the Capitol building of the Puerto Rican legislature, his bronze and lead casket draped with the flags of Catalonia and Puerto Rico. Thousands filed by to pay their last respects to the world-famous cellist who'd made the island his final home. The Puerto Rico Symphony Orchestra played Beethoven's *Eroica* funeral march as the casket was carried down the great steps of the Capitol to the hearse, and from there to the Church of Nuestra Senora de la Piedad, where Casals and Marta had been married sixteen years earlier. Crowds lined the route of the funeral cortege, flags were flown at half-mast, policemen saluted, workers doffed their caps, and cars came to a spontaneous stop, their occupants emerging in mournful silence.

At the church a simple requiem was followed by the sound of Casals' cello, his recording of "The Song of the Birds," the arrangement of that ancient Catalan lullaby that in his hands had become a plea for peace. He was buried nearby at the Puerto Rico Memorial Cemetery, not far from the sea.

But it was a burial place meant to be temporary. Casals had always aimed to be buried in his homeland as soon as politics would allow for his return. That hinged on the death of Franco and the restoration of democracy to Catalonia. Franco's death came in 1975, but it was another four years before new elections and a referendum made Catalonia an autonomous territory. With these conditions met, the Spanish consul sealed the casket in a ceremony in Puerto Rico, and Marta accompanied Casals' remains back to Spain.

Forty years after he was forced to leave Spain, Casals was buried in the small cemetery on the outskirts of Vendrell. Not far away, past the olive groves leading to the Mediterranean, an elegant museum was created to house his memory and artifacts in his villa in San Salvador.

On the centenary of his birth in 1976, Mstislav Rostropovich, who himself knew the anguish of political exile, performed three cello suites at the Villa Casals with the queen of Spain in attendance. By then there was a Spanish stamp, a street in Barcelona, a coastal highway, a bronze bust in the United Nations, and music festivals from Prades to Puerto Rico all bearing his name. Casals' tombstone in the Vendrell cemetery could have been inscribed with any number of great accomplishments. But his most enduring legacy, had there been space for it on the simple stone monument, would have shown every last note of the six suites for solo cello.

GIGUE

Doing the six suites in a row is a hypnotizing experience
for both the player and the listener. I remember years
ago when I was playing them and getting this weird
feeling as I was getting near to the end of No. 6—a feeling
of weightlessness and gratitude.

PIETER WISPELWEY

I HAD PICKED UP the business card in a music store during my stay in Brussels. I took the card because it advertised a shop called Prelude that sold sheet music. Prelude, naturally, made me think of the Cello Suites. It seemed as good a destination as any, and I set out to find the store one afternoon.

It turned out to be a lengthy walk through streets lined with handsome century-old art nouveau townhouses before I finally arrived at the shop, a bare-bones, desultory setup with an old man smoking a pipe at the back and a black dog snoozing nearby. There were bins of second-hand vinyl, a few shelves of books, a showcase with a handful of tuners, metronomes, and a few classical guitars hanging from a wall.

It was difficult to imagine the cash register at Prelude ever ringing. One wall of metal shelves was devoted to aged, musty stacks of sheet music. The piles were categorized by instrument as indicated by strips of handwritten white tape. They were mostly for piano and violin, with only two meagre piles for cello. I started to go through them: Duport, Dotzauer, etc., all ancient pedagogues of the instrument whose publications, inscribed with fanciful title pages, would have been the backdrop to Casals' early education.

Then a bound volume with a gold monogram in an upper corner—L. W.—and a white label with a scrawled *"Exercises de Duport & Suites de Bach."* I turned the thick pages and it hit me like a wave: the Grützmacher edition! The same edition that Casals discovered in 1890 in Barcelona, in a musty second-hand shop not unlike this one, the edition that was based on the Anna Magdalena manuscript. I admired its elegant title page, printed in Leipzig, with its soft red frame filled with nymphs and maidens and harps.

The cash register rang up a sale: six euros. This was the prelude scene for Casals that I had always imagined. I had stumbled into my own prelude.

DISCOVERING THE GRÜTZMACHER edition was a spine-tingling thrill in my personal search for the Cello Suites, but it was not a major find that was going to shake the world of Bach scholarship. The one mystery that totally eluded me—the one that inspired me in the first place to think there was a story behind the suites—remained Bach's missing manuscript. The composer's autograph manuscripts of the *St. Matthew Passion*, the Brandenburgs, *The Art of the Fugue*, *The Well-Tempered Clavier*, the *Goldberg Variations*, scores of cantatas, the solo violin works, and much more all survived. How is it that the Cello Suites manuscript slipped through the cracks of history? I had always assumed the answer would reveal itself, or that the manuscript would turn up before I finished the book. I imagined racing off to a high-stakes auction at Sotheby's in London, the elegant raison d'être to the story of the Cello Suites laid bare with all the drama one could hope for.

A pipe dream, maybe. But a glance at the history of Bach discoveries makes it feel entirely possible. One of the earliest discoveries was reported in 1879, when a London *Telegraph* article appeared under the headline "Manuscript Works of Bach Found in an Old Trunk and Used for Padding Fruit Trees." Apparently a composer by the name of Robert Franz was visiting a country mansion in Saxony when he noticed that the stakes being used to tie up fruit and ornamental trees were fastened with manuscript paper.

"What was his joy, what his horror," reported the newspaper, "upon recognizing Bach's well-known and beautiful notation upon this paper padding!" The gardener informed him that there was an old trunk full of manuscript paper that was proving horticulturally useful. As a result, the newspaper reported, many of Bach's long-lost "tune gems" were in the process of being discovered. Alas, there were losses too, as "rain and snow have expunged from this inestimable 'padding' some of the noblest music that ever issued from the brain of a mighty master." Yet there was no subsequent mention in the press, suggesting that the alleged discovery was probably a false alarm.

But Bach treasures do have a habit of popping up, sometimes in unlikely places. A long-standing anecdote says that Felix Mendelssohn's teacher, Carl Friedrich Zelter, found the score of the *St. Matthew Passion* in a cheese shop, where it was being used as wrapping paper. It is a curiously similar story to one reported by Georg Poelchau, the Bach manuscript hunter, who claimed to have found in 1814 the autograph manuscript of the violin sonatas and partitas in a St. Petersburg butter shop, again in the form of wrapping paper.

These accounts seem to stretch the truth. But they are no less improbable than the story of an original flute part for one of Bach's cantatas being discovered in 1971 at a construction site near Water Street in New York City. The Lower Manhattan discovery in fact happened when a music-loving pedestrian noticed a sheet of paper jutting out from a pile of construction debris. The alert passerby, recounts biographer Martin Geck, received "permission from the nearest workman to take not only the score but the rubble with it!"

Other essential Bach treasures have surfaced in far-flung places. Spitta, the nineteenth-century biographer, tracked down that most personal of Bach's letters to his friend Erdmann in the Moscow state archives. Bach's personal copy of the Bible, the three-volume Calov edition with annotations in his own hand, turned up in a St. Louis seminary after following an unknown route. And the best authentic portrait of Bach, the Hausmann painting currently in New Jersey, surfaced publicly only after the Second World War.

During the war many Bach manuscripts went missing and in some cases had to be rediscovered all over again. A large number of manuscripts had been housed in the Prussian State Library, a baroque building located in Berlin on the stately Unter den Linden. The library was first hit by a surprise British raid in 1941. The damage was minimal (wreckage was to come later in the war), but it jolted library authorities into taking action. They developed an elaborate plan to stash precious library holdings in castles, monasteries, mines, and other unorthodox storage areas.

Things did not always go smoothly. The original manuscript of the *Brandenburg Concertos*, for example, came under aerial bombardment when a Berlin librarian was transporting it by train to a Prussian castle. He hid the score under his coat and dashed into a forest, diving to the ground for cover as the bombers returned to attack. The story would be more moving had not so many people been liquidated by the Nazis with similar dedication. (The same Berlin librarian would later charm angry Russian soldiers by playing Bach fugues on a village organ. Music had "nothing to do with Hitler," he told the soldiers.)

The Anna Magdalena manuscript also got caught up in the war. Of twenty-nine evacuation sites used by the Prussian State Library for the music manuscripts, one was the Benedictine monastery of Beuron, near Württemberg. Two hundred and fifty boxes were sent to the monastery, including the Anna Magdalena manuscript. The Cello Suites were in illustrious company: the shipment included about fifty Beethoven scores, eighty-three of Mozart's, twenty of Schubert's, and the world's most expensive book—a parchment copy of the Gutenberg Bible. The suites also shared storage space with the most impressive Bach compositions, among them the *St. Matthew Passion*, the Mass in B Minor, the sonatas and partitas for solo violin, the *Little Clavier Book of Anna Magdalena Bach*, and numerous cantatas.

The Beuron monastery was in what became the French zone of postwar-occupied Germany. In 1947 the music manuscripts were transferred to Tübingen, where the Anna Magdalena manuscript was placed in the university library. Following the unification of Germany, the manuscript entered the German State Library in Berlin, where it remains carefully stored in a high-security vault, catalogued as "Mus. ms. Bach P269." It is in good company; the library houses about eighty percent of all the Bach autograph manuscripts known to exist.

Various Bach manuscripts have been discovered since the war years, including those that were scattered during the 1940s. The pre-eminent Bach scholar Christoph Wolff tracked down the musical estate of C. P. E. Bach, lost during the Second World War when Red Army trophy brigades grabbed the massive collection that had been stashed away by the Nazis. Wolff found the estate, which also includes some works by J. S. Bach, in the Ukrainian central archives in 1999. Twenty-four years earlier Wolff had also played a key role in verifying Bach's personal copy of the *Goldberg Variations*, including fourteen—there's that Bachian number again—previously unknown canons for the work that were in the hands of a Strasbourg Conservatory professor.

As recently as 2005 scholars discovered the "shoebox aria" that Bach composed as a birthday present to his Weimar patron, Duke Wilhelm Ernst (the same duke who later threw Bach into prison). The manuscript had been gathering dust in a shoebox along with other poems celebrating the duke's birthday in 1713. By chance the box was removed from the library in Weimar where it was stored, a year before a fire ravaged the building.

And more manuscripts of the Cello Suites also saw the light of day. In the 1960s, Russian cellist and scholar Dimitry Markevitch discovered two manuscripts of the suites. "After searching for a long time for the most reliable documents I could find," he recounted, "I had the good fortune to locate two copies in Marburg am Lahn, Germany, made by two Bach enthusiasts which had eluded the attention of musicologists for over a century."

One of the manuscripts, prepared by an unknown copyist, was originally in the collection of an eighteenth-century Hamburg organist and music dealer by the name of Westphal. The other manuscript originated sometime around 1726, when a young organist from the tiny German village of Gräfenroda made a copy, though not an entirely complete one, of the Cello Suites. The organist was Johann Peter Kellner, known in his day as an organ virtuoso, teacher, and composer, but remembered today solely for his collection of Bach manuscripts.*

But the Anna Magdalena manuscript remains the most authoritative source for the Cello Suites, having been copied directly from Bach's original manuscript. As for the original manuscript in Bach's hand—not a trace. I am still hoping it

---

* How Kellner got his hands on the Cello Suites remains fuzzy. Whether he was friends with Bach or studied under him, or whether they even met, is unclear. Why he wanted music for an instrument he appears not to have played is also unknown. One noteworthy aspect of this manuscript is that it is intended for a "Viola de Basso," which could be a viola-type instrument held on the arm, not unlike a violoncello piccolo.

turns up. Not that it would change anything much at this point. The wide interpretations of the Cello Suites—from period performances to Romantic to jazz to African, and versions on every instrument under the sun—mean that so much has already been reimagined.

Perhaps proof might surface that Bach meant the suites for another instrument, say the violoncello piccolo, or the lute. Or that there's a seventh suite—improbable, considering his era's penchant for publishing in sets of six. The music might be altered here and there, but given the manuscript copies that have survived, none of which differs tremendously when it comes to the actual notes (bowings, dynamics, ornaments, yes, but not the notes), that too is unlikely.

So there may be no practical reason to want to see the manuscript rediscovered. But there would be the thrill of the chase, the detective story behind it, the possibility that a manuscript with secrets to tell has been lodged in a salt mine or is biding its time in a dilapidated German castle.

There is a further twist, though. A great number of Bach's original manuscripts have been slowly disintegrating because of the ink that he used—iron-gall ink, which is highly acidic. And the acid in the ink is disintegrating the paper. The note heads fall away, leaving holes in the paper and a manuscript that resembles Swiss cheese. About half of the Bach manuscripts in the German State Library have been severely damaged in this way. A repair process has been developed whereby the damaged pages are split and a thin leaf of alkaline material is inserted to neutralize the acidic ink. But it is a very expensive process, and the library has laboured to raise funds to get it done.

So if the Bach manuscript of the Cello Suites is somewhere out there awaiting discovery, it is also more than likely disintegrating, its secrets dissolving, forcing cellists or lutenists or violoncello piccolo players, and even listeners, to find their own way in the music.

270 - THE CELLO SUITES

The story distilled from the Cello Suites will change radically over time, as more material comes to light about the many mysteries of Bach and as new takes on the music are created. Musically, the future success of the Cello Suites hinges on their survival skills. And if the past is any indication, the odds are heavily in their favour; endurance and timeless relevance are woven into the very fabric of the music.

This final gigue, the thirty-sixth movement, as played by Casals is a ceiling-spinning jig full of staggering merriment, the sort of earthy music scratched out by a medieval tavern fiddler—somewhat unsteady on his feet but with the sound of a miniature orchestra at his fingertips, scattering the seeds of so many half-conscious harmonies, running out of breath only as he reaches the last note of the last melody, cleanly, simply, without any grand flourish—and suddenly, a little too suddenly, finishing right there.

NOTES

SUITE NO. I

Prelude
The epigraph is taken from program notes written by Laurence Lesser for his recitals of 26 and 27 October 2000 in Toronto. Lesser's name might draw a blank with the uninitiated, but he is a past president of the New England Conservatory and a leading cellist who has soloed with numerous top orchestras. Lesser unknowingly inspired this book with a spellbinding performance of the suites on his 1622 Amati cello.

The high-altitude cello player was profiled in "Cellist Takes Bach to Summit of Mount Fuji," 18 June 2007, Earthtimes.org, http://www.earthtimes.org/articles/show/73738.html.

Suites No. 1 and 6, the second of three instalments by Casals on the Victor label, were released in 1941. The review in the *New York Times* was by critic Howard Taubman (16 March 1941, x6). A concert review in the *New York Times* by John Rockwell suggested that the suites have an intensity that approaches the Japanese but which represents "the apex of Western musical creativity" (7 May 1979, c16).

Allemande
Bach, showing an unsurprising flair for symmetry and interweaving, designed his personal seal himself. To see what it looks like, visit the admirable *Bach Bibliography* website at http://www.mu.qub.ac.uk/tomita/bachbib/.

There is no shortage of Bach biographies, though the non-specialist will have to negotiate some forbidding musicological terrain. The best of the contemporary accounts, all of which I have relied on greatly, are Christoph Wolff, *Johann Sebastian Bach: The Learned Musician* (New York: W.W. Norton, 2000); Malcolm Boyd, *Bach* (New York: Oxford University Press, 2000); Martin Geck, *Johann Sebastian Bach: Life and Work*, trans. John Hargraves (New York: Harcourt, 2006); and Peter Williams, *The Life of Bach* (Cambridge: Cambridge University Press, 2004).

For the story behind Walter Jenke's ownership and sale of the Bach portrait, I spoke on the phone with his gregarious son Nicholas Jenke, who lives in England. Detailed information on the provenance of the portrait can be found in Werner Neumann, *Pictorial Documents of the Life of Johann Sebastian Bach* (London: Basel Tours, 1979). See also Stanley Godman, "A Newly Discovered Bach Portrait," *Musical Times* (July 1950).

Classical music commentator Miles Hoffman profiled Bach on a fun segment of National Public Radio's *Morning Edition* marking the composer's 317th birthday on 21 March 2002, http://www.npr.org/programs/morning/features/2002/mar/bach/.

Courante
The epigraph from Pierre Rameau is quoted in Meredith Little and Natalie Jenne, *Dance and the Music of J. S. Bach* (Bloomington: Indiana University Press, 2001), 115.

The quote from an eighteenth-century diplomat that not a dog barks in Europe without the permission of Louis XIV, and much other excellent history, can be found in Tim Blanning, *The Pursuit of Glory: Europe 1648–1815* (London: Penguin, 2008), 543.

The description of Eisenach's municipal character is colourfully chronicled by Percy M. Young in *The Bachs: 1500–1850* (London: J. M. Dent & Sons, 1970), 63–64.

The excerpts from Bach's job contract at Anstadt can be found, along with all Bach primary documents, in Hans T. David and Arthur Mendel, eds., *The New Bach Reader: A Life of Johann Sebastian Bach in Letters and Documents*, revised and expanded by Christoph Wolff (New York: W.W. Norton, 1998), 41.

A discussion on Bach's brawl with a "nanny goat bassoonist" and the various ways of translating the German insult is found in Sara Botwinick, "From Ohrdruf to Mühlhausen: A Subversive Reading of Bach's Relationship to Authority," *Bach* (*Journal of the Riemenschneider Bach Institute*) 35, no. 2 (2004): 1–59. The translation of the same German words as not "greenhorn bassoonist" but "passing wind after ingesting green onions" is found in Geck, 53. The same work contains Bach's quote about wanting to "understand various things in his art," 49.

The reference to the city of Mühlhausen clinging to its "old fashions and customs" is by Bach's great nineteenth-century biographer Philipp Spitta in *Johann Sebastian Bach: His Work and Influence on the Music of Germany*, trans. Clara Bell and J.A. Fuller-Maitland, vol. 1 (New York: Dover, 1951), 357.

The notion that Bach might have first got the idea of music for solo cello from Westhoff in Weimar was suggested to me by the Bach scholar Christoph Wolff, in an interview he graciously granted when I showed up unannounced at the Bach-Archiv in Leipzig.

The description of Bach's musical duel with Marchand, written by Johann Abraham Birnbaum in 1739 (and, in the absence of any independent documentation of the event, thought to derive from Bach's own version of the story) is cited in David and Mendel, *New Bach Reader*, 79–80.

The old account that Bach started writing *The Well-Tempered Clavier* while in the clink stems from Ernst Ludwig Gerber, a music lexicographer whose father, Heinrich Nicolaus, was a student of Bach's in the 1720s. See Geck, 96, and David and Mendel, 372.

Johann Mattheson's quote from 1739 about the allemande appears in the text volume of the Bärenreiter edition of the suites: Bettina Schwemer and Douglas Woodfull-Harris, eds., *J. S. Bach: 6 Suites a violoncello solo senza basso* (Kassel: Bärenreiter, 2000). I leaned on this comprehensive work for the provenance of the suites and their individual movements. Peter Eliot Stone eloquently describes the sarabande in his liner notes to Anner Bylsma, *The Cello Suites*, Sony Essential Classics, 1999.

The terse lines regarding Bach's imprisonment and discharge are in the Weimar court secretary's report, reprinted in David and Mendel, 80.

Bach's statement that Prince Leopold "both knew and loved music" (from a rare letter he wrote to friend Georg Erdmann in 1730) is translated in Wolff, 202.

Sarabande
Anyone writing about Casals is hugely indebted to Kirk, H.L. *Pablo Casals: A Biography* (New York: Holt, Rinehart and Winston, 1974). Another superb account of the cellist is Robert Baldock, *Pablo Casals* (Boston: Northeastern University

Press, 1992). Casals was generous with his time to a number of biographers. I have drawn on the following works:

Blum, David. *Casals and the Art of Interpretation*. California: University of California Press, 1980.

Corredor, J. Ma. *Conversations with Casals*. Translated by André Mangeot. London: Hutchison, 1956.

Kahn, Albert E. *Joys and Sorrows: Reflections by Pablo Casals, as told to Albert E. Kahn*. New York: Simon and Schuster, 1970.

Littlehales, Lillian. *Pablo Casals*. Second Edition. New York: W. W. Norton, 1948. (Originally published in 1929.)

Taper, Bernard. *Cellist in Exile*. New York: McGraw-Hill, 1962.

The section on Spanish history is informed by Gerald Brenan, *The Spanish Labyrinth: An Account of the Social and Political Background of the Civil War* (Cambridge: Cambridge University Press, 1969). The quote from Casals following his encounter with a cello for the first time is cited in Littlehales, 24.

Minuet

The story of Casals' discovery of the Cello Suites was pieced together from a variety of sources, including his recollections in *Joys and Sorrows* and "The Story of My Youth," *Windsor Magazine* (1930). I was able to view the Holy Grail of the story, the tattered pages of the Cello Suites that he found in 1890, among his papers at the Arxiv Nacional de Catalunya (Catalan National Archives), located in San Cugat, a suburb north of Barcelona. Ambles though the old port district of Barcelona provided the architecture. The history of the Catalan capital is masterfully told in Robert Hughes, *Barcelona* (New York: Vintage, 1993).

The source material for Casals from 1893, when he moved to Madrid, to 1900, when he launched his international career in Paris, comes largely from the Kirk biography, with additional information gleaned from Baldock, Corredor, Kahn, and Littlehales. Excerpts from the two newspaper reviews of concerts in Spain during 1893–94 and the review in *Le Temps* in Paris are found in Kirk. The Spanish newspaper that heralds Casals as "a national glory" is cited in Baldock. The anecdote about the king of Spain as a youngster wanting guns more than music is in Corredor.

A glimpse of Barcelona in the late nineteenth century was provided by *Baedeker's Spain and Portugal*, 1901. Statistics regarding social and economic conditions in Spain in the wake of the Spanish-American War are taken from Antony Beevor, *The Battle for Spain: The Spanish Civil War 1936–1939* (London: Phoenix, 2007).

Gigue
The excerpt from the author's review of the U2 concert in Montreal appeared in "U2 Lost in Pop Mart," *The Gazette* (Montreal), 3 November 1997, EI.

The New Yorker magazine's Alex Ross—a beacon to anyone looking to discover classical music—has held forth on the needless stuffiness of classical concerts. See, for example, his essay "Listen to This: A Classical Kid Learns to Love Pop—and Wonders Why He Has to Make a Choice," *The New Yorker*, 16/23 February 2004, 146–55.

SUITE NO. 2

Prelude
The epigraph is from a charmingly idiosyncratic book by the renowned Dutch cellist Anner Bylsma, *Bach, the Fencing Master: Reading Aloud from the First Three Cello Suites* (Amsterdam, 2001).

The musings about "implied harmony" are informed by several sources, including Peter Eliot Stone's liner notes for the disc by Anner Bylsma, the text volume of the Bärenreiter 2000 edition of the suites, and interrogation of cellists. The Bylsma quote was heard at a master class given by the cellist at Domaine Forget, a music academy in Quebec's highly scenic Charlevoix region.

The theory that Bach composed the Partita in D Minor for solo violin as an epitaph for his deceased wife has been championed by violin pedagogue Helga Thoene. She sets out her case in the liner notes of a very successful recording by the Hilliard Ensemble, *Morimur*, ECM Records, 2001.

The suggestion that Bach's sarabande and minuet borrow from Couperin's "La Sultane" is made by Mark M. Smith in a compelling article, "The Drama of Bach's Life in the Court of Cöthen, as Reflected in His Cello Suites," *Stringendo* 22, no. 1, 32–35.

Allemande
The epigraph by Johann Mattheson, originally printed in his *Der Vollkommene Capellmeister*, 1739, is cited in the Bärenreiter 2000 edition of the suites.

For the rise of Prussia from backwater to upstart kingdom to leader of Germany, several sources were relied on: Alexandra Richie, *Faust's Metropolis: A History of Berlin* (New York: Carroll & Graf, 1998); Hajo Holbron, *A History of Modern Germany: 1648–1840* (New York: Alfred A. Knopf, 1971); R. R. Palmer and Joel Colton, *A History of the Modern World* (New York: Alfred A. Knopf, 1978); and the above-mentioned work by Blanning.

For Bach's dedication of his *Brandenburg Concertos* to the Margrave of Branden-burg, I have used the translation provided by Malcolm Boyd in *Bach: The Brandenburg Concertos* (Cambridge: Cambridge University Press, 2003). In his biography of Bach, Boyd makes the point that the composer wrote undemand-ing bass viol parts for Prince Leopold in the sixth Brandenburg concerto (*Bach*, 90), an idea I have borrowed to shed possible light on the Cello Suites.

Courante
The epigraph is from Percy Young's fine book *The Bachs: 1500–1850*, 155.

For the story of Bach's fame, David and Mendell's *New Bach Reader* contains two key essays, "Johann Sebastian Bach: A Portrait in Outline" and "Bach in the Romantic Era," which includes the quote by Mozart and describes Beethoven's connection to Bach, 488–91. The same book devotes much space to Bach's pio-neer biographer, Johann Nikolaus Forkel, noting that the printing plates of Forkel's scores for old music were melted down to make bullets during the Napoleonic Wars. The two quotes from Forkel's own biography are recycled in David and Mendell, 419 and 479.

The statement about the silence surrounding Bach's compositions is taken from Friederich Blume, *Two Centuries of Bach: An Account of Changing Taste*, trans. Stanley Godman (London: Oxford University Press, 1950), 19–20.

For the famous 1829 performance of the *St. Matthew Passion* in Berlin, a polished account is Celia Applegate, *Bach in Berlin: Nation and Culture in Mendelssohn's Revival of the St. Matthew Passion* (Ithaca, NY: Cornell University Press, 2005). The underwhelmed reactions of Heine and Hegel are taken from Applegate's book, as well as the quote about Mendelssohn's "German-Jewish-Christian" symbiosis, 247.

The theory that Mendelssohn's cuts to the *St. Matthew Passion* reflected his sensi-tivity to anti-Jewish content is persuasively argued by Michael Marissen in his article "Religious Aims in Mendelssohn's 1829 Berlin-Singakademie Perfor-mances of Bach's St. Matthew Passion," *Musical Quarterly* 77 (1993): 718–26.

The generational links showing that Mendelssohn was a great-grand-pupil of Bach's are shown in Eric Werner, *Mendelssohn: A New Image of the Composer and His Age* (New York: Free Press of Glencoe, 1963), 98. Werner also cites the remark attributed to Mendelssohn that it took a Jew (working together with an actor, Mendelssohn's friend Devrient) to revive the world's greatest Christian music, 99. For connections between Bach's sons and Mendelssohn's great-aunt Sara Levy, see Peter Wollny, "Sara Levy and the Making of Musical Taste in Berlin," *Musical Quarterly 77* (1993): 651–726.

The quote from Mendelssohn's letter that Bach was considered an "old-fashioned wig stuffed with learning" is cited in Barbara David Wright, "Johann Sebastian Bach's 'Matthews Passion': A Performance History, 1829–1854," Ph.D. diss., University of Michigan, 1983, 155. Some background on the 1829 performance was also taken from Henry Haskell, *The Early Music Revival: A History* (New York: Dover, 1996), 13–25.

Sarabande
Rostropovich's solemn epigraph is taken from his musings in *J.S Bach: Cellon Suites*, VHS recording, EMI classics, 1995.

The bee-buzzing quote by George Bernard Shaw is found in Taper, 37.

The way is which Casals revolutionized cello-playing technique is summed up by Tully Potter in the liner notes for a two-volume disc on the Pearl label, *The Recorded Cello: The History of the Cello on Record* (from the incomparable collection of Keith Harvey). Casals discusses his technique in Corredor, 24, and Baldock explains it on page 30. For the new kind of star cellist Casals became when he launched his career, I am indebted to Baldock, 56–57.

The curious remark from Casals after he injured his hand is taken from Kirk, 163. That a New York manager promised higher fees for Casals if he started wearing a wig is also in Kirk, 178.

The Philadelphia review of 1904 and the Liverpool review of 27 October 1905 were found in the Catalan National Archives (box 40). *The Strad* review from 1908–9 is from Daniel Philip Nauman, "Survey of the History and Reception of Johann Sebastian Bach's *Six Suites for Violoncello solo senza basso*," Boston University, September 2003. Clippings from the Spanish newspapers *Diario de Barcelona* and Madrid's *El Liberal* in October 1901 were found in the Catalan National Archives.

That Casals played entire suites in more than half a dozen cities during 1903 and 1904 is shown primarily in concert programs in the Harold Bauer Collection of papers in the Library of Congress, Music Division, Washington, DC. Casals informed biographer Kirk that the first suite he ever played in public was Suite No. 3, in Barcelona. That information was found in Kirk's research notes in the Herbert L. Kirk Collection, also housed in the Library of Congress, Music Division.

The Casals quote about the new world opened up by his discovery of the Bach suites is in Taper, 33.

The quote from Grieg after he heard Casals is in Kirk, 247; the quote from Röntgen to Grieg is in Kirk, 243; and the quote from Edward Speyer about Casals' performance of the third suite in London in 1905 is quoted at more length in Kirk, 264.

The recording of Klengel playing the sarabande of Suite No. 5 can be heard on *The Recorded Cello*, vol. 2. The anecdote of Harold Bauer's chat with a Spanish stagehand moved by Casals' playing was recounted in his autobiography, *Harold Bauer: His Book* (New York: Greenwood Press, 1969), 93.

The letter from Pilar Casals is quoted in Kirk, 114. That Suggia only played Suites No. 2 and 3, the rest belonging to Casals "until the angels take over," is quoted in Baldock, 86. The description of the foreboding Casals experienced at the moment of his father's death is in *Joys and Sorrows*, 132.

The characterization of Casals' relationship with Suggia is provided by Anita Mercier, *Guilhermina Suggia: Cellist* (Burlington, VT: Ashgate, 2008). The quote is found on page 16.

The quote from Tovey's biographer about the hot summer with Suggia and Casals is taken from Mary Grierson, *Donald Francis Tovey: A Biography Based on Letters* (London: Oxford University Press, 1952), 161.

The anecdote about Tovey leaping out of his bath comes from Tully Potter in the liner notes to *The Recorded Cello*. The story allegedly comes from Tovey himself, as reported by violinist Adolf Busch. See Mercier, 25–26. Casals' melancholic telegram to Suggia is quoted in Baldock, 37; Casals' line about "the most cruelly unhappy episode" is from a letter he wrote to Julius Röntgen, quoted in Kirk, 292.

Minuet
The exclusive story in *Musical America* is quoted in Kirk, 293. The background of the Casals-Metcalfe relationship also comes from Kirk, 293–97, and from

information graciously provided by George Moore of Los Angeles, who two decades ago discovered a number of personal letters through a Hollywood music dealer.

The letter of May 1915 that Metcalfe wrote to Casals is in the Susan Metcalfe and Pablo Casals Letter Collection, 1915–1918, Archives of American Art, Smithsonian Institution, Washington, DC. The letter written by Susan Metcalfe's mother to Pilar Casals is in the same collection, as is the draft letter Casals wrote to Metcalfe in 1917. The quote that Casals felt "Germany covets the earth" is in the Emmet Family Papers, 1729–1989, Archives of American Art, Smithsonian Institution.

The description of Casals' home in San Salvador comes largely from Kirk, as well as a personal visit to the villa, now the enchanting Pau Casals Museum.

The political situation in Spain following the First World War has been stitched together from the following books: Hugh Thomas, *The Spanish Civil War* (New York: Penguin, 1977); Beevor, *Battle for Spain*; and Raymond Carr, *Spain: 1808–1939* (London: Oxford University Press, 1966). The colourful description of Primo de Rivera is found in Thomas, 27.

That the Spanish queen was like a "second mother" to Casals comes from his own words, *Joys and Sorrows*, 217.

Gigue
The glowing review of Maisky from *The Times* is found in the artist's profile on the Deutsche Grammophon website. The bad review — if Dostoevskyian can be considered bad — was by Benjamin Ivry, *International Record Review* (reprinted in Andante.com. http://www.Andante.com).

SUITE NO. 3

Prelude
The happy epigraph is from Hans Vogt, *Johann Sebastian's Chamber Music: Background, Analyses, Individual Works*, trans. Kenn Johnson (Portland, OR: Amadeus Press, 1988), 181.

The historical record (scanty as it is) for Bach and Anna Magdalena prior to their marriage comes primarily from Wolff, 216–18. Wolff raises the possibility that Bach might have asked Anna Magdalena's father for her hand while passing through Schleiz.

The lyrics for this mysterious aria of secret love, attributed to Giovannini, were taken from the booklet of *The Notebook of Anna Magdalena Bach*, CD, Nonesuch, 1981. The quote from Bach that his wife sings a "good, clear soprano" is in that tell-all letter to Georg Erdmann written in 1730 and reproduced in David and Mendell, 151–52. The quote showing Anna Magdalena's joy over a gift of carnations was from Bach's nephew, who worked as a personal secretary to the composer for two years; it appears in Wolff, 394. And see the musings of Percy M. Young on the love between Bach and Anna Magdalena, 136.

Allemande

The epigraph comes from Bylsma, 125. Bach's description of the *amusa* is found in the above-mentioned letter he wrote to Erdmann. Geck, however, casts doubt on the *amusa* allegation, 113. The facts surrounding budget cuts at court are outlined in Wolff, 218–19. The likelihood that Bach was looking forward to better schooling for his children is set out in Wolff, 219; Geck, 114; and the delightful if dated Charles Sanford Terry, *Bach: A Biography* (London: Oxford University Press, 1950). On the death of Bach's brother Jacob in Sweden and how his thoughts might have turned to the future of his children, see Davitt Moroney, *Bach: An Extraordinary Life* (London: Royal School of Music, 2000), 53. Bach's letter bellyaching about Leipzig is found in (where else?) his much-quoted letter to Erdmann in David and Mendell.

Courante

The epigraph from the prolific Johann Mattheson, a composer and music theorist who was a contemporary of Bach, is cited in the text volume of the Bärenreiter 2000 edition of the suites.

For the unceremonious departure of the king of Spain see Carr, 601, and Brian Crozier, *Franco: A Bibliographical History* (London: Eyre & Sottiswoode, 1967). The polo quote, as well as Alfonso's feeling "out of fashion," come from Carr, 601. Casals' enthusiasm for the Republican government is outlined in Kirk, 377–79, and Baldock, 141–44. The arrest of Luis Casals is mentioned in Baldock, 153.

The story of Casals' rehearsal in Barcelona on the fateful day July 18, 1936, is recounted in Kirk, 398, with the Casals quote in Littlehales, 165. The facts surrounding the outbreak of the civil war are taken mostly from Beevor and Thomas. The quote from Beevor is on page 89. The remark from Casals about the threat posed to his home and safety from both the right and the left was found in the Herbert L. Kirk Collection (box 35), Library of Congress, Music Division.

Sarabande

The epigraph is from Rostropovich, spoken in Russian but with English subtitles, in a combined interview and performance of the Cello Suites, *J. S. Bach: Cello Suites*, VHS recording, EMI Classics, 1995.

The quote from Baldock about Casals needing to play despite the danger and turmoil is found on page 157. That Casals loathed the "steel monster" of recording is stated by his friend Maurice Eisenberg, "Casals and the Bach Suites," *New York Times*, 10 October 1943.

The historical background for the civil war is taken primarily from Thomas and Beevor.

Casals' quote that the arms embargo by the Western democracies was unfair because Franco was well stocked with firepower is in Littlehales, 167. The quote from Casals' radio broadcast in 1939 warning about Hitler is in *Joys and Sorrows*, 227. The circumstances of Casals' life in the aftermath of the civil war in 1939 are based mostly on Kirk and Baldock.

Quotes from Casals about the threat from General Queipo de Llano and his depression in Paris after the Republican defeat are in *Joys and Sorrows*, 226 and 231, respectively.

Bourrée

The epigraph from Casals is in Blum, 101.

Two letters, dated 5 June and 5 July 1939, about how physically draining and difficult Casals found recording the suites to be, are located in the EMI Group Archive Trust in London. The discs were released in England earlier than in North America, with the first two installments appearing in 1938 and the third in 1948.

The praise from Norman Lebrecht is found in *The Life and Death of Classical Music: Featuring the 100 Best and 20 Worst Recordings Ever Made* (New York: Anchor Books, 2007), 173.

The quote from Rostropovich on how long it took him to record the suites is seen and heard on the VHS recording *J. S. Bach: Cello Suites*. Matt Haimovitz is quoted from the booklet for *6 Suites for Solo Cello*, CD, Oxinglale Records, 2000. Janos Starker's comment is in his published edition of the music, *Six Suites for Unaccompanied Violoncello*, rev. ed. (Peer International, 1988).

Pieter Wispelwey made his "barometer" remark to me in an interview follow-ing a Montreal recital. Mischa Maisky explained how he felt compelled to re-record in an interview at his home in Belgium. The review of Wispelwey's recital is by Jeremy Eichler, *New York Times*, 8 April 2003, E3. The anecdote about Piatigorksy was related by Maisky.

Gigue
My one-time cello teacher Hannah Addario-Berry is now a member of the San Francisco–based Del Sol String Quartet. The obituary for Walter Joachim, written by Arthur Kaptainis, was printed in the Montreal *Gazette*, 22 December 2001, D11.

SUITE NO. 4

Prelude
The epigraph by the arcane composer Sorabji appears in Jeremy Nicholas, *Godowsky: The Pianists' Pianist* (Southwater, Sussex: Corydon Press, 1989), 117.

Wispelwey made his tantalizing comments about the prelude while giving a cello master class at McGill University. Tortelier's impressions are in the liner notes of his recording *Bach: Cello Suites*, EMI, 1983.

The brief but oddly precise item reporting Bach's arrival in Leipzig appeared in a Hamburg newspaper and is found in David and Mendell, 106.

Two revealing works that deal with the Leipzig of Bach's time are Carol K. Baron, ed., *Bach's Changing World: Voices in the Community* (Rochester University Press: 2006), and Tanya Kevorkian, *Baroque Piety: Religion, Society, and Music in Leipzig*, 1650–1750 (Burlington, VT: Ashgate, 2007). Descriptions of Leipzig, including its oil lamps and night watchmen, were taken from Terry, 151–75; Wolff, 237–40; and Peter Washington, *Bach* (New York: Knopf, 1997), 83–89.

Schweitzer's crestfallen quote regarding Bach's working conditions is found in his two-volume biography, Albert Schweitzer, *J. S. Bach*, trans. Ernest Newman, vol. 1 (Boston: Bruce Humphries, 1962), 112.

Ideas about whether the Cello Suites were planned as a unified cycle derive in part from the text volume of the Bärenreiter 2000 edition of the suites, 9, and from the volume of the suites edited by Egon Voss, *Sechs Suiten. Violoncello Solo*, (Munich: G. Henle Verlag, 2000) BWV 1007–12.

Allemande

For the history of public executions in Leipzig I am entirely indebted to the excellent, if gruesome, essay by Peter Williams, "Public Executions and the Bach Passions," in *Bach Notes*, the noble newsletter of the American Bach Society, no. 2 (Fall 2004). My description of the steel sword is also taken from the article. The subject is similarly discussed in the superb (and remarkably slim) biography by Peter Williams, *The Life of Bach* (Cambridge: Cambridge University Press, 2004), 118. The same book contains the quote musing about how congregants reacted to the *St. John Passion* in 1724 when it was first heard, 116.

The main work cited on the question of anti-Semitism and the *St. John Passion* is Michael Marissen, *Lutheranism, Anti-Judaism, and Bach's St. John Passion* (New York: Oxford University Press, 1998). Marissen's suggestion that Bach was not well acquainted with anyone Jewish is on page 22. A telephone conversation in 2008 with Raymond Erickson, professor of music at Queen's College, City University of New York, added more details to the section about the Jewish presence in Leipzig during Bach's lifetime. Additional background was fleshed out by Baron and Kevorkian. Richard Taruskin's views on the *St. John Passion* are found in his exhaustive *The Oxford History of Western Music*, Volume 2 (New York: Oxford University Press, 2005), 389–90.

Courante

The epigraph, which describes the difficult key of E-flat, is found in the brilliant work by Daniel Heartz, *Music in European Capitals: The Galant Style, 1720–1780* (New York: W. W. Norton, 2003), 317.

Bach's famous quote about "vexation, envy, and persecution" is from his letter to Erdmann, quoted in David and Mendell, 151–52.

That Bach was hired in Leipzig as the absolutist candidate representing August the Strong, as opposed to the estates faction, is set out by Ulrich Siegele, "Bach and the Domestic Politics of Electoral Saxony," trans. Kay LaRae Henschel, in John Butt, ed., *The Cambridge Companion to Bach* (Cambridge: Cambridge University Press, 2000), 17–34. Siegele continues the argument in "Bach's Situation in the Cultural Politics of Contemporary Leipzig," ed. Carol K. Baron, trans. Susan H. Gillespie with Robin Weltsch, in Baron.

Bach's Dresden concert in September 1725 received a two-sentence review in the Hamburg *Relationscourier*, reprinted in David and Mendell, 117. The description of Prince Leopold's funeral is drawn from Wolff, 206.

Bach's sensitivity about not having a university education is raised by Moroney, 66–67.

A handy book that profiles both Bach's forebears and his children is *The New Grove Bach Family* (New York: W.W. Norton, 1983). Bach's presenting Friedemann with a certificate marking his registration at university is mentioned in a chapter by Eugene Helm, 239. The quote about the father/son relationship glimpsed in the *Little Clavier Book for Wilhelm Friedemann Bach* is in Williams, 85. Bach's trips to Dresden to attend the opera with his eldest son were first reported in Forkel's early biography; the quote is supplied by Wolff, 363. C.P.E.'s precocious playing of his father's music is described by Helm, 251.

The possibility that Bach was suffering from a sort of midlife crisis at age forty-two and on the verge of a "breaking point" with his work disputes is floated by Moroney, 73–76. Boyd, 118, argues that Bach was temperamentally unsuited for the job of cantor.

Sarabande
The epigraph of 1690 by James Talbot, an English writer of music, is cited in Little and Jenne, 94–95.

The atmosphere of Prades uses material from "Letter from Prades," a charming piece in *The New Yorker* with a byline reading simply "Genêt," 17 June 1950, 81–88, as well as information from Baldock, 166–67, and Kirk, 418.

The Nazi visit to Casals is recounted by Littlehales, 192–95; in *Joys and Sorrows*, 244–47; and in Kirk, 419. The *New York Times* report that Casals was "living in seclusion" in France is cited in Baldock, 168; the blank cheque is described in Bernard Taper, "A Cellist in Exile," *The New Yorker*, 24 February 1962, 69. The immediate postwar period for Casals, including his return concerts in England and his eventual decision to mute his cello, is detailed in Kirk, 425–41. The quote from Casals' correspondence, in which he describes the progress he was making on cello after the Germans left town, is reported in Littlehales, 167.

Bourrée
Casals accompanied his line about a string sounding best when it's about to snap with a phrase in French: *"le chant du cygne"* —swan song. The quote appears in Taper, "Cellist in Exile," 76. Taper subsequently parlayed this in-depth profile into his book *Cellist in Exile: A Portrait of Pablo Casals*.

The description of Casals' cello, a Bergonzi-Gofriller made in Venice sometime around 1700 that he purchased in 1908, is found in "Letter from Prades," 87. The same article paints a picture of the Prades Festival. *Life* magazine also ran a lengthy piece, Lael Wertenbacker, "Casals: At Last He Is Preparing to Play in Public Again," photographs by Gjon Mili, 15 May 1950. The *Life* article contains the Casals quote about England and America letting him down politically. The line about "managers, officials and admirers" pleading for Casals to return to the concert hall is by Howard Taubman, "The Best Who Draws a Bow," *New York Times Magazine*, 28 May 1950, 118. The "heavy silk" sound of Casals' cello is taken from "Letter from Prades," 82. I have also borrowed from Kirk on the festival, 453–61, and Baldock, 182–93.

Gigue

For the Canadian Amateur Musicians website and news on its courses and retreats in bucolic settings, see http://www.cammac.ca.

The recording of the cantata *Brich dem Hungrigen dein Brott* (BWV 39) was impressively recorded live by the Monteverdi Choir and the English Baroque Soloists conducted by John Eliot Gardiner: John Eliot Gardiner, *Bach Cantata Pilgrimage*, vol. 1, SDG. Among Gardiner's deep connections to Bach is the fact that the Hausmann portrait of the great composer hung in his father's home for a time after its German owner, Walter Jenke, placed it there for safekeeping following its retrieval from Nazi Germany in 1937.

SUITE NO. 5

Prelude

The epigraph is from Godowsky's foreword to his piano transcription of three cello suites, reprinted in Jeremy Nicholas, *Godowsky: The Pianists' Pianist* (Southwater, Sussex: Corydon Press, 1989), 116. For the captivating transcriptions, consider the recording by Carlos Grante, Music and Arts, 1999.

Some provenance information on the lute manuscript is set out in notes to a published reproduction of the manuscript by Godelieve Spiessens. I'm the proud (and legal) owner of the manuscript, a facsimile containing Bach's bona fide swirls and squiggles purchased at the Royal Belgian Library; *Suite Pour Luth en Sol Mineur*, BWV 995, Collection Fontes Musicae Bibliothecae Regiae Belgicae, Bibliothèque Royale Albert 1er, Bruxelles, 1981.

Allemande
The epigraph is from Vogt, 184.

The history of Saxony under August the Strong has been culled from various sources. A book that is as splendiferous as its subject matter is Daniel Heartz, *Music in European Capitals: The Galant Style, 1720–1780* (New York: W. W. Norton, 2003). For music-making at Dresden, see pages 295–349. Bach doesn't figure in the story, but Heartz devotes fascinating chapters to two of his sons, as well as to the semi-enlightened despot Frederick the Great. The quote on the thumb-biting infighting in the Dresden *Capelle* is found on pages 304–5.

More material on the music and musicians surrounding the Saxon court is found in the early-music magazine *Goldberg*: Brian Robins, "Dresden in the Time of Zelenka and Hasse," *Goldberg* 40 (June/August 2006): 69–78. For the history of Saxon absolutism, much can be learned from Blanning.

Bach was accused of "doing nothing" and of being "incorrigible" in the minutes of the Leipzig town council meeting of 2 August 1730. The minutes are excerpted in David and Mendell, 144–45. Bach's lengthy memorandum to the council in which he envies the state of music-making in Dresden is in David and Mendell, 130. Bach's candid letter to Erdmann in 1730 is found in the same source, 151–52.

Boyd, 165–67, makes the point that Bach "went out of his way" during this period to form closer ties with Dresden, possibly hoping for a permanent post, and that even after the death of August the Strong, Bach's new compositions were aimed at flattering the Dresden court.

After so much seriousness in Bach, it is refreshing to come across a work as fun as the *Coffee Cantata*. For more on the controversial caffeinated establishments in Leipzig, see Katherine R. Goodman, "From Salon to *Kaffeekranz*: Gender Wars and the *Coffee Cantata* in Bach's Leipzig," in Baron, 190–218. Another stimulating discussion is found in Hans-Joachim Schulze, "Ey! How Sweet the Coffee Tastes: Johann Sebastian Bach's Coffee Cantata in Its Time," *Bach* 32, no. 2 (2001): 2–35.

The title page of the libretto for *Cleofide* is quoted in Heartz, 322.

The brief review from a Dresden newspaper about Bach's organ recital is in David and Mendell, 311. The poem that accompanied the review begins with wordplay on Bach's name: "A pleasant brook..." *Bach* in German means "brook."

Bach's petition for a royal title is reprinted in David and Mendell, 158.

The description of the market square concert before the royal couple, as well as the trumpeter's death, appear in Wolff, 360–61, in a section dealing with the special concerts Bach was producing (and making decent money for) to honour the Saxon dynasty during the 1730s.

For more on the keyboard player Goldberg (who gave his name not only to an immortal composition but also to an early-music magazine), see Peter Wollny, "Johann Gottlieb Goldberg," *Goldberg* 50 (February 2008): 28–38.

That Bach was finally named royal court composer "because of his ability" is taken from Geck, 182.

The footnote describing Bach's emphasis on new "catchy tunes" in the mid-1730s quotes William, 132.

Courante
The epigraph by Fétis, an "ebullient, Balzacian personality who thrived on controversy," is found in Harry Haskell, *The Early Music Revival: A History* (Mineola, NY: Dover, 1996). His career is summarized on pages 19–20.

The passage about Wilhelm Friedemann's new position in Dresden reflects the ideas of Helm, 239–40.

The heart-rending letter that Bach wrote about the disappearance of his son Gottfried Bernhard is quoted from a translation that appears in Boyd, 171–72.

To hear the soothing lute sonatas of Weiss, look for the nine separate discs performed by Robert Barto on the budget Naxos label. Sonata No. 37 in C Major is in places reminiscent of a Bach cello suite: *Silvius Leopold Weiss: Sonatas for Lute*, vol. 4, Naxos, 2001. For the latest research on the life of Weiss, see Daniel Zuluage, "Sylvius Leopold Weiss," *Goldberg* 47 (August 2007): 21–29.

The mystery of "Monsieur Schouster" was more or less solved in an article by the eminent German musicologist and Bach expert Hans-Joachim Schulze: "'Monsieur Schouster': Ein vergessener Zeitgenosse Johann Sebastian Bachs," in *Bachiana et Alia Musicologica: Festschrift Alfred Dürr zum 65*, ed. Wolfgang Rehm (Cassel, 1983), 243–50. I am indebted to Ilke Braun for translating the article for me. The letter from Weiss that helped unravel the mystery was published by Schulze under the title "Ein unbekannter Brief von Silvius Leopold Weiss," *Die Musikforschung* 21

(1968): 204. The same letter is in English on the Web at *Classical Net,* trans. Douglas Alton Smith, http://www.classical.net/music/comp.lst/articles/weiss/bio/php.

Information about the recipient of Weiss's letter, Luise Adelgunde Gottsched, was generously provided in a telephone interview with Katherine R. Goodman, professor of German Studies at Brown University. The statement that Luise Gottsched was the German nation's "most learned woman" comes from Goodman's article about gender wars in Baron. Useful background about the city of Danzig was also furnished by Goodman's article "Luis Kulmus' Danzig," *Diskurse der Aufklärung* (2006): 13–35.

Boyd, 95, raises the possibility that the tuning of the lute (in fourths) may be connected to the *scordatura* tuning of the fifth cello suite. If the lute suite was composed first, he writes, "it might also explain why the cello version sometimes seems to need completion by another strand."

The solo cello of Domenico Gabrielli can be heard on *Italian Cello Music,* a beguiling CD on the Accent label. Information on how Gabrielli tuned his cello was provided in the disc's liner notes by Marc Vanscheeuwijck, trans. Christopher S. Cartwright. The CD contains sixteen tracks by Gabrielli in addition to cello music by Marcello, Bononcini, Alessandro Scarlatti, and De Fesch. Gabrielli's cello works have a meandering, relaxed quality, and sound like the sort of raw material Bach mined for his highly structured suites.

Sarabande
Epigraphs for this unique movement are easy to come by. The Rostropovich line is extracted from his commentary/performance on the EMI Classics video.

The description of Capdevila as a "pleasant grey-haired housekeeper" was reported by Wertenbacker, *Life,* 161. In fact, Capdevila was the daughter of a wealthy Catalan furniture manufacturer; she received cello lessons from Casals in Barcelona when she was seventeen years old and he was two years older; Kirk, 102. The quote from Kirk about the marriage being a chivalrous gesture is on page 473; the description of the return to Spain is on pages 473–74. The payment to the Franco government for his villa as constituting "ransom" according to Casals is quoted in Taper, "Cellist in Exile," 63.

Marta Casals Istomin recounted in a 2008 telephone interview her first impressions of meeting Casals in Prades. The description of Marta's becoming close to Casals derives from Kirk, 475–80. Information about the trip to Puerto Rico was taken from Kirk, 482–88, and Baldock, 213–19. The letter from Casals to Schneider is quoted in Baldock, 219. The Puerto Rico festival rehearsal and heart attack are described by Baldock, 222.

Casals later attributed his heart attack to thoughts about his orchestra in Barcelona on the day the Spanish Civil War erupted; *The New Yorker*, 19 April 1969, 123. That Casals came to consider the heart a marvel that can heal itself is found in Kirk, 497, although his sister-in-law was concerned that it might not be "safe" for a man in his condition to have a pretty young girl around him, 495.

The quote from Marta explaining her motivation for marriage was taken from Anna Benson Gyles, dir., *Song of the Birds: A Biography of Pablo Casals*, Kultur/BBC, VHS, 1991.

Casals' comment about how much Marta reminded him of his mother appeared in "An Interview with Pablo Casals," *McCall's*, May 1966.

Gavotte
The epigraph by Rousseau is quoted in Boyd, 187.

The story of how Casals came to play before the United Nations is recounted by Baldock, 234–36, and Kirk, 505–10. Baldock called it the most "widely broadcast musical event in history." Baldock also coined the memorable phrase "geriatric superstar" for Casals at this point in his career.

The postwar relationship between Franco's Spain and the Western coalition is outlined in H. Stuart Hughes, *Contemporary Europe: A History*, 5th ed. (Englewood Cliffs, NJ: Prentice-Hill, 1981), 505–9.

The description of Casals' appearance at the U.N. is based on Lindesay Parrot, "Throng at U.N. Hails Performance by Casals," *New York Times*, 25 October 1958, 1. The report in the TV section of the same edition was by Jack Gould. The brilliant music critic Harold C. Schonberg reviewed the performance on page 2 under the headline "Music of Casals Retains Its Vigor."

Excerpts from the recorded statement Casals made to the U.N. are reproduced in Kirk, 506–7.

Gigue
The epigraph was extracted from Dimitry Markevitch, *Cello Story*, trans. Florence W. Seder (Miami: Summy-Birchard, 1984), 160. Markevitch was a distinguished cellist and scholar of the Bach suites.

The story about the nefarious "swinging" of Bach appeared under the headline "'Swinging' Bach's Music on Radio Protested," *New York Times*, 27 October 1938, 1.

Glenn Gould's ecstatic reaction to the Swingle Singers is taken from Mike Zwerin, "Giving Fugues to the Man in the Street," *International Herald Tribune*, 28 April 1999. http://www.iht.com/articles/1999/04/28/ward.t.php.

Observing the Procol Harum court case was Rod Liddle, "J.S. Bach Should Claim the Royalties," *The Spectator*, 15 November 2006. http://www.spectator .co.uk/the-magazine/cartoons/26422/js-bach-should-claim-the-royalties. thtml.

Harold C. Schonberg's quote about suffering "deep cultural shock" over *Switched-On Bach* appeared beneath the headline "A Merry Time with the Moog?" *New York Times*, 16 February 1969, D17. *Time* magazine likened the many spins on Bach to translations of Homer; "Swing, Swung, Swingled," 6 November 1964.

The story surrounding Robert Schumann's work on the Cello Suites is outlined by Joachim Draheim in the Breitkopf edition; *Suite 3 for Violoncello and Piano*, arr. Robert Schumann, ed. Joachim Draheim (Wiesbaden: Breitkopf & Härtel, 1985), 7–9.

Leopold Godowsky's experience transcribing the suites is recounted in Nicholas, 115–19.

The quote from Casals about stringing notes together is found in Blum, 19.

Allen Winold, in a musicological deconstruction of the Cello Suites, has identified the B-A-C-H theme in the third suite. See Allen Winold, *Bach's Cello Suites: Analyses & Explorations*, Vol. 1, *Text* (Bloomington: Indiana University Press, 2007), 62.

For Danny "DV8" Stratton see "Bach Fugue Gets the DJ Treatment," NPR.org, 18 May 2006, http:/www.npr.org/templates/story/story.php?storyId=5402905.

The system Bach was using, also known as the natural order number alphabet, assigns the same value to letters I/J (9); and U/V (20). Thus *J.S. Bach* adds up to forty-one; and *Bach* makes fourteen.

SUITE NO. 6

Prelude
The epigraph on Bach's ideal instrument is in Schweitzer, 385.

The passage from Forkel about Frederick the Great summoning Bach to his palace is reprinted in David and Mendell, 429. The report from the Berlin newspaper on Bach's visit is found in the same source on page 224; Bach's dedication to the king is on page 226.

The ways in which Bach and Frederick the Great confronted each other as the "embodiments of warring values" is described with panache by James R. Gaines, *Evenings in the Palace of Reason: Bach Meets Frederick the Great in the Age of Enlightenment* (New York: Fourth Estate, 2005), 6–8. Gaines recounts how comfortable the composer Hasse was with the enemy occupier Frederick the Great, 208–9. The fact that Bach never relinquished his Eisenach citizenship is discussed in Wolff, 310.

The footnote likening Frederick's challenge to sixty blindfolded games of chess is taken from Douglas R. Hofstadter, *Gödel, Escher, Bach: An Eternal Golden Braid* (New York: Vintage, 1989), 7.

Boyd, 201, nicely sums up the esoteric final phase of Bach's career, "alone with the impenetrable mysteries of his art." The quote from the Saxon prime minister anticipating Bach's death was taken from Wolff, 442. The description of Dr. Taylor's entourage is found in Gaines, 250.

The comments from C. P. E. Bach are extracted from what's known as "the obituary" in the Bach literature. Written by C. P. E. together with J. F. Agricola in 1750 and published in 1754, it is reproduced in David and Mendell; the quotes employed are on page 303.

The details of Bach's estate, including the notion of "ideal" value, are succinctly outlined in Wolff, 454–58.

Allemande
The epigraph from C. P. E. about Bach's manuscripts drifting to and fro is from a letter he wrote to biographer Forkel in 1774, reprinted in David and Mendell, 388.

The quote from C. P. E. characterizing his brother Gottfried Heinrich is in Wolff, 398.

The portrayal of Bach's youngest son, John Bach, comes primarily from Charles Sanford Terry, *John Christian Bach* (London: Oxford University Press, 1967); Heartz, 883–929; and Ernest Warburton in *The New Grove Bach Family*. For vivid portraits of both John Bach and Abel see the paintings by their close friend

Thomas Gainsborough.
The biographical sketch of C. P. E. is based on Hans-Günter Ottenberg, *C. P. E. Bach* (Oxford: Oxford University Press, 1967); Young, 167–81, 207–22; Heartz, 389–424; and Helm. Frederick the Great's uneven sense of rhythm is cited in Young, 169.

The section on Bach's eldest son, Friedemann Bach, relied on Young, 183–206; Helm, 238–50; and Gerhard Herz, "The Human Side of the American Bach Sources," *Bach Studies* 1 (1989): 323–50. For Friedemann's relationship with his father see the psychological ruminations of Williams, 198–202. The posthumous part of the story comes courtesy of Christoph Wolff, "Descendants of Wilhelm Friedemann Bach in the United States," *Bach Perspectives*, vol. 5, ed. Stephen Crist (Chicago: University of Illinois Press, 2002).

The biography of the little-known "Bückeburg Bach" is based on Young, 223–35, and Helm, 309–12. His share of Bach's estate is outlined by Wolff, 458–60. Provenance details for the autograph manuscript of the solo violin works are found in Vogt, 21–22.

W. F. E. (grandson of Bach) is ranked as a minor composer by "stretching courtesy," in the words of Young, who nonetheless extends the courtesy on pages 275–76.

Courante
The frolicking epigraph is from Little and Jenne, 114.

The quote purportedly by Bach's second wife appears in Esther Meynell, *The Little Chronicle of Anna Magdalena Bach* (London: Chapman and Hall, 1954). The author's name was not put on the title page when the book appeared in 1925, making it look like a bona fide diary. It still fools people. As recently as April 2008 an edition of the glossy French magazine *Guitar Acoustic Classic* printed an article that contained only one reading recommendation to shed light on Bach's life: *The Little Chronicle of Anna Magdalena Bach*.

The *Telegraph* article was by Barbie Dutter and Roya Nikkhah, "Bach's Works Were Written by His Second Wife, Claims Academic," 22 April 2006. Isserlis was cited in the same article.

The details surrounding the copy made for Schwanenberger are outlined in the Bärenreiter 2000 edition of the suites, with additional background in Geck, 164, and Wolff, 375. The provenance of the Anna Magdalena Bach manuscript is further elucidated in the edition of the music edited by Egon Voss, *Six Suites for Violoncello Solo* (G. Henle Verlag). See also the edition by Kirsten Beisswenger (Leipzig: Breitkopf & Hartel, 2000).

Key pieces in the puzzle were provided in a demystifying dissertation by Bradley James Knobel, "Bach Cello Suites with Piano Accompaniment and Nineteenth-Century Bach Discovery: A Stemmic Study of Sources," treatise submitted to the College of Music, Florida State University, 2006. Knobel notes that in 1841 the Royal Library in Berlin (later renamed the Prussian State Library) acquired the Anna Magdalena Bach manuscript, which was still "taken for that of Bach himself." Knobel also reveals that Grützmacher's edition was based on the Anna Magdalena manuscript. The quote from Knobel appears on pages 33–34 of his treatise.

Details of Grützmacher's career were taken from Lev Ginsburg, *History of the Violoncello*, trans. Tanya Tchistyakova (Montreal: Paganiniana Publications, 1983), 65–69. The irate letter Grützmacher wrote to his publisher is quoted in Markevitch, 61–62.

Sarabande
The epigraph falsely attributed to Anna Magdalena Bach is in fact from Meynell, 82.

The "unsolved riddle" about the sixth suite is quoted from the Bärenreiter 2000 edition of the suites, text volume, 16. For a full discussion of the cello in Bach's day and the mystery of the sixth suite, see pages 14–18.

Dmitry Badiarov has since relocated to Tokyo. His website is http://www.violadabraccio.com.

Excellent background on the violoncello piccolo was provided by Mark M. Smith, "Bach's Violoncello Piccolo," *Australian String Teacher* 7 (1985), 93–96.

The quote from Mozart's father about the violoncello is found in Leopold A. Mozart, *Treatise on the Fundamental Principles of Violin Playing*, translated by Editha Knocker, second edition (New York: Oxford University Press, 1985), 11.

Gavotte
The epigraph is in Wilfrid Mellers, *Bach and the Dance of God* (New York: Oxford University Press, 1981), 31.

The performance at Kennedy's White House is detailed in Baldock, 329–42, and Kirk, 519–22, and reported by Harold C. Schonberg, "Casals Plays at White House," *New York Times*, 14 November 1961, 1.

The newspaper story of Casals cutting a "dashing figure" at age ninety is from
Henry Raymont in the *New York Times*, 16 April 1966, 57. The fact that Casals' portable oxygen tank was used more for "elderly ladies overcome with emotion" at
his concerts is reported in Kirk, 538. The quote about "coaxing the orchestra"
was in another *New York Times* article by Raymont, 31 May 1967, 51.

Norman Cousins's visit to Casals is poignantly described in his book *Anatomy of
an Illness as Perceived by the Patient* (New York: W. W. Norton, 1979), 72–79.

Casals' daily routine for playing the Bach suites, as well as his visualizing the
sixth suite as a vast cathedral, was related in an interview by Marta Casals
Istomin.

Information from Casals' trip to Israel is found in Baldock, 256, and Kirk, ix, and
was recollected by Marta Casals Istomin. The Casals quote about giving "the
meaning of notes" is supplied in Blum, 49. Mischa Maisky recalled his playing for
the maestro in an interview.

Casals' illness was described in an interview by Marta Casals Istomin and is in
Baldock, 256–57; Kirk, ix–x; and the *San Juan Star*, 22 October 1973, 11. Casals'
quote about divinity was printed in *McCall's*, May 1966. Details about his funeral
are based on Baldock, 259–62; Kirk, x–xi; Marta Casals Istomin; and the *San Juan
Star*, 24 October 1973, 1.

Gigue
Wispelwey's heady epigraph comes from Peter Goddard, "Dutch Cellist Has
Suite Dreams on His Mind," *Toronto Star*, 15 October 1998, G5.

The *Telegraph* article about Bach manuscripts found as padding for fruit trees
was printed in the *New York Times*, 9 February 1879, 8. The freakish discovery of
a Bach manuscript at a Manhattan construction site is mentioned in Geck, 31.

The story of Bach's manuscripts, particularly about those housed at the Prussian
State Library getting caught up in the Second World War, is deftly told in Nigel
Lewis, *Paperchase: Mozart, Beethoven, Bach...The Search for Their Lost Music*
(London: Hamish Hamilton). The quote from the Berlin librarian is on page 54.
To piece together the postwar fate of the Cello Suites manuscript, information
was gleaned from Richard S. Hill, "The Former Prussian State Library," *Notes*
(*Journal of the American Music Library Association*) 3, no. 4 (September 1946): 327–50,
404–10; as well as P.J.P. Whitehead, "The Lost Berlin Manuscripts," *Notes* 33, no. 1
(September 1976): 7–15.

For the gumshoe work of Christoph Wolff in tracking the lost musical estate of C. P. E. Bach, see Sarah Boxer, "International Sleuthing Adds Insight about Bach," *New York Times*, 16 April 1999; Joseph P. Kahn, "A Bach Score," *Boston Globe*, 30 September 1999; and Michael Ellison, "Search Uncovers Lost Bach Treasures," *The Guardian*, 6 August 1999.

The tale of the "shoebox aria" was reported in Luke Harding and Charlotte Higgins, "Forgotten Bach Aria Turns Up in Shoebox," *The Guardian*, 8 June 2005, 3; and in the liner notes by Michael Maul (the discoverer), trans. Stephanie Wollny, in the premiere recording, *Bach Alles mit Gott*, John Eliot Gardiner conducting the Monteverdi Choir and the English Baroque Soloists, SDG, 2005.

The quote from Markevitch about his discovery of the Westphal and Kellner manuscripts is contained in his book *Cello Story*, 157–58. Details surrounding Kellner are fleshed out in Russell Stinson, *The Bach Manuscripts of Johann Peter Kellner and His Circle: A Case Study in Reception History* (Durham, NC: Duke University Press, 1989).

The mortal threat to Bach's immortal music was explained to me by Bach-Archiv scholar Peter Wollny in Leipzig. The story was reported by John Hooper, "Fund Shortage Blocks Efforts to Repair Deteriorating Scores," *Sun-Times* (Chicago), 23 January 2000.

BIBLIOGRAPHY

Applegate, Celia. *Bach in Berlin: Nation and Culture in Mendelssohn's Revival of the St. Matthew Passion*. Ithaca: Cornell University Press, 2005.

"Bach Fugue Gets the DJ Treatment." National Public Radio. NPR.org. 18 May 2006. http://www.npr.org/templates/story/story.php?storyId=5402905.

Baedeker's Spain and Portugal, 2nd ed., 1901.

Baldock, Robert. *Pablo Casals*. Boston: Northeastern University Press, 1992.

Baron, Carol K., ed. *Bach's Changing World: Voices in the Community*. Rochester: Rochester University Press, 2006.

Bauer, Harold. *Harold Bauer: His Book*. New York: Greenwood Press, 1969.

Beevor, Antony. *The Battle for Spain: The Spanish Civil War 1936–1939*. London: Phoenix, 2007.

Blanning, Tim. *The Pursuit of Glory: Europe 1648–1815*. London: Penguin, 2008.

Blum, David. *Casals and the Art of Interpretation*. Berkeley: University of California Press, 1980.

Blume, Friedrich. *Two Centuries of Bach: An Account of Changing Taste*. Translated by Stanley Godman. London: Oxford University Press, 1950.

Botwinick, Sara. "From Ohrdruf to Mühlhausen: A Subversive Reading of Bach's Relationship to Authority." *Bach* 35, no. 2 (2004): 1–59.

Boxer, Sarah. "International Sleuthing Adds Insight about Bach." *New York Times*, 16 April 1999.

Boyd, Malcolm. *Bach*. New York: Oxford University Press, 2000.

———. *Bach: The Brandenburg Concertos*. Cambridge: Cambridge University Press, 2003.

———, ed. *Oxford Composer Companions: J. S. Bach*. New York: Oxford University Press, 1999.

Brenan, Gerald. *The Spanish Labyrinth: An Account of the Social and Political Background of the Civil War.* Cambridge: Cambridge University Press, 1969.

Butt, John, ed. *The Cambridge Companion to Bach.* Cambridge: Cambridge University Press, 2000.

Bylsma, Anner. *Bach, the Fencing Master: Reading Aloud from the First Three Cello Suites.* 2nd ed. Amsterdam: 2001.

Carr, Raymond. *Spain: 1808–1939.* London: Oxford University Press, 1966.

Casals, Pablo. "The Story of My Youth." *Windsor Magazine,* 1930.

"Casals Buried near Isla Verda Home." *San Juan Star,* 24 October 1973, 1.

"Cellist Takes Bach to Summit of Mount Fuji." Earthtimes.org. 18 June 2007. http://www.earthtimes.org/articles/show/73738.html.

Corredor, J. Ma. *Conversations with Casals.* Translated by André Mangeot. London: Hutchison, 1956.

Cousins, Norman. *Anatomy of an Illness as Perceived by the Patient.* New York: W.W. Norton, 1979.

Crozier, Brian. *Franco: A Bibliographical History.* London: Eyre & Spottiswoode, 1967.

David, Hans T., and Arthur Mendel, eds. *The New Bach Reader: A Life of Johann Sebastian Bach in Letters and Documents.* Revised and expanded by Christoph Wolff. New York: W.W. Norton, 1998.

"Discovery of Missing Music: Manuscript Works of Bach Found in an Old Trunk and Used for Padding Fruit Trees." *London Telegraph,* 25 January 1879. Reprinted *New York Times,* 9 February 1879, 8.

Eichler, Jeremy. "A Cellist Tethered Lightly to Bach and Britten Solos." *New York Times,* 8 April 2003, E3.

Eisenberg, Maurice. "Casals and the Bach Suites." *New York Times,* 10 October 1943.

Ellison, Michael. "Search Uncovers Lost Bach Treasures." *The Guardian,* 6 August 1999.

Gaines, James R. *Evenings in the Palace of Reason: Bach Meets Frederick the Great in the Age of Enlightenment.* New York: Fourth Estate, 2005.

Gay, Peter, and R.K. Webb. *Modern Europe to 1815.* New York: Harper and Row, 1973.

Geck, Martin. *Johann Sebastian Bach: Life and Work.* Translated by John Hargraves. New York: Harcourt, 2006.

Ginsburg, Lev. *History of the Violoncello.* Translated by Tanya Tchistyakova. Montreal: Paganiniana Publications, 1983.

Goddard, Peter. "Dutch Cellist Has Suite Dreams on His Mind." *Toronto Star,* 15 October 1998, G5.

Goodman, Katherine R. "Luis Kulmus' Danzig." *Diskurse der Aufklärung* (2006).

Harding, Luke, and Charlotte Higgins. "Forgotten Bach Aria Turns Up in Shoebox." *The Guardian,* 8 June 2005, 3.

Haskell, Henry. *The Early Music Revival: A History*. New York: Dover, 1996.

Heartz, Daniel. *Music in European Capitals: The Galant Style, 1720–1780*. New York: W.W. Norton, 2003.

Hill, Richard S. "The Former Prussian State Library." *Notes* [*Journal of the American Music Library Association*] 3, no. 4 (September 1946): 327–410.

Hofstadter, Douglas R. *Gödel, Escher, Bach: An Eternal Golden Braid*. New York: Vintage, 1989.

Holbron, Hajo. *A History of Modern Germany: 1648–1840*. New York: Alfred A. Knopf, 1971.

Hooper, John. "Fund Shortage Blocks Efforts to Repair Deteriorating Scores." *Sun-Times* (Chicago), 23 January 2000.

Hughes, H. Stuart. *Contemporary Europe: A History*. 5th ed. Englewood Cliffs, NJ: Prentice-Hill, 1981.

Hughes, Robert. *Barcelona*. New York: Vintage, 1993.

"An Interview with Pablo Casals." *McCall's*, May 1966.

Kahn, Albert E. *Joys and Sorrows: Reflections by Pablo Casals*. New York: Simon & Schuster, 1970.

Kahn, Joseph P. "A Bach Score." *Boston Globe*, 30 September 1999.

Kaptainis, Arthur. "Walter Joachim Was MSO Cellist." *Gazette* (Montreal), 22 December 2001, DII.

Kevorkian, Tanya. *Baroque Piety: Religion, Society, and Music in Leipzig, 1650–1750*. Burlington, VT: Ashgate, 2007.

Kirk, H. L. *Pablo Casals: A Biography*. New York: Holt, Rinehart and Winston, 1974.

Knobel, Bradley James. "Bach Cello Suites with Piano Accompaniment and Nineteenth-Century Bach Discovery: A Stemmic Study of Sources." Treatise submitted to the College of Music, Florida State University, 2006.

Lebrecht, Norman. *The Life and Death of Classical Music: Featuring the 100 Best and 20 Worst Recordings Ever Made*. New York: Anchor Books, 2007.

"Letter from Prades." *The New Yorker*, 17 June 1950, 81–88.

Lewis, Nigel. *Paperchase: Mozart, Beethoven, Bach . . . The Search for Their Lost Music*. London: Hamish Hamilton, 1981.

Liddle, Rod. "J. S. Bach Should Claim the Royalties." *The Spectator*, 15 November 2006.

Little, Meredith and Natalie Jenne. *Dance and the Music of J. S. Bach*. Bloomington: Indiana University Press, 2001.

Littlehales, Lillian. *Pablo Casals*. 2nd ed. New York: W.W. Norton, 1948.

Marissen, Michael. *Lutheranism, Anti-Judaism, and Bach's St. John Passion*. New York: Oxford University Press, 1998.

———. "Religious Aims in Mendelssohn's 1829 Berlin-Singakademie Performances of Bach's St. Matthew Passion." *Musical Quarterly* 77 (1993): 718–26.

Markevitch, Dimitry. *Cello Story.* Translated by Florence W. Seder. Miami: Summy-Birchard, 1984.

Marshall, Robert L. "Toward a Twenty-First Century Bach Bibliography." *Musical Quarterly* 84: 497–525.

Mellers, Wilfrid. *Bach and the Dance of God.* New York: Oxford University Press, 1981.

Mercier, Anita. *Guilhermina Suggia: Cellist.* Burlington, VT: Ashgate, 2008.

Meynell, Esther. *The Little Chronicle of Anna Magdalena Bach.* London: Chapman and Hall, 1954.

Moroney, Davitt. *Bach: An Extraordinary Life.* London: Royal School of Music, 2000.

Nauman, Daniel Philip. "Survey of the History and Reception of Johann Sebastian Bach's *Six Suites for Violoncello solo senza basso.*" Unpublished paper submitted as part of Ph.D. requirements. Boston University, September 2003.

The New Grove Bach Family. New York: W. W. Norton, 1983.

Nicholas, Jeremy. *Godowsky: The Pianists' Pianist.* Southwater, Sussex: Corydon Press, 1989.

Ottenberg, Hans-Günter. *C. P. E. Bach.* Oxford: Oxford University Press, 1967.

"Pablo Casals, as Told to Albert E. Kahn." *McCall's,* April 1970.

"Pablo Casals' Condition Stabilizes." *San Juan Star,* 22 October 1973, 11.

Palmer, R.R., and Joel Colton. *A History of the Modern World.* New York: Alfred A. Knopf, 1978.

Parrott, Lindesay. "Throng at U.N. Hails Performance by Casals." *New York Times,* 25 October 1958, A1.

Raymont, Henry. "Casals, 89, Is a Dashing Figure with 2-Continent Schedule." *New York Times,* 16 April 1966, 57.

———. "Casals Prepares Puerto Rico Fete." *New York Times,* 31 May 1967, 51.

Richie, Alexandra. *Faust's Metropolis: A History of Berlin.* New York: Carroll & Graf, 1998.

Robins, Brian. "Dresden in the Time of Zelenka and Hasse." *Goldberg* 40 (June/August 2006): 69–78.

Rockwell, John. "Bach Cello Suites by Neikrug." *New York Times,* 7 May 1979, C16.

Ross, Alex. "Escaping the Museum." *The New Yorker,* 3 November 2003.

———. "Listen to This." *The New Yorker,* 16 & 23 February 2004, 146–55.

Sadie, Julie Anne, ed. *Companion to Baroque Music.* Berkeley: University of California Press, 1990.

Schonberg, Harold, C. "Casals Plays at White House." *New York Times,* 14 November 1961, A1.

———. "A Merry Time with the Moog?" *New York Times,* 16 February 1969, D17.

————. "Music of Casals Retains Its Vigor." *New York Times,* 25 October 1958, A2.

Schulze, Hans-Joachim. "Ein unbekannter Brief von Silvius Leopold Weiss." *Die Musikforschung* 21 (1968): 204.

————. "Ey! How Sweet the Coffee Tastes: Johann Sebastian Bach's Coffee Cantata in Its Time." *Bach,* 32, no. 2 (2001): 2–35.

————. "'Monsieur Schouster': Ein vergessener Zeitgenosse Johann Sebastian Bachs." In *Bachiana et Alia Musicologica: Festschrift Alfred Dürr zum 65,* edited by Wolfgang Rehm, 243–50. Cassel, 1983.

Schweitzer, Albert. *J. S. Bach.* Translated by Ernest Newman. 2 vols. Boston: Bruce Humphries, 1962.

Schwemer, Bettina, and Douglas Woodfull-Harris, eds. *J. S. Bach: 6 Suites a Violoncello Solo senza Basso.* Text vol. Kassel: Bärenreiter, 2000.

Smend, Friedrich. *Bach in Köthen.* Translated by John Page. St. Louis, MO: Concordia, 1985.

Smith, Dinitia. "Collector Assembles a Rare Quartet of Bibles." *New York Times,* 10 June 2002.

Smith, Mark M. "Bach's Violoncello Piccolo." *Australian String Teacher* 7 (1985).

————. "The Drama of Bach's Life in the Court of Cöthen, as Reflected in His Cello Suites." *Stringendo* 22, no. 1: 32–35.

Spitta, Philipp. *Johann Sebastian Bach: His Work and Influence on the Music of Germany,* vol. 1. Translated by Clara Bell and J. A. Fuller-Maitland. New York: Dover, 1951.

Stinson, Russell. *The Bach Manuscripts of Johann Peter Kellner and His Circle: A Case Study in Reception History.* Durham, NC: Duke University Press, 1989.

"Swing, Swung, Swingled." *Time,* 6 November 1964.

Taper, Bernard. "A Cellist in Exile." *The New Yorker,* 24 February 1962.

————. *Cellist in Exile: A Portrait of Pablo Casals.* New York: McGraw-Hill, 1962.

Taubman, Harold. "The Best Who Draws a Bow." *New York Times Magazine,* 28 May 1950.

————. "Pablo Casals: He Is Heard in Bach Suites Nos. 1 and 6 for 'Cello Alone.'" *New York Times,* 16 March 1941, X6.

Terry, Charles Sanford. *Bach: A Biography.* London: Oxford University Press, 1950.

Thomas, Hugh. *The Spanish Civil War.* 3rd ed. New York: Penguin, 1977.

Tingaud, Jean-Luc. *Cortot-Thibaud-Casals: Un Trio, Trois Soloistes.* Paris: Éditions Josette Lyon, 2000.

Vogt, Hans. *Johann Sebastian's Chamber Music: Background, Analyses, Individual Works.* Translated by Kenn Johnson. Portland, OR: Amadeus Press, 1988.

Washington, Peter. *Bach.* New York: Knopf, 1997.

Werner, Eric. *Mendelssohn: A New Image of the Composer and His Age.* New York: Free Press of Glencoe, 1963.

Wertenbacker, Lael. "Casals: At Last He Is Preparing to Play in Public Again." *Life*, 15 May 1950.

Whitehead, P. J. P. "The Lost Berlin Manuscripts." *Notes* 33, no. 1 (September 1976): 7–15.

Williams, Peter. *The Life of Bach*. Cambridge: Cambridge University Press. 2004.

———. "Public Executions and the Bach Passions." *Bach Notes* 2 (Fall 2004).

Winold, Allen. *Bach's Cello Suites: Analyses and Explorations*. 2 vols. Bloomington: Indiana University Press, 2007.

Wolff, Christoph. *Johann Sebastian Bach: The Learned Musician*. New York: W.W. Norton, 2000.

Wollny, Peter. "Johann Gottlieb Goldberg." *Goldberg* 50 (February 2008): 28–38.

———. "Sara Levy and the Making of Musical Taste in Berlin." *Musical Quarterly* 77 (1993): 651–726.

Wright, Barbara David. "Johann Sebastian Bach's 'Matthews Passion': A Performance History, 1829–1854." Ph.D. diss., University of Michigan, 1983.

Young, Percy M. *The Bachs:* 1500–1850. London: J. M. Dent & Sons, 1970.

Zuluage, Daniel, "Sylvius Leopold Weiss." *Goldberg* 47 (August 2007): 21–29.

Zwerin, Mike. "Giving Fugues to the Man in the Street." *International Herald Tribune*, 28 April 1999.

SUGGESTED LISTENING

RECORDINGS OF THE CELLO SUITES

Pablo Casals, *Cello Suites* (EMI)
Pieter Wispelwey, *6 Suites for Violoncello Solo* (Channel Classics)
Steven Isserlis, *The Cello Suites* (Hyperion)
Pierre Fournier, *6 Suites for Solo Cello* (Deutsche Grammophon)
Matt Haimovitz, *6 suites for Cello Solo* (Oxingale Records)

TRANSCRIPTIONS AND ARRANGEMENTS OF THE CELLO SUITES

Three Suites for Solo Violoncello, Transcribed and Adapted for Piano by Leopold Godowsky, Carlo Grante (Music and Arts)
Suiten BMV 1007–1009 (marimba), Christian Roderburg (Cybele)
Six Suites for Violoncello Solo (guitar), Andreas von Wagenheim (Arte Nova)
Bach on the Lute, Nigel North (Linn Records)
Works for Cello and Piano (Robert Schumann's arrangement of Suite No. 3 for cello and piano), Peter Bruns and Roglit Ishay (Hänssler Classic)
Bach Bachianas (works by Heitor Villa-Lobos and Bach), The Yale Cellos of Aldo Parisot (Delos)

MORE MUSIC FROM THE STORY OF THE CELLO SUITES

Italian Cello Music (including Domenico Gabrielli), Roel Dieltiens (Accent)
Anna Magdalena Notebook, Nicholas McGegan / Lorraine Hunt Lieberson
(Harmonia Mundi)
Cantatas with Violoncello Piccolo, Christophe Coin / Concerto vocale de
Leipzig / Ensemble baroque de Limoges (Naïve)
Bach Cantatas, vol. 1 (including *Brich dem Hungrigen dein Brot*, BWV 39), John Eliot
Gardiner / Monteverdi Choir / English Baroque Soloists (SDG).
Sylvius Leopold Weiss: Sonatas for Lute, vol. 4, Robert Barto (Naxos)
Carl Philipp Emanuel Bach: Viola da Gamba Sonatas, Dmitry Kouzov / Peter Laul
(Naxos)
Gamba Sonatas, Riddle Preludes, Baroque Perpetua, Pieter Wispelwey / Richard
Egarr / Daniel Yeadon (Channel Classics)
Cello Sonatas, Mischa Maisky / Martha Argerich (Deutsche Grammophon)
Music of Bach's Sons, Bernard Labadie / Les Violons du Roy (Dorian)
Bach Transcriptions, Esa-Pekka Salonen / Los Angeles Philharmonic (Sony
Classical)
Jacques Loussier Plays Bach (Telarc)
Lambarena: Bach to Africa (fusing Bach with music from Gabon, including a
cello suite gigue) (Sony Classical)

The catalogue system for Bach's works identifies the Cello Suites as BWV 1007–1012
(1007 for Suite No. 1 and so on, until 1012 for Suite No. 6). BWV is an abbreviation for
Bach Werke Verzeichnis, which in turn is short for the unwieldy Thematisch-
systematisches Verzeichnis der musikalischen Werke von Johann Sebastian Bach.

ACKNOWLEDGEMENTS

THIS BOOK HAS benefited from the finest ensemble of critics a writer could hope for. Daniel Sanger, Aaron Derfel, Norm Ravvin, Mark Abley, Noah Richler, and Francesca Lodico all read portions of the manuscript at various stages. At my stellar publisher Grove/Atlantic, I'm very grateful to Joan Bingham, Emily Cunningham, Jodie Hockensmith, Alex Littlefield, and to designer Charles Woods for making the cello come alive on the jacket. I also owe a huge debt of gratitude to my Canadian publisher, House of Anansi Press, and in particular to Sarah MacLachlan, Lynn Henry, Matt Williams and my tireless editor Janie Yoon. Thanks also to the first reader to get from opening prelude to final gigue — my agent, Christy Fletcher, and her colleague Swanna MacNair.

Every cellist I managed to buttonhole after concerts, in cafés, or via email was unfailingly generous with his or her time, in particular Mischa Maisky, Pieter Wispelwey, Anner Bylsma, Tim Janof, and Matt Haimovitz, who was waylaid, cello in hand, on the steps of a music faculty. I have yet to meet cellist Laurence Lesser, whose performance of the suites first put the idea of this book into my head, but he graciously answered many questions by way of email. The late Walter Joachim put an unforgettable human face on the music and spurred me on.

From the worlds of Bach scholarship and German studies, Christoph Wolff, Raymond Erickson, Katherine R. Goodman, Teri Noel Towe, and Peter Wollny were all extremely helpful and tolerant of my amateur questions.

For assistance chronicling the career of Pablo Casals, I am thankful to Marta Casals Istomin in Washington, DC, to biographer Robert Baldock in London, and to George Moore in Los Angeles, who provided sage advice. Núria Ballester of the Pau Casals Museum guided my way through the faded newsprint at the Catalan National Archives in Sant Cugat. In London, Jennifer Pearson searched for clues in the EMI archives and helped decode the provenance of Bach's 1748 portrait.

The mysterious "Monsieur Schouster" would still be mysterious to me without Ilke Braun, who translated a key article from German. My good friend Nathalie Lecoq helped translate and decipher the mostly French correspondence among Casals, Susan Metcalfe, their respective mothers, and the painter Lydia Field Emmet.

Finding a story in a piece of music was enhanced by all the words I was given access to in the Catalan National Archives, the Smithsonian Institution's Archives of American Art, the EMI Group Archive Trust, the Library of Congress Music Division, and McGill University's Marvin Duchow Music Library.

INDEX

AUTHOR PHOTO: MARCIE RICHSTONE.

ABOUT THE AUTHOR

ERIC SIBLIN is an award-winning journalist and filmmaker, and was the pop music critic at the Montreal *Gazette*. He made the transition to television in 2002 with the documentary *Word Slingers*, which explores the curious subculture of competitive Scrabble tournaments. The film aired in Canada and the U.S. and won a Jury Award at the Yorkton Short Film and Video Festival. He also co-directed the documentary *In Search of Sleep: An Insomniac's Journey*, which aired in Canada and Europe. *The Cello Suites* is his first book.